THE WOW! FACTOR

WITHDRAWN
WRIGHT STATE UNIVERSITY LIBRARIES

D0890808

HOW TO
CREATE IT,
INSPIRE IT,
&
ACHIEVE IT

A COMPREHENSIVE GUIDE FOR PERFORMERS

BY DR. STEVE ZEGREE

ISBN-13: 978-1-42346-813-4

Copyright © 2010 by Hal Leonard Corporation

All rights reserved. No part of this book may be reproduced in any form or by any electronic or mechanical means including information storage and retrieval systems without permission in writing from the publisher, except by a reviewer, who may quote brief passages in a review.

Published by Hal Leonard Corporation
7777 W. Bluemound Road
P.O. Box 13819
Milwaukee, WI 53213

Library of Congress Cataloging-in-Publication Data

Zegree, Stephen.
  The wow factor : how to create it, inspire it, and achieve it / By Dr. Steve Zegree. -- 1st ed.
    p. cm.
  1. Music--Vocational guidance. 2. Practicing (Music) 3. Music--Performance. I. Title.
  ML3795.Z44 2010
  780.23--dc22
                          2010014168

Printed in the U.S.A.

First Edition

Visit Hal Leonard Online at **www.halleonard.com**

THE WOW FACTOR

TABLE OF CONTENTS

ACKNOWLEDGMENTS

Although writing a book certainly requires copious amounts of alone time for the author, it is by no means a solitary project. Ultimately there are numerous people involved in the project, most of whom work behind the scenes and generally do not receive the credit they deserve.

My personal growth and development of *Wow Factors* has been a lifelong endeavor with myriad influences, role models and mentors. In addition, as a performer I have been blessed with a wide variety of performance opportunities and travel experiences that have spanned five continents. As a professor, I have been equally blessed with and inspired by students who are not only talented, but also motivated, and perhaps most importantly, fun people to be around.

First, to all of my former, current and future students in the Gold Company Program at Western Michigan University, thank you for teaching me at least as much as I have taught you. My goal has always been to have a positive effect on your musical, professional and personal lives.

In my professional life as pianist and conductor I have been fortunate to interact with audiences that have included students and teachers throughout the world in concert, clinic, festival and master class settings. Although these encounters may have been brief and less personal, I thank you for the gift of wonderful memories, plus your part in adding and contributing to the factors contained in this book.

I am deeply humbled by my personal friends and professional colleagues who graciously agreed to be interviewed for this book. Your tremendous insights and experiences will educate and inspire every reader.

Thank you to my extraordinary friends and colleagues at Western Michigan University whose musical and personal contributions make the School of Music a special place: Diana Spradling, Duane Davis, Michael Wheaton, Trent Kynaston, Tom Knific, Scott Cowan, Keith Hall, Tim Froncek, Billy Hart, Fred Hersch, David Colson, Carl Doubleday, Margaret Hamilton, Kevin West, Joan Bynum, Gail Otis Birch and Margaret Merrion. Also, thanks to "mon ami" Jean-Claude Wilkens for literally bringing greater harmony to the world of choral music.

Special thanks to Duane Davis for his support and involvement in the Gold Company Program, and for agreeing to direct Gold Company for a year, allowing me a sabbatical and the desperately needed time to complete this project.

For the development and presentation of this book I am grateful to:

Emily Crocker and my friends at Hal Leonard Publishing, including Dan Stolper, Tom Anderson, and Janet Day, for their support and for always doing their best to make me look (and sound) good!

Denise Savas for her invaluable insights and suggestions as an "objective" reader, and offering perspectives that enhanced my vision of what this book could and should be.

Susan Rice for her initial editorial input (and especially her expertise in eliminating ellipses…).

Dulcie Shoener: Editor Extraordinaire. Dulcie not only is a wiz in terms of crossing "t's" and dotting "i's"; she is competent, conscientious and creative, and also has wonderful musical intelligence—in addition to her gift for making the written page (and my message) much more clear and concise.

To my favorite sis and B-I-L, Joan and Spider, thanks for keeping it alive.

Finally, to my daughter Sarah and son Nat, who cause me to have a *wow* experience on a daily basis, thank you for the gift of joy and laughter. I love you more than all the world.

Dr. Steve Zegree

INTRODUCTION

I have had an ongoing relationship with music for essentially my entire life. My earliest musical memories involve sitting at the piano with my father when I was just 3 years old. My father would play the melody and harmony of the first two measures of the "Blue Danube Waltz" by Johann Strauss, and I would play the famous two-note motive in melodic response. From a very early age I was aware of my ability to play melodies and harmonies "by ear" at the piano.

My formal musical training began with piano lessons when I was 7. My piano teacher recognized my ability to play by ear, and encouraged and fostered that creative ability (with equal amounts of traditional study that included classical repertoire and traditional music theory). I will always be grateful to my first piano teacher for allowing me the freedom to play non-classical music. In retrospect, I believe that freedom was significant in maintaining my interest in piano lessons throughout my formative years (combined with the fact that my mother did not allow me to quit!).

With formal piano lessons came the requisite solo piano performances at recitals and other musical functions. Therefore I was asked to (and I agreed to) perform

> I will always be grateful to my first piano teacher for allowing me the freedom to play non-classical music.

from a very young age. Although I got nervous prior to a performance—and still do!—I learned the basics of how to perform, focus, concentrate and even bow, all in the second grade, thereby establishing the roots of my career as a performer.

I formed my first band when I was in the seventh grade in San Mateo, California. The band included the best players from the eighth-grade class and even two high school students. Perhaps in deference to the keyboard player, we were called "The Zigs." OK, there, I confessed it—but at least the name was catchy! We were offered and accepted professional performances like school dances and casual gigs at country clubs and private parties. As I reflect back, it seems as though I was quite young to be playing "professionally," but it was a great opportunity to learn a bit about "professionalism" at a tender age and what that meant in every sense of the word.

As a college student I had the opportunity to perform with a wide variety of celebrities ranging from Bob Hope to Dave Brubeck. Because of my education, hard work and being in the right place at the right time, I was truly fortunate to collaborate with some extraordinary personalities. In every instance, not only was I interested in and fascinated by the performer from the audience's perspective, but I always had an even greater curiosity as to how the celebrities acted in rehearsals and then backstage—where they were more inclined to reveal their true personalities—when they were *not* in the spotlight. To this day I still enjoy the opportunity to get to know a performer both on and off the stage.

I have met and worked with performers who are dazzling while onstage and anything but when offstage. It can be quite enlightening (and potentially disappointing) when performers reveal their "real" selves and their true characters emerge. In the pages that follow, I discuss not only effective ways to pursue *The Wow Factor* in auditions and performances, but also how to carry that distinction offstage, where it can play an equal (if not more important) role in how you want to be known and remembered by others.

I wonder if you are like me—I can't be a "regular" audience member when attending any performance. Indeed, I "know too much," and at times I am not sure whether this is a blessing or a curse! As a member of the audience, I am always making note of the lights, staging, technical setup, etc. I am curious to know all the details and inner workings of the how and why and the "behind the scenes," and as a result of this curiosity, I have received a great education. If you can relate to this and feel similarly "blessed" or "cursed," perhaps you might consider that in fact you have grown into a sensitive, sophisticated, intelligent and insightful audience member, and that your "curse" actually enables you to soak in and savor the performance with even greater appreciation for all the preparation required.

I have always had this natural curiosity—I tend to ask questions about everything. As a child, I wanted to know *how* things work and *why* they work. This incessant curiosity continues to translate into all aspects of my musical performance, and it has served me quite well as a professional. It is a trait that I appreciate and value and, hence, try to develop in others.

There are a few parts of (or, perhaps "holes in") my personal professional biography that you might find interesting, and perhaps even curious. First, I have never appeared onstage as a singer, actor or dancer in a drama or musical production—not in high school, in college or in any other venue. Although I have served as musical director of several productions and played piano and keyboards in the "pit" of numerous national touring Broadway shows, I did not benefit from the experience of being "directed" (in terms of acting, staging and choreography) in my formative years.

Although some people who may *think* they know me might find this hard to believe, I describe myself as having a more "retiring" personality than the outgoing stage persona I display in a performance setting. Should you see me in that role (as conductor or ensemble director), you should know that it is a stage persona and therefore essentially a "character" that I have developed over time—to exude an impression of comfort and confidence (not arrogance or cockiness!) to the audience. Comfort and confidence are stage attributes that will cause an audience to be more at ease, receptive and therefore

> As performers, it is our obligation to strive for confidence in whatever and wherever we perform. As ensemble directors and conductors, we must strive for musical excellence and elevated artistic standards.

more inclined to enjoy a performance, regardless of genre. As performers, it is our obligation to strive for confidence in whatever and wherever we perform. As ensemble directors and conductors, we must strive for musical excellence and elevated artistic standards.

I am frequently asked by students, teachers and professional colleagues how or why so many students who have been a part of our program at Western Michigan University have gone on to achieve success and careers in so many varied areas of the music profession, including jazz performance, Broadway, recording studio performing and production, composing, arranging, audio and stage technical work, and music education at all levels.

So how do I respond? Could it be coincidence? Am I quite simply the best teacher in the world, or do I have the best network of professional contacts and connections? The answer to all of the above is, of course, no! However, I teach some fundamental philosophies and concepts—in *addition* to music—that I believe are essential to a person's growth and development, and important and integral factors that will help contribute to a successful professional life. From this point on I will refer to these elements as *Wow Factors*.

Wow Factors can be achieved through a combination of competencies including formal education, but they involve *so much more* than just teaching the basics, sticking to a prescribed curriculum, and getting in front of an audience to go through the motions of what you did in rehearsal.

Are *Wow Factors essential* to achieving career success? Perhaps not, but in a competitive world they can make a distinctive and significant difference. You will experience the difference between standing ovations and polite audience applause; the difference between receiving college scholarship offers and being put on the waiting list; or the difference between being cast in a leading role and being asked to merely reaudition at the next opportunity—or worse yet, being rejected outright.

Creating *"wow"* takes a lot of hard work and requires an investment of time, effort, discipline and energy to accomplish and master. Is it worth it? My experiences as a performer and teacher have taught me that not only are the *Wow Factors* "worth it," but they are a crucial and indispensable part of my teaching, and significant contributing factors to the success of my students. They are also an inseparable part of how I choose to live my own professional and personal life, and in so doing I hope to lead by example.

I encourage you to consider utilizing as many of the *Wow Factors* found in these pages as apply to your

> One of the most wonderful things about music is that, after learning the right notes in a composition, there are no absolutes.

personal and professional situation. They work for me and they work for my students. The "proof" can be measured by the successes of former students as they pursue their careers, goals and dreams in their own professional lives. As you read this book, you will be subjecting yourself to my personal and professional philosophies of life and teaching. Please realize that these philosophies and opinions are based upon years of research and experiences, and that I have reasons and justifications for *everything* that I teach. I simply ask you to consider the personal, philosophical and pedagogical points that follow, and to embrace all that might apply to you and your students. Also I encourage you to disagree with any of the writings that follow, as this creates opportunity for discourse, dialogue, discussion and even debate.

One of the most wonderful things about music is that, after learning the right notes in a composition, there are no absolutes. The values and "rules" that are "right" or "wrong" to one person may be the exact opposite for someone else, or you have the option and right to *change* what is "right" or "wrong" or the "truth" in music, as *you* grow and change. It is essential that you keep an open mind, be at least receptive to the *possibility* of change, and remember that it is the *process* that is most important. Enjoy the process, enjoy your growth and progress, and, above all, have some fun!

CHAPTER ONE
THE WOW FACTOR
THE FRAMEWORK

At the least, experiencing "wow" is encountering the unexpected. At the most it's encountering the unbelievable. —Eph Ehly

• • •

Some people walk away from a concert or performance and sum up their entire experience with only one word: *"Wow..."* How can a single word so fully express something so deeply felt, so wonderfully satisfying, so amazing and extraordinary? *"Wow"* can be an exclamation that expresses astonishment as well as admiration. It can mean one is impressed and excited, and also can mean that something is sensationally successful. Can you think of any concerts, performances, auditions, jam sessions or even rehearsals that left you saying *"wow"*—either as a performer, as a director or as an audience member?

When I recall *wow* concerts that I've attended, four events stand out in my memories—representing different genres in different locations. I know I will never forget these *wow* performances that live on so vividly in my mind.

> "Wow..." How can a single word so fully express something so deeply felt, so wonderfully satisfying, so amazing and extraordinary?

- Leonard Bernstein conducting the New York Philharmonic in a performance of Mahler's Symphony #5 at Avery Fisher Hall in New York City.
- Fred Waring and the Pennsylvanians in concert, when I was in my 20s.
- Liza Minnelli performing her Tony Award-winning solo show, *Liza's at The Palace*, at the Palace Theatre in New York City.

- Sharing a Gold Company concert with Johnny Mathis at the Rosemont Theatre in Chicago.

What are the individual elements that create a *wow* performance? Are there certain general factors that are common to all performers, regardless of idiom, genre or style? What are they for me personally, both as a performer and an audience member?

I was in New York City, at Avery Fisher Hall at Lincoln Center, to hear Leonard Bernstein conduct the New York Philharmonic Orchestra in a performance of Gustav Mahler's fifth symphony. Bernstein's love and affinity for the music of Mahler was legendary. The occasion was Bernstein—the former music director of the New York Philharmonic, and perhaps the person singularly responsibly for bringing worldwide exposure and appreciation for the Mahler symphonies—conducting the entire cycle of Mahler symphonies. Bernstein was well into his 70s at the time, and he was universally revered as an international conducting icon. Audience expectations were high, as it was thought that this could very well be the final time that Bernstein would conduct the Mahler symphonic cycle. The concert was sold out. A buzz was in the air; this was truly an event. Both Mahler and Bernstein were former music directors of the New York Philharmonic. Both were composers and conductors, and both were hyperromantic, though they never knew each other. (Bernstein was born eight years after Mahler died.)

The concert began auspiciously when the Maestro entered the stage to a round of thunderous and extended applause. It was as though the audience thanked him for an entire career of musical gifts. The orchestra played their hearts out. Perhaps it was for the music, perhaps for Mahler, perhaps for Bernstein, perhaps for their own individual and collective reputations, or perhaps simply because they are highly paid professionals, and that is their job—it is what they are *supposed* to do.

Bernstein was in constant motion throughout the performance. His hyperkinetic, fully absorbed conducting style may have been a distraction to some, but I was spellbound and mesmerized. He was as fresh, passionate, committed and vital as any conductor I had ever seen. Even if he was conducting this piece for the 100th time and the orchestra had performed it a similar number of times, I would have never known. The applause at the conclusion was equally memorable. There was a spontaneous standing ovation, complete with cheers and screams of "bravo." The audience insisted that Maestro Bernstein return to the stage for five curtain calls and as many bows for the orchestra. I knew that I was in the midst of a historic moment.

I also remember being in the audience for a concert given by Fred Waring and The Pennsylvanians in Indianapolis, and being similarly blown away. At the time I was in graduate school and not exactly sure what caught my attention and caused me to classify the Fred Waring Show as a *"wow"* experience. However, I remember making the following observations: It was primarily a choral concert—with excellent instrumental accompaniment. The performance lasted nearly 2 hours and 45 minutes (with a 10-minute intermission—precisely 10 minutes!), yet the entire concert seemed to me as if only 45 minutes had passed. It included choreography, staging and lighting plus a variety of costume changes. And there were several medleys. In addition, the show was infused with humor and had a clever and witty host—Mr. Waring himself. I was struck by the wide variety of music, styles and programming. So much variety, in fact, that I thought everyone in the audience might not have liked everything they heard, but everyone would have liked something that they heard.

Liza Minnelli has won a Tony, an Oscar, an Emmy and a Grammy. In addition to being the daughter of Judy Garland, she is an iconic performer in her own right who has transcended every idiom. I attended her show *Liza's at The Palace*—appropriately held at the famed Palace Theatre in New York City. I must say, in complete candor, that my primary motivation in attending was to see one of my former students, who was one of

> I thought everyone in the audience might not have liked everything they heard, but everyone would have liked something that they heard.

Liza's four backup singer/dancers and also played some piano in the show.

It had been several years since Liza had presented a solo show in New York City, so again, the audience's expectations were high. First, there is her family legacy: Her mother gave historic performances at the Palace Theatre. Both mother and daughter have legions of fans because of their legendary show-business careers that have included singing, dancing, and acting in movies, on stage and on television.

Quite simply, I was totally *wowed* by this performance. I attended the concert with my two children, who were not particularly familiar with Liza and her legacy. They counted no fewer than 13 standing ovations *during* the show. The audience started cheering when the *houselights* started to dim! At the top of the show, the main curtain parted and a fabulous Big Band appeared at the sides of the stage, seated on movable platforms that rotated and brought the musicians together as one unit at center stage. Then a pin spotlight hit the star and silhouetted her in her classic white outfit and the equally classic Bob Fosse pose, resulting in another standing ovation. Then Liza simply walked from upstage to downstage center—where, for the first time, the audience could see her face and her smile—and yet a third standing ovation erupted, all within the first 2½ minutes of the show! Could this love-fest possibly be sustained for the next 2½ hours? Of course! Liza didn't simply "phone it in." She worked and worked and worked and *performed* two halves with an intermission. Working solidly for more than two hours, she never let up in terms of focus, energy and entertainment for even one second. And Liza was clearly loving the performance, perhaps as much as the audience was adoring her. It was all about "give, give, give," and she kept giving. Three Zegrees and about 2,000 others were clearly won over that day.

> She never let up in terms of focus, energy and entertainment for even one second.

Johnny Mathis has a singing career that has spanned more than 50 years. His *Greatest Hits* album spent an unprecedented 490 consecutive weeks (almost 10 years!) on the Billboard Top Album chart. Western Michigan University's Gold Company shared a concert in Chicago with Johnny Mathis and the Chicagoland Pops Orchestra. My natural curiosity caused me to want to know more about the audience for this concert, so before the performance I sneaked into the lobby of the theater and people-watched. I could sense the anticipation of the people as they entered, and I was struck by the fact that the *average* age of the audience was about 75. So I assumed we were in for a mellow evening of music.

I could not have been more wrong. Mr. Mathis made his stage entrance without the typical hype and verbal introduction that one might expect. The houselights dimmed and he simply walked onstage. What followed blew me away. The sold-out audience of nearly 4,000 people collectively screamed and cheered. The ovation was deafening. I thought I was at a rock concert! The response to Mr. Mathis was similar to what I have observed for The Beatles or Bruce Springsteen.

And then it struck me: This audience had listened to the music of Johnny Mathis when *they* were teens and young adults, and when he appeared they were magically transported to that period in their lives. So even though their bodies may have been of "senior citizen" vintage, their minds

> When he appeared they were magically transported…

were more like those of seniors in high school. Mr. Mathis spoke very little. His performance consisted primarily of one man singing great songs, and that was all his audience needed or wanted.

None of these was a typical or average concert. In each case something went way beyond the presentation of the music—and in

> In each case something went way beyond the presentation of the music.

fact not just one aspect but rather a *combination of factors* helped create *"wow."* It was certainly not random nor was it accidental. There was a significant amount of forethought, and every aspect of the performance was addressed, from the first note to the last—in fact, from the initial stage entrance to the final bows and exit. These all had **The Wow Factor**.

How would *you* like to *create "wow," inspire* it in others, and *achieve* it in every performance opportunity in your future? What are some of the unique factors that can cause your auditions, rehearsals, concerts and performances to be memorable? What separates the average from the *"wow,"* and how can you achieve it? There are no shortcuts. Let's start with attention to every detail of the performance and combine that with hard work, *and* add healthy doses of discipline, *and* dedication, *and* energy, *and* passion, *and* patience, *and* imagination, *and* commitment, *and* stamina, *and* adventure and even some risk.

This book is for ensemble directors, teachers (and future teachers!), students, parents, and people seeking the qualities, standards and values that are inherent in excellence. What follows is an in-depth exploration and examination of the essential elements that will help you evolve your performances from mundane to magical, from dull to dazzling and from ordinary to extraordinary.

This is the framework. Now, ladies and gentlemen, let the fun and hard work begin!

CHAPTER TWO
HOW TO PRACTICE
AND REHEARSE FOR
THE WOW FACTOR

"… once a musician has enough ability to get into a top music school, the thing that distinguishes one performer from another is how hard he or she works. That's it. And what's more, the people at the very top don't work just harder than everyone else. They work much, much harder."
—Malcolm Gladwell, Outliers

"Rehearsal is the rent you pay to earn attention." **—John Jacobson**

"We never know when an individual has a 'wow' moment, but it can come at any time, from any rehearsal." **—Weston Noble**

● ● ●

In master classes and clinic sessions, aspiring young student-musicians often ask me, "What is the shortcut to achieving my goal of success in the music profession?" I am always eager to share my "secret" answer to their question: After a big build-up, I inform them, simply, "Hard work." Although this may not be the answer the student wanted to hear, it is the most honest, realistic answer to the question. For every day that a student delays her music practice or puts off time devoted to developing his art and craft is one day longer toward realizing that goal.

Musicians and performers who have serious aspirations for success in the professional world of music must first establish tangible goals to accomplish and then determine how and when to achieve those goals. I chose the word "serious" in the previous sentence with great care, because if you intend to pursue a career in music, you are undertaking a task that comes with a huge responsibility and cost. There is a direct relationship of hard work and practice to the achievement of *The Wow Factor*.

This chapter has two sections, the first of which addresses ensemble rehearsal techniques and suggestions, and the second, individual (solo) practice.

One of the most serious pursuits in the music profession—requiring a significant amount of time, energy, responsibility and devotion—is that of music educator. I am extremely fortunate to have been the beneficiary of excellent music teachers. I would not be writing this book were it not for the motivation, inspiration and education I received from my former piano teachers, band and choir directors, and music professors. I was taught from an early age the importance of practice. I learned that if I wanted to make progress I should practice only on the days that I ate! (And I had—and still have—a voracious appetite!) As a youth, although I was aware of the noteworthiness of practice, the "how to" often eluded me. Consequently, I have devoted a great deal of time, effort and energy in my professional life developing rehearsal efficiency, both as a soloist and as an ensemble conductor. I believe effective and efficient rehearsals are a key to success as a music educator.

I have the greatest admiration for my colleagues who teach music at the high school and middle school levels. And, quite simply, elementary music teachers are my heroes, because at this level the seeds are planted in young minds and the groundwork is laid for what can develop into a lifetime appreciation of music, culture and the arts. Another reason that I have such a healthy appreciation for my music-teaching colleagues is that, as a college professor, their good work ultimately keeps me employed! I love "inheriting" the brightest, most talented graduate and undergraduate students from my esteemed colleagues in the music education profession, and subsequently assisting that student with his or her musical and personal growth and development.

One of the most meaningful and important gifts that I can bestow on my students is teaching them "how to practice." There is no doubt that if effective practice skills and techniques are learned early in life, a terrific reward awaits both the student and the teacher at the higher level. It is important that all music teachers, regardless of level, instill in their students the discipline and benefits of effective practice.

ENSEMBLE PRACTICE

A True Story

I recall being invited to serve as a guest conductor for a high school festival that included a residency whereby I visited all of the area high schools and rehearsed each choir individually, prior to the massed ensemble rehearsal. I arrived (15 minutes early, of course!) at one participating school on the prearranged day of my 50-minute rehearsal with the choir, during fourth hour (11 to 11:50 a.m.). After meeting the director, I sat and patiently waited to work with the choir. The singers casually assembled shortly after 11 and at 11:05 the director yelled above the din and asked the choir members to be seated. At that point the director started talking—first about the choir's performance for the Rotary Club the past week, then about a performance at the elementary school next week, followed by information about the next choir fund-raiser. (This year they will sell candles instead of wrapping paper.) While I understood that all of these discussions were probably important to the director and the ensemble, as I continued to patiently sit and wait for the opportunity to rehearse I wondered why they had to happen on that particular day. I endured nearly 20 minutes of listening to the director, after which I was introduced to the choir at just after 11:20 (not that I was paying attention to the clock!). Of course, the singers had not yet sung a note and needed to warm up. I asked the director to warm up the ensemble, as I can learn a great deal about a director and an ensemble simply by observing the warm-up. The "warm-up" lasted 10 minutes, and, not surprisingly, most of those 10 minutes consisted of the director talking and the ensemble not singing. I stepped in front of the ensemble at just after 11:30, leaving me about 18 minutes with the ensemble. And the ensemble was not vocally, physically nor mentally prepared to sing, especially after sitting and being talked at for the first half of "rehearsal." It came as no surprise that the ensemble was underrehearsed and not sufficiently prepared on the literature for the festival.

> ...a great rehearsal should always be the primary goal.

I have often reflected on that experience and wondered what might have motivated the director to manage time more efficiently and to more effectively inspire the singers. Not only was the rehearsal time management disrespectful to the guest, the primary task at hand—making music—was largely ignored. As previously mentioned, I believe one must continually be open to self-assessment and re-evaluation. Over time, a director can develop habits that are counterproductive to an efficient rehearsal, and lose sight of the fact that a great rehearsal should always be the primary goal. Consistently superb, skilled and passionate rehearsals beget great performances and *"wow."*

Prepare for Excellence

You must develop several abilities to best and most efficiently prepare your ensemble for excellence in performance—regardless of level or age group—including:

Understand the Theory. Have a thorough and functional knowledge of traditional music theory. If you rehearse a jazz or show choir, knowledge of jazz/pop music theory and vernacular will also be helpful. I am not certain why, but it seems as though college music theory classes are the bane of many music educators' existences. Perhaps it is how the classes were taught, or because the students struggle to find practical or functional uses for the theoretical information they were given. Regardless, traditional music theory is the backbone—or the vocabulary—for the musical language, and the ability to speak this language is an essential skill for every competent musician. Jazz and pop theory can be thought of as a subset of traditional music theory. The general facts remain the same in both (the key of G still has one sharp!). Although the theory is essentially the same in both idioms, jazz theory illustrates traditional theoretical principles in clearer ways that many students find easier to comprehend and more practical to apply.

Know the Score. There is no substitute for an ensemble director doing his or her homework prior to the first rehearsal with the ensemble. This homework includes comprehensive research on all historical aspects of the music and detailed score study and preparation. Score study includes a complete formal and harmonic analysis of the music, combined with a thorough functional understanding of all horizontal and vertical structures in the piece. Vertical structure analysis will help you know who is singing what part of each chord, and whose parts are "more important" than the others. For example, if the basses are singing the third of a chord and the tenors are singing the seventh, not only should those parts be in tune (as they define the quality of the chord), but they should also slightly predominate, in order to achieve the ideal balance within the ensemble.

Some suggested steps:

- Study the history of the piece.

- Know about the lives of the composer and lyricist.
- Learn about the times and conditions under which the piece was written.
- Mark your score with indications that include tempos, phrase structure and dynamics.

The more details you cover and the better prepared you are before the first rehearsal, the better your ensemble will sound and the sooner you will achieve *"wow!"*

Develop Keyboard Skills. You might think that I believe keyboard skills are important because of my formal piano training. And you may have a point—in part! I agree that my piano studies form an important (and, for me, indispensable) part of my overall musicianship. However, I also firmly believe that, at the very least, functional keyboard skills are an essential part of an ensemble director's collection of skills. In my own rehearsal preparation of a choral score, I play each individual vocal line to learn what each section will encounter, and to anticipate places in the score that might present technical problems or musical challenges for individual singers. These include challenging melodic intervals, extremes in range or tessitura, or the aural challenges that can appear when one choral part is sung simultaneously with other parts, especially when involving intervallic relationships of minor seconds, major sevenths, and, of course, the dreaded tritone. Also you can get an idea of how the piece should sound—so that if it doesn't sound that way when it is sung, you are best prepared to make quick and efficient corrections in rehearsal.

Develop Effective Hearing Skills. One of the most important functional uses of your well-developed keyboard skills is the ability to play all of the choral parts simultaneously so that you can hear them as vertical structures, and then how they relate to one another as horizontal structures. For me, there is no better way to learn and memorize a score. I practice the choral parts (and the accompaniment) until I commit them to memory, thereby also memorizing how each chord is supposed to sound. The next step is to develop the ability to quickly make any and all necessary corrections and modifications (based on what you hear), and effectively and efficiently communicate these changes to your ensemble. Ensemble directors must learn how to *listen*, both analytically and evaluatively. This is a crucial skill that can be developed over time. Are you able to perceive and comprehend all that you hear? You might be able to hear all of the notes, but do you hear the *music?* You need to have a sonic model in your mind— the "perfect" sound or performance. Not only must you know what it

> You need to have a sonic model in your mind—the "perfect" sound or performance.

is, but you must also learn how to efficiently explain and/or demonstrate exactly what you would like to hear.

Be Efficient. Rehearsal efficiency is a complex, multidimensional goal that requires discipline, self-assessment and continual re-evaluation. In addition, just like piano competence, it is a skill that can be achieved only through practice. Directors must therefore display due diligence and patience in their pursuit and development of excellent rehearsal efficiency. I find it a bit ironic that one must invest a significant amount of time and energy practicing how to become an efficient practicer and rehearsal technician. And, like so many great things in life, this can be learned only through experience. Develop your ability to quickly and efficiently recognize mistakes, succinctly correct them, then have the ensemble repeat (correctly, several times) until you are satisfied with the consistency.

Maximizing your rehearsal efficiency can manifest itself in many ways on many levels. This checklist of guidelines can help you meet this goal.

- **Avoid excess verbiage.** In other words, talk less! This includes all of the typically unnecessary (and ultimately distracting and annoying) verbal pauses including "You know," "Um," "Uh" and "OK." Think about what needs to be said and determine how to say it using the absolute minimum number of words.

- **Stick to 80/20.** I believe the best ratio for an efficient rehearsal is 80/20. This means that the ensemble is performing 80 percent of the time and you are speaking 20 percent of the time, or less. In any five-minute interval, your ensemble should be singing (or playing) for four of the five minutes: a task much easier said (or written!) than done.

- **Avoid unnecessary repetition of words.** One quick path to achieving efficiency is to avoid repeating yourself. You may be surprised at the number of directors who will utter the exact same phrase twice in a row, such as "Very good. Very good." Teach your ensemble members to listen to directions and to get it the first time, thereby eliminating the need for you to repeat yourself. If you say everything twice, or ramble on (and on and on), then the rehearsal is needlessly filled with your speaking. Make your point. Be concise. Move on.

- **Keep up the pace.** Keep things moving. Have you been in a rehearsal where you glance at the wall clock and note the time, then rehearse for what seems like an eternity—then look at the clock again and see that exactly five minutes have passed since the last clock-check? As a director, if you keep everyone's attention and minds actively occupied in the rehearsal (especially at the times when they are not immediately involved), then time will fly by. One of my favorite moments in a productive rehearsal is when, after two hours of rehearsing, both the students and the director look at the clock and cannot believe that two hours have passed—and all want to continue rehearsing.

- **Know when to fold.** There will be times when, in spite of your best efforts, the ensemble hits a brick wall, and nothing you do can advance the cause. Although unpleasant, this is a natural and common occurrence. Don't beat the proverbial dead horse: Simply move on, and return to that section at your next rehearsal.

- **Set a timetable.** Determine a schedule for your rehearsal period whereby the ensemble repertoire is memorized and prepared to perform *well ahead* of the actual concert date. Essentially, build in a "false" concert date, then you can *practice every aspect of the performance*. Remember, in order to create **The Wow Factor**, your *performance* must be *practiced*, many times and well in advance of the actual concert. Your performance is not only about singing and playing the right notes.

- **Be an inspiration.** *You* must have it, and be able to successfully pass it along to your students. Inspiration can be found in many places and manifests itself in myriad ways. Perhaps you love the text of a piece, or the harmonic content, or the style of the arranger or composer. You must determine what excites you and fuels your passion, and then communicate that to your ensemble in ways that will ignite their passion as well. Your actions will speak louder than

> If you are excited about the music, it will be infectious.

words. If you are excited about the music, it will be infectious. Your singers will become excited, and your musical results will improve.

- **Do it again! Repetition, repetition, repetition.** I know—very clever use of words! It's just like the punch line of the joke about the tourist sightseeing in New York City for the first time who wants to visit all of the famous landmarks. He needs directions and asks an elderly woman on the street, "Excuse me, ma'am, can you tell me how to get to Carnegie Hall?" Her reply: "Practice, practice, practice."

When presenting a new piece of literature to my ensemble, I typically have more than one plan of attack, mostly to maintain a varied pace and variety in the rehearsal. Here are some suggestions to try:

- Have the ensemble sight-read the piece at or near performance tempo from start to finish, just to give them an idea of the degree of difficulty.

- Start by rehearsing the most challenging sections of the piece first, thus allowing you to maximize the amount of time that the singers are exposed to the problematic parts.

- Start rehearsing the piece at the end and work in reverse order to the beginning of the piece. I realize that this is the opposite of a more traditional approach, but this method has several benefits. Oftentimes the complexity and degree of difficulty in compositions and arrangements increase as the piece progresses, with a climax occurring at or near the end of the piece. By working backward, you are likely addressing the most challenging sections first. Plus, after working this way, the end will be more satisfying to the singers and instrumentalists when you run the piece from start to finish. Knowing the ending can provide a big psychological lift, especially in the initial phases of learning a new piece. There is no need to keep repeating and rehearsing the early, simple sections of the piece when the challenging places are not yet mastered. This is simply a waste of precious rehearsal time.

> Knowing the ending can provide a big psychological lift, especially in the initial phases of learning a new piece.

A phrase that is often heard in my rehearsals is "Good! Do it again," typically repeated four to five times in a row as the ensemble performs the same phrase quite well several times. I enjoy anticipating the inevitable question from the novice ensemble member: "If it is so good, how come we have to 'do it again' so many times?" Consider: In the initial learning phase of the rehearsal process, the ensemble will most likely spend more time rehearsing and performing inaccurately (with "mistakes") than they will perfectly (or as close to your model of sonic perfection as you are able to achieve). Unless you have a group of perfect sight readers, the ensemble will most likely be inaccurate on individual lines, and then have "issues" with intonation, blend and balance as more than one part sounds simultaneously. For example, a group may rehearse a phrase nine times in a row, and, though each time it improves, the ensemble doesn't get it "right" until the 10th attempt. This means that the consistency rate of the ensemble is just 10 percent. The odds are that the next time it will not be "right." Therefore, to achieve consistency (and, as a result, confidence), it is important to "do it again" as many times as necessary until the ensemble can perform that phrase correctly several times in a row.

- Each time you repeat a phrase, ask the ensemble for something even more musical.

- Remind them of what they already know.

- Remember to reinforce the positive, praise the things that they do well, and offer constructive criticism on the aspects needing improvement.

- Once the challenging section is secure, move to another section of the piece, or perhaps even another piece of repertoire. Then return to the challenging section and see if the musicians have retained their ability to perform that section a few minutes later. If not, it needs to be repeated some more.

- A visit to the same section in rehearsal the next day will most likely yield a regression in the retention rate of the ensemble, especially if extreme harmonic or rhythmic complexities or technical challenges are found in that section.

- Don't be disappointed; be determined. There will be days when you will wonder whether you are listening to your angelic ensemble or their evil twins. Stay on task and do not lose sight of your goal of artistry and excellence.

> Don't be disappointed; be determined.

- Repeat the process over and over until you find the consistency that the ensemble needs in order to perform confidently.

- Be patient. This can sometimes be a long and tedious process.

In addition to the requisite repetitions, experiment rehearsing in different settings. Try placing your ensemble in different choral positions, in sections, randomly mixed, spread out all over the room, in a circle, facing one another, mixed couples, tight quartets, singing with the lights off, singing silently, using different tempos, or going to the stairwell, to the auditorium or outside. Use your imagination and figure out ways to make the important and serious task of repetition fun!

Anticipate the problem spots in every piece of music in advance of your rehearsal and determine the most efficient way to solve them. Oftentimes, ensuring that each section can confidently sing or play its individual line will not solve all musical challenges. Many times the musical problem is *how that line relates to some or all of the other parts*. Therefore it is good to practice repetition in the following ways:

- All parts *a cappella* individually, starting slowing and incrementally working up to tempo.
- Women's parts alone.
- Men's parts alone.
- Outside parts (soprano and bass).
- Inside parts (alto and tenor).
- Building chords and lines from the top down, adding one more part with each repetition.
- Building from the bottom up, adding one part at a time.
- Adding accompaniment instruments when appropriate, starting with bass line, then piano, then drums and other instruments.

Use your connections. A frequently ignored rehearsal problem is the vocal, tonal, physical and technical adjustment that singers and instrumentalists must make from the end of one phrase to the start of the next. Try a section of repetitions by starting at the end of a previous phrase so that the musicians can gain confidence in connecting phrases and sections of the piece. It is also good to repeatedly move back and forth between two challenging chords or phrases, thus ensuring confidence and consistency in the ensemble. Once the immediate connection is mastered, add a few measures on either side of the problem, thereby rehearsing the approach to and departure from the difficult section.

Be aware. As a professional educator, be aware of what you know and do well, and more importantly, be aware of what you *don't* know. Nobody likes a "know-it-all," and, in fact, there is no such thing—because no one *can* know it all. Don't be afraid to admit what you don't know, especially to your students! Be honest and open to change, new input and (appropriately timed) suggestions from your students. Many times students have great ideas, plus it gives them a feeling of responsibility and ownership in the creative and rehearsal process. You can always learn new things, regardless of your age and experience. This is a concept that everyone should embrace.

Incorporate technology. In case you have not been paying attention, computers and the Internet are here to stay. It was not that long ago that the most familiar reference to the word "google" was from a comic strip and in the lyrics of an old nonsense song ("Barney Google"). And now, in a relatively short period of time, it is a common verb used in our daily communication and teaching. Research every aspect of your performance by googling important terms. Find music software that can be used to make rehearsals more fun and interesting to the students. Use mp3 recordings, iTunes and YouTube to inspire your singers through listening and sonic modeling. It is important to both embrace technology and change (as change is inevitable), and to still retain important *values* and educational philosophies, because the best of those are timeless.

Detailing. Perhaps I can be accused of rehearsal extremes, but I believe a significant portion of the success of our ensemble program comes from attention to detail—in all aspects of the rehearsal and performance—from the matching earrings the ladies wear to unified vocal entrances and cutoffs, to the font and design of publicity posters, and especially to "don't go to your face!" (More on this later!) The more articulate and specific you are in your directives, and the more details that you include, the better your ensemble will perform.

Have a plan for the band. Unless your vocal ensemble performs exclusively *a cappella*, you will need to rehearse with your instrumentalists at some point before your performance. The important issues that you need to address are who the players are and when they play. If you are fortunate enough to be able to hire (and afford) a professional piano accompanist, then he or she is expected to be at your rehearsal when wanted and needed, as the accompanist is being compensated for his or her time.

If your vocal ensemble includes student instrumentalists, develop a plan and routine, and communicate them effectively. You must be efficient with the use of your band and their time. Don't make them sit around needlessly; plan ahead. Rehearse your *a cappella* literature first, then bring the band in. While you are concentrating on your vocal rehearsal, you might send the band to a practice room for a sectional, or, if they know your repertoire well, have them learn and practice new repertoire, even if it is not related to the ensemble. Most importantly, keep the band playing! They live to play and they love to play.

If you need the services of professional string or brass players, one or two rehearsals prior to the performance should suffice. Typically, well-trained, professional classical and jazz instrumentalists need far less rehearsal time to learn music than most vocal ensembles, in part because of well-developed sight-reading skills. Make sure that one of those rehearsals is a dress rehearsal in the actual performance space, so that you can determine appropriate balance, levels, staging and lighting. When the paid instrumentalists are on stage, do your best to ensure they are playing and not sitting needlessly while you rehearse *a cappella* vocals—your work with the vocal ensemble should be completed by this point. Have clean, legible and clearly marked instrumental parts, and make sure in advance that all measure numbers and rehearsal letters are consistent with the vocal parts and master score.

Be punctual. Start and end on time. This applies to your work with your singers as well as your instrumentalists, but is especially true if you are working with professionals. If the players are members of the musicians union, they will expect to be paid more if you exceed the negotiated rehearsal times, so plan ahead, and stay on schedule and within your budget! If you are working with amateur or student instrumentalists, be respectful of their time as well. In return, it is within your rights to expect your student instrumentalists to be punctual, prepared and professional in their presentation. It is also quite likely that these players are in demand with busy schedules. Your ability to be organized and efficient with your use of rehearsal time will help make the collaboration a pleasant and musical experience for the players, and, as a result, enhance your reputation and cause the instrumentalists to look forward to future collaborations with you.

Typically there is a slightly different vocabulary and phraseology that can and should be used to more effectively communicate with instrumentalists. Knowing and using that terminology can cause you to better relate to and earn respect from "the band," establish a professional relationship and to create a more effective and efficient rehearsal.

Some Golden Particulars
In Gold Company, in addition to the 16 singers and the sound crew, I work with an ensemble of eight instrumentalists. The instrumentation for the Gold Company Band includes piano, bass (both double bass and electric bass), drum set and guitar. The GC Horns consist of two trumpets,

saxophone and trombone. This is common instrumentation for combo horns, and many published arrangements include this particular configuration of instruments. For larger shows I sometimes add an auxiliary percussionist (conga drums, timbales, tambourine, etc.) and an auxiliary keyboard player (synthesized strings, special effects, etc.). In Gold Company I require the instrumentalists to memorize their music—just as the singers are required to do. Memorization sets a new standard for the instrumentalists and ultimately causes them to perform with much more confidence and creativity, have more fun and interact better with the director, the ensemble and one another. Although these players are registered for the class and fully participate in the ensemble, I do not require them to attend every rehearsal. Quite simply, this would be a waste of their time.

I audition my ensembles (singers and instrumentalists) at the start of every academic year. No one (even singers and players who have participated in the ensemble in the past) is guaranteed a place in the new ensemble. Each performer must prepare an audition each year, and selection and participation in the new ensemble is predicated upon the success of that audition. This causes anyone and everyone interested in being in Gold Company to do his or her best in the audition, regardless of past history. Plus, it is fair: It gives all students (returning and new) the same opportunity.

When the new ensemble is selected, the singers have a rather steep learning curve, whereby they are required to learn and memorize a large amount of varied repertoire in a relatively short amount of time. Typically I like six weeks of rehearsal time before the entire ensemble is prepared to perform a 45-minute program that will include vocal jazz, pop and choreography. The majority of time in that initial six weeks is spent learning and rehearsing vocals and choreography. There is no need to have the instrumental ensemble in those rehearsals, because they will not play a note. I do not need an accompanist in my own rehearsals because I either work from the piano or have the singers rehearse *a cappella*. Therefore, the issue becomes, what to do with your band while the singers get their "act" together? In Gold Company, I post a rehearsal schedule on Monday morning for the entire week. This informs all students what the assignments and expectations are before every rehearsal. Assignments typically include the specific repertoire to be learned and/or memorized by a specific date, plus other musical projects including transcriptions, arrangements, solos and listening reports. An example of the assignment sheet follows:

Thursday:

6:00 p.m. Singers set up PA system, warm up

6:30 p.m. Listening assignment #6 due
Rehearse group vocals: "Unwritten" memorized (sing
in mixed quartets for grade); "They Say It's Wonderful"
learned; practice "I Wish You Love," "Once Upon A Time"
and "Friends in Low Places."

7:45 p.m. GC Band in: "Friends in Low Places"

8:00 p.m. GC Horns in: "Unwritten"

8:15 p.m. Full ensemble business meeting

8:30 p.m. Everyone strike and put away PA system

I realize that as an ensemble director you are most likely bound to a rehearsal schedule that has been previously determined, and that the specifics of the example schedule may not apply to you. However, that is not necessarily the point! Several important points are implied in the posting of this schedule:

- It is the responsibility of the ensemble members (not the director nor only the tech crew) to set up the PA system, *prior to* the official start of the rehearsal at 6:30, and to have completed a sound check.

- It is the responsibility of the singers to be vocally and physically warmed up *prior to* the official start of the rehearsal at 6:30. This important task can be an individual responsibility, or it can be assigned to a section leader, but it is a wonderful opportunity to develop professionalism and responsibility in your students.

- When the rehearsal begins (promptly) at 6:30, the ensemble is expected to be physically ready to sing and mentally focused on the task at hand. The ensemble will be singing by 6:31.

- When I walk into the rehearsal just before 6:30, I have several expectations, including those listed above. One of my favorite moments in the rehearsal is when I walk into the room just prior to the official start of the rehearsal and the ensemble is *already* rehearsing (perhaps led by a section leader). One of the telltale signs of an ensemble whose members love to sing together is when they sing at times they do not *have* to. In other words, they are so serious about the musical development of their ensemble that they *choose* to sing and rehearse, rather than socialize.

Setting standards. Don't settle for a rehearsal or performance that is only OK, average or mediocre. Have a realistic set of expectations for yourself and your ensemble and insist that your group rise to whatever level of excellence you wish to establish. I believe that all students want to do well and would prefer to work hard in a rehearsal rather than be part of an average ensemble. Instill a sense of pride in the work ethic of your students. This will help develop confidence in your individual singers and the ensemble. It may take some time for them to get to the place you are seeking, but do not give up on your ideal and your perfect sonic model. Most importantly, do not lower your standards or reduce expectations to bring things down to your students' level. Have a vision and establish a philosophy for your ensemble. Set general and specific goals for yourself, your students and the ensemble. Announce to your ensemble at the start of your rehearsal: "In the next 45 minutes our goals are…" Make your list of tasks *more* than what can realistically be accomplished in 45 minutes, but at the end of the period, review with your ensemble what *was* accomplished, and the things that still need improvement.

I clearly communicate my philosophies and expectations for the ensemble to the entire ensemble in a general business meeting at the start of the school year. In addition to the posted weekly rehearsal schedule (that everyone can see, therefore there is no room for excuses and misinterpretations!) I also send group e-mails to all members of the ensemble that serve as updates and reminders. By being consistent in all of the above, you can establish a tradition and a pattern of expectation and excellence that is then passed from the returning students to the entering students. There is no substitute for quality leadership from within the ensemble and the positive example and influence that can be demonstrated by veteran ensemble members. Once you have established your expectations, your path to "*wow*" will be paved.

> There is no substitute for quality leadership from within the ensemble

"It's NOT All About Me"

In addition to excess verbiage, one of my rehearsal pet peeves has to do with "me, myself and I." I am reminded of the joke about the solipsistic person at a party, who, after 30 minutes of nonstop talking about himself, pauses and says to his bored and irritated "conversation partner," "I've been talking about myself all this time, why don't you tell me what *you* think of *me?*"

Here's a suggestion: Record yourself and check your rehearsal vocabulary. If you are inclined to say things like:

"Give *me* a big crescendo at measure 23" or "I want you to sing louder at Letter B"

then I suggest that you delete the "me" and "I" from your rehearsal vocabulary, and substitute those words with ones that are more inclusive, such as "let's" or "we":

"Let's crescendo at measure 23" *or* "Can we sing louder at Letter B?"

I believe it is better to maintain a rehearsal attitude that is all about the *music* and not about *me or you*! As conductors or rehearsal technicians, we are simply the vehicle for the composer or arranger to help interpret and bring his or her music to life. This can also mean giving up some of your own ego for the greater good.

Our ultimate goal in rehearsal is to achieve musical and personal confidence and competence in each individual member of the ensemble. When you have achieved this goal (through excellent rehearsal technique), your group will be well on its way to achieving **The Wow Factor**. Remember, one method that I use to instill individual confidence in Gold Company is to require memorization of all parts *well before* the concert by establishing a false deadline, thereby building in a cushion of time to improve and gain even more performance confidence as an ensemble. If the musicians' heads are out of the music, it leaves more "ear space" for listening, reacting and interacting.

My ultimate test is to hear each individual singer perform his or her part as a solo, *a cappella*, from memory, in tempo, on a microphone—counting rests when not singing and staying on pitch, with the correct rhythms, dynamics and articulations. In addition the singers must exhibit the appropriate physical involvement. If the piece is in a "medium swing feel," then they need to do all of the above while snapping their fingers on beats 2 and 4 and smiling if it is a happy text. This "individual performance opportunity" can be presented for me alone, or in front of the entire ensemble. Then try putting your singers into mixed quartets and sing (and perform) for one another. If your ensemble members can successfully do all of the above, then they should be able to sing their repertoire anywhere, in any hall, for any audience. The performance will be better and most likely more fun for your ensemble.

In any performance setting, when I walk on stage as conductor of my ensemble, I want to have an inner confidence (not to be confused with a cocky or egomaniacal attitude) that all members of the ensemble are *also* confident of their own parts and how each will contribute to the success of the performance. If I know that *they* are confident, then I, in turn, can be confident, and that creates a *great* feeling for all involved, and as a byproduct achieves the sometimes-elusive peace of mind prior to a performance. The inner confidence that the ensemble exudes also crosses over to the audience, as they sense a confident performer, and that puts the audience more at ease and more receptive to whatever the ensemble or performer has to offer. This preparation will contribute significantly toward a *"wow"* performance.

How important and necessary are you, the conductor? Ultimately, some of my best "conducting" in a concert is done when I step to the side of the stage and watch my ensemble perform with a confident energy and pure joy. By taking yourself out of the equation you transfer the responsibility of a great performance to your students and ensemble. If you have done your job in rehearsal, and your ensemble is well-prepared and confident, they will do theirs in performance. By this time, the vast majority of your work has been completed, and there is not much that your presence in front of your group can add. You must decide whether it is *necessary* for you to be in front of the group at *all* times. Perhaps when you conduct an *a cappella* ballad, you then have the option of true artistic expression and subtle variety for each performance, as opposed to a less musical, more robotic autopilot performance that some groups strive to achieve. But on a song that has a contemporary pop groove or a more traditional swing feel, it is likely that your placement in front of your ensemble beating a traditional four pattern will detract from rather than enhance the overall performance. Remember, *The Wow Factor* is more about the music than it is about *you*!

> If I know that they are confident, then I, in turn, can be confident...

So, as an educator, in fact, it *is* really "all about *me*," as I don't want to lose sleep over whether my ensemble is "ready" to perform! More importantly, by investing this amount of effort into your ensemble's preparation, you will help ensure a positive performance experience for your students, and that is one of the most precious gifts you can give.

INDIVIDUAL PRACTICE

Individual practice for a director, conductor, student or aspiring soloist can sometimes impose a greater challenge than does the ensemble rehearsal. Whereas ensemble directors are specifically trained to produce psychic inspiration and musically stimulating rehearsals, soloists are often clueless when it comes to "how to practice." In an ensemble setting, the students' "job" is to simply follow the directions and suggestions of the director. Essentially they are "victim" to the director's rehearsal technique, but typically they fall into a regular routine of what to expect, how to react, how much effort will be required, and the amount of time they need to commit. If their ensemble rehearses from 11 a.m. to noon, Monday through Friday, the students know where they need to be and how long they will be there. They also develop a sense of responsibility and obligation, especially if this is a required class and they earn a grade in the process.

Even though the ensemble rehearsal or music class can be part of a students' daily routine as early as elementary school, rehearsing outside of the ensemble can be analogous to the proverbial "horse of a different color." Speaking of horses, there is an old saying that "you can lead the horse to water, but you can't make it drink." I prefer a slightly different take on that saying: "You can lead the horse to water, then figure out how to make it thirsty."

Singers vs. Instrumentalists

Solo singers often find themselves at a musical and music theory compre-hension disadvantage when compared with their instrumental counterparts. Typically, instrumental students are given the option of joining the school band program in fifth or sixth grade. They each choose an instrument, get on a monthly payment plan to own the instrument, and commence with daily rehearsals at school. The initial sounds from the aspiring instrumental-ist are not very satisfying, but are quite rewarding nonetheless. Instrumental students must learn to vibrate reeds, buzz mouthpieces and saw wood, and in the process learn the essentials of music theory, including the develop-ment of sight-reading skills. They participate in an ensemble that, even in the early stages, can perform "cool" repertoire like "Theme From Jaws" or "The Pink Panther"! The students get excited by the power and potential of the ensemble, and improve incrementally through the daily rehearsal process. Some students are fortunate to begin private instrumental studies as early as first or second grade, or even earlier through the Suzuki method.

Now let us jump ahead several years; the instrumentalists are high school seniors who have played their instruments for eight years. They studied privately, participated in concert band, marching band, jazz band or orchestra, solo and ensemble contests, and summer music camps, and not only mastered their instruments, but also became proficient in music theory, sight-reading and basic keyboard fundamentals. Individual solo practice has become a part of their daily routines. They now would like to pursue their musical studies at the collegiate level. Their private study, solo and ensemble experience and theory skills have all combined to prepare them for excellent auditions. They can quickly identify all time and key signatures, write and play all major and minor scales and intervals, and recognize chord qualities. The instrumentalists have been in training for years for successful college music auditions.

Aspiring vocal students can typically follow a different path of musical preparation. Consider this scenario: A student shows no interest in music, especially singing, throughout the elementary and middle school years. In the student's sophomore year of high school, a guidance counselor puts the student in choir (as a last resort) to fill a curricular requirement, much to the student's displeasure.

To everyone's surprise, when the student sings, a lovely, free, natural and vibrant sound emerges. Unfortunately, the student is musically illiterate and does not know the difference between a sharp and a flat. But we can't allow an unimportant detail like this to be a deterrent! In fact, because of a good, natural ear, the student can learn his or her choral part by listening to other singers, and whatever is not picked up that way is reinforced by the director—by rote. The student decides to pursue music as a major in college—because choir class was so much fun in high school—and such little work—and, because of the naturally beautiful voice, the singer is accepted into a school of music—without being able to read a note of music. What is worse, the student has never learned how to practice, and, in fact, has never been asked to do so. In spite of a lack of knowledge and discipline regarding music, the student continues and succeeds in collegiate voice studies because once again, he or she is coddled by professors and accompanists, all because of the lovely, natural voice.

Of course this scenario is completely fictitious and would never happen in reality! At Western Michigan University, all auditioning potential music students are required to take a Basic Music Qualifying Exam that tests the students' knowledge of the rudiments of key signatures, scales, intervals, triads and time signatures. In addition, they are tested on aural recognition including identifying intervals, triads, short melodies and rhythms, and aural performance including singing major and minor scales, matching pitches, call and response melody and rhythm, and basic melodic and rhythmic sight-reading. In the past, more than 50 percent of the instrumentalists who take this test pass, with more than half of those earning a grade of A. Only about 20 percent of the vocalists pass this basic skills exam. While the result of this exam is just one of many factors considered for prospective students, it is a good indicator of their potential success (or failure) in the requisite core music curriculum that includes theory and ear-training courses. At the very least, those students who are accepted into the School of Music with deficiencies in music fundamentals will be delayed by a semester in completing their required coursework. Based on past statistics, a number of them will not end up remaining as music majors.

You Can't Fake It!

We have made a compelling case as to why instrumentalists can tend to have a disciplined, habitual approach to individual practice and why singers sometimes have not had the opportunity to develop a similar discipline. Is there any wonder that, at times, in the world of instrumentalists there can be found a less-than-positive attitude toward singers?

For the less disciplined singer, this work ethic can manifest itself in many ways. For example, I suspect some of our readers can relate to preparing for a major exam in high school or college. Perhaps you chose to not make that class a priority, and did not study until the night before the exam. You spent a good part of the night memorizing facts and cramming the specific knowledge into your brain, and, as a result, did very well on the exam the next morning. The specific material was probably forgotten shortly after the exam was over. I have observed a similar work ethic in many collegiate vocal music majors. Some vocalists will not practice their assigned repertoire and technical exercises until the day before (or even the day of!) the lesson, at which time they quickly learn the melody and lyric of their assigned pieces, and thereby achieve passing results for the applied private lesson. There is no way to hold them accountable for such lackadaisical practice habits, and this becomes their modus operandi.

Conversely, if I assign one of my piano students a new Bach prelude and the first movement of a Beethoven sonata for next week's lesson, I *know* the amount of time, effort and the practice procedure that are required to prepare this literature. The *only* way to achieve success and learn this music is through regular, daily practice. There is *no way* that a student could learn the literature and perform it well at his or her lesson, even if he or she pulled an "all-nighter" the day before the lesson. It would be silly to even think this way, and, more importantly, the students like this would be only cheating themselves out of their own opportunities for growth and development.

> The *only* way to achieve success and learn this music is through regular, daily practice.

Solo Practice

It is interesting to note the similarities and differences between solo and ensemble practice. Several factors must be considered when approaching an individual practice session:

- The student must develop a love for practicing. In my case, I went through a transformation from 1) hate; to 2) love/hate; to 3) love. When I began piano studies at age 7, I could not stand to practice. In fact, I had great difficulty sitting on the bench and practicing! My mother had to use bribes to keep me at the piano for even 15 minutes. The thought of playing outside and engaging in athletic activity with my friends had much greater appeal for me at that time. This aversion to practice continued even through my high school years. It was not until I became a music major in my third year of college (after deciding not to pursue the law career that my father had charted for me) that I realized the importance and necessity of regular, daily practice. Having obtained the exalted status of "college student" and the requisite maturity that accompanies that status, I slowly developed a love of practice that eventually supplanted my long-standing habit of not enjoying the experience. I realized that the reason for my "hate" was that practicing is a solitary endeavor, unlike the sense of "ensemble" that is achieved in a group rehearsal.

- The solitary nature of practice is something that should not be overlooked. In order to be most effective, solo practice should be done alone, with no distractions or interruptions. If you are a socially active person, you will need to find ways to resist the temptation to use your telephone or any other distraction during your prescribed practice session. I suggest you hang a "do not disturb" sign on your door, turn off all electronic devices, set a specific amount of time and do nothing but practice until that time has expired.

- Initially, the music-making is not particularly rewarding and satisfying, especially in the early phases of practice, when a person is incapable of performing well. Only later, in my professional life, did I achieve a true love of practicing, which holds true to this day. My current professional life is quite active, and consists of teaching, traveling, performing, writing and recording music, and countless other activities—none of which easily includes regular daily practice. I now long for the luxury of time that I had in my student years. I only wish I had known then what I know now, for I *thought* I had a busy schedule when I was a student. In fact, I had an abundance of time, and now I regret not using it more wisely! When I hear my students tell me how "busy" they are and that they "have no time," although I am not unsympathetic, I try to help them *find* more time in their daily routine, and also let them know that they have more time now as students than they ever will once they enter the professional world.

- The love of practice comes from the satisfaction you attain from knowing that you have made a concentrated, focused effort to improve yourself, and from the enjoyment of observing your own growth and development. This growth occurs through studying, learning and memorizing new literature, and from reading and listening, plus the confidence, maturity, sophistication and experience gained through the process.

- We have already established that repetition is the best way to achieve consistency. Remember: We perform the way we practice, whether as a soloist or as an ensemble. I have found more similarities than differences in ensemble versus solo practice. Essentially, practice is practice, regardless of style, forces, age group, demographics or location. Of course a wonderful acoustic space where singers can hear themselves is preferable for a choir rehearsal to an unpleasant, unresonant and small room, and a new concert grand piano is a preferable instrument to a studio spinet. However, if you are faced with the latter as your only option, be grateful to have a space and an instrument, and make the best of your situation, even if it is challenging or even at times unpleasant. Never allow less than desirable rehearsal circumstances to deter you, and especially never use it as an excuse.

> We perform the way we practice, whether as a soloist or as an ensemble.

In solo practice, your goal is to achieve technical and artistic consistency in performance. This is achieved through dedicated and disciplined daily practice. Just as in the ensemble rehearsal, initially, you will sing or play your repertoire incorrectly many more times than you will get it "right." Therefore when you get to that phase where you are starting to master the music, use that as the launching point to make numerous repetitions of how the piece is *supposed* to sound and feel when performed.

Here are some practical suggestions that may help you make more efficient use of your practice time:

1) Know what you intend to accomplish and set specific practice goals. For example, if you are learning four new pieces and you intend to practice for 60 minutes, then allocate 15 minutes practice time for each piece. Set a timer and when the 15 minutes expire, move to the next piece, regardless of what has just transpired.

2) I ask my piano students to not allow their hands to leave the keyboard when they practice. This is a way to ensure that they will be playing and achieving the requisite repetitions. If their fingers are not moving, they are not practicing! The same philosophy applies to singers. They must get into the habit of creating the appropriate vocal sounds on a regular, daily basis.

3) Vary tempos. In particular, if the repertoire is in a slower tempo, then practice it faster. You will complete more repetitions in the 15 minutes that you have, plus the piece will seem much easier to perform when you return to the original (slower) tempo.

4) Try playing or singing the piece a half step above and below the original pitches. In both classical and jazz styles, there is no substitute for being able to function in more than one tonal center.

5) For pianists working on memorization, play the right hand alone from memory with the left hand behind your back, then switch. It will become obvious just how well you have mastered the material.

6) Include some form of warm-up and/or technical exercises in your daily routine. These warm-ups should involve physical movement and stretching (especially earlier in the day) and then include a variety of musical drills (scales and arpeggios, etc.) that will not only warm up your entire range (from bottom to top) but also stretch your ear.

7) Do not allow any interruptions or distractions in your one-hour practice.

8) When the hour is complete, take a quick, brisk walk, drink some water and refresh your brain. If you have the physical, musical and men-

tal stamina to continue, then begin your second hour by revisiting the most technically and musically challenging section of each piece that you practiced in the previous hour.

9) Maintain an intense, fervent, determined focus to your practice. Challenge and push yourself to be as proactive and productive a practicer as possible.

10) There will be days when things do not go as well as you might hope or expect. The emotions you may feel can include frustration, exasperation, annoyance, irritation and even anger. Learn to embrace "the joy of frustration." It is an important part of the process.

If you have the privilege of rehearsing an ensemble on a regular basis, then it is also your responsibility to master your skills, refine your rehearsal technique, be organized and communicate effectively, and perhaps most importantly, know when to get out of the way. For individual practice, first cultivate your love of practice, then embrace the solitude. Set challenging yet realistic goals, and develop a plan to achieve them. Be persistent, disciplined and determined.

There is much truth in the old adage "Practice makes perfect." The sooner you develop a strong work ethic and an effective, regular practice routine, the sooner you will achieve *The Wow Factor* in your ensemble and solo performances.

CHAPTER THREE
HOW TO PREPARE A
"WOW" AUDITION

"Be prepared. Because when luck meets preparation, you win! If luck comes along and you're not prepared—that's it." —*Liza Minnelli*

"Prepare and rehearse to the point that no one is aware of the preparation." —*Mac Huff*

• • •

One of the most challenging requirements of a developing musician is the ability to prepare for an audition. In the music and theater world, auditions are a basic fact of life, though of course auditions are not limited to the arts. You can think of a job interview as another type of audition, so developing your ability to audition well may be an important factor in your ultimate employability—whatever path you choose!

Auditions can begin as early as elementary school for roles in school productions or solos within concerts, or for child roles in community, high school or professional theater productions. Opportunities to audition continue through middle school and high school, and, in fact, never end. If a person has a desire to perform, it is in his or her best interest to develop an ability to audition well as early as possible.

This chapter will offer tips and discuss specific ways to prepare for various types of auditions, including:

- How to prepare for a college music department audition.
- How to prepare for a musical theater audition (high school, collegiate, professional, Broadway, theme park, cruise ship), or for a specific role in a production.
- What is essential to every audition.

You must realize that it takes years of practice to develop one's abilities to perform a great audition and that there is no substitute for experience. How does one gain experience? From repetition, specifically, a commitment to hard work in the practice and preparation phase, followed by auditioning as often as possible in the performance phase.

Tough Odds: The Reality Check

Out of more than 100,000 high school basketball players annually, fewer than 4,000 male college students play basketball in the NCAA, and about 50 get drafted to the NBA each year. The chance of a high school male athlete being drafted by the NBA is about 5 in 10,000, or 0.05 percent. With odds like that, I think it is best to have at least one "backup" plan.

On the other hand, never let these odds *dis*courage you from trying to achieve your dreams, especially while you are young with few or no responsibilities. This is the ideal time in your life to work hard and go for it.

The same kinds of statistics and odds apply to high school and college singers who might aspire to be cast in a leading role in a Broadway show. My friend Timothy Noble is Distinguished Professor of Voice at Indiana University. He is one of the leading operatic baritones in the world. His voice students are accomplished singers, but, in Tim's words to his students, "you have to be better than *me*." And when Tim says "better," he means not only vocally better, but also better in terms of musicianship, and *all the other* **Wow Factors** *that go beyond the music and upon which reputations are built:* professionalism in rehearsal, reliability, punctuality, attitude, work ethic, flexibility and adaptability, discipline and reputation. If all of these attributes are excellent, then why not select the person with the proven track record? Therefore it is even *more challenging* for a newcomer to successfully audition for a role.

WHAT TO KNOW TO "WOW"

In your preparation for an audition, nothing substitutes for knowledge and intellect. These can be lifelong quests, starting with the pursuit of a formal education. Depending on one's goals and aspirations, a formal education can consist of (minimally) a high school diploma, and (preferably) an earned college degree. Masters and doctoral programs are options for those who choose to pursue even more degrees!

As an aspiring musician, you have the task of acquiring special knowledge, training and experience that far exceed the requirements of your nonmusical colleagues. This should include private study on an instrument or voice and knowledge of music theory and history, accompanied by copious amounts of specialized listening and reading, starting with, but not limited to, your specific areas of interest.

In addition, I cannot overemphasize the importance of listening to all types of music—especially those that are *not* your favorite—as much as possible. Be able to quickly answer these questions:

"Who do you listen to, and why?"

"What's on your iPod?"

Try to explore and learn about as many different genres and styles of music as you can and open yourself to new input. I sincerely believe that the more versatile you are, the more marketable you are, and therefore you will be more interesting and valuable to a prospective employer.

What follows are suggestions within specific genres and styles for ways to increase your knowledge and sophistication, prepare for an audition, and improve your chances of creating *"wow."*

Classical

Work to develop a solid technique. Without technique we do not have the tools and ability to create.

Know the basic and standard repertoire for your instrument. For example, a pianist should be able to perform from memory a representation of repertoire from the Baroque era (for example, a Bach Prelude and Fugue from the *Well-Tempered Clavier*), the Classical era (a Haydn, Mozart or Beethoven sonata), the Romantic era (a work by Chopin, Schumann, Liszt or Brahms) and the 20th century (Debussy, Rachmaninoff, Bartok or Gershwin), plus develop some basic skills in improvisation and harmonization. For example, you should be able to play "Happy Birthday" or another simple melody with your own creative accompaniment—in any key.

A singer should be able to perform several memorized selections reflecting a variety of music from the standard repertoire, including Italian art songs, German lied, French chansons, and art and folk songs in English. Make sure your choices are age-appropriate (in terms of technical challenges, tessitura, degree of difficulty and the strain the selection can put on your voice). If you aspire to a career in opera, know the great operas and composers. Listen to recordings. Know some of the great singers, both current and past. Be able to name two to three singers in each vocal category that you like, and be able to state why.

Jazz

Just as in classical music, you must develop a solid technique. Jazz is simply a style of music, and will be played and sung successfully only after you have mastered the ability to play or sing well.

Students of jazz are *obligated* to be familiar with the entire history of this classic American art form, not just music recorded in the recent past. To accomplish this, you must devote a significant amount of time exclusively to listening to the great artists and famous recordings. The addition of and access to iPods and YouTube in our daily lives make this important investment of your time much easier and more fun.

In addition to knowledge attained through listening, you should know the basic forms used in jazz, jazz theory, the greatest artists on your instrument, common repertoire (the "standard" songs from the Great American Songbook) and specific recordings. A great source for historical information is album (CD) liner notes. I suggest reading everything on the CD, including the names of all of the performers, where and when it was recorded, the engineer, composers and arrangers, tributes and thanks.

If asked, be able to state some of your favorite artists and specific recordings.

Musical Theater

As in jazz, there is a long and wonderful history and tradition in the American musical theater. Again, the aspiring student must be familiar with the entire history of musicals, not just the music from the most recent or current popular Broadway shows.

You should be familiar with the names of the great composers and lyricists, classic and contemporary. Know the standard repertoire—from classics including George Gershwin, Richard Rodgers, Irving Berlin and Cole Porter to more contemporary composers such as Stephen Sondheim.

Watch the classic MGM musicals. Know what a Fred Astaire dance looks like and how it differs from one by Gene Kelly.

Try to see current Broadway productions. Make a road trip to New York City, or catch the national tours when they come to a city near you, or rent a DVD, or see it on YouTube, but *don't* be ignorant—it will appear that you do not care or are not sophisticated, mature or motivated.

Musical theater performers must be a "triple threat"—singer, dancer and actor—so you must develop your skills in all three areas. Study dance and develop technique (and know the different dance styles), develop your vocal technique (breath management, range, styles, support) and have a repertoire that includes a wide variety of musical styles. A good and fun way to develop your acting skills is by participating in school plays or community theater productions.

> Musical theater performers must be a "triple threat"—singer, dancer and actor—so you must develop your skills in all three areas.

Choral

Study the basic repertoire and representative composers and forms from various historical eras including Renaissance, Baroque, Classical, Romantic, 20th century and contemporary (including world and vocal jazz literature). Listen to recordings of great choirs and choral conductors and be familiar with the classic masterworks.

Know the names of important choral composers, arrangers and publishers.

GENERAL AUDITION POINTS

Repertoire

This is perhaps one of the most basic and important decisions that you will make. Decide what repertoire to learn, practice and perform after completing your own research. Do your homework by making an educated and informed decision based on facts and what you know (or what you can learn) about your desired audition goal. Here are some questions that you might ask:

- **What repertoire is appropriate** for this performance opportunity (gig)? What repertoire might be *in*appropriate? (Generally, I am a strong proponent of age-appropriate repertoire. For example, one would need to know the history and original setting of the great Cole Porter standard "Love For Sale" to decide whether it is the most appropriate audition choice for a middle school girl.)

- **Are there required pieces?** It is your responsibility to know if there is repertoire that is required of all people auditioning.

- **What style of music is performed on the gig?** (Jazz, classical, musical theater, pop) It would be in your best interest to prepare repertoire in the style that is required by the audition panel or the performance venue. However, it is also important to be honest and true to who *you* are. If someone suggests that you sing a Mariah Carey song, but that song (or style) does not represent you very well, then it is not in your best interest to try to cover Mariah's voice and style. Do what you do well, and do it with conviction. If you are auditioning as a jazz singer, but have little or no experience with improvisation or scat singing, make that clear to the panel prior to your performance.

- **Specific skills** (such as jazz improvisation) take months and years of practice to develop. Competence must be earned, and it cannot be faked—so don't even try! If you would like to develop your skills and abilities in a specific area of expertise (such as scat singing), then you must put yourself on a disciplined course of study that includes regular daily practice and listening to recorded examples of people who excel in the idiom.

What to Wear

- Plan ahead when determining what to wear for an audition. It is said that you have one chance to make a first impression. And, whether you like it or not, people make evaluations based on appearance. Generally, it is good to dress up, look nice, and choose tasteful and appropriate clothes that flatter you. Try not to be too trendy, and make sure that your outfit fits well and is comfortable (especially your shoes!).

- As obvious (and perhaps old-fashioned) as this may sound, be clean and neat, and have your clothes pressed, shoes shined, tie tied straight, hair combed and out of your eyes, and facial hair trimmed.

- Select clothes that are not too warm or cold. If you are in doubt, wear layers so that you can adjust to changes in room temperature. Your goal in an audition is to be as relaxed as possible, and to feel good—both physically and mentally. Your ultimate success can be predicated upon factors that include just how well you are feeling, both on the inside *and* out.

- In the jazz world, there once was a stereotype that jazz musicians had little regard for fashion, and even less regard for their audience. While there may be some credence to this stereotype (perhaps perpetuated by Miles Davis), it is now quite antiquated. You are more likely to see Wynton Marsalis in a designer suit than in jeans. Making an effort and dressing up also will indicate that you have respect for the music, for the audition and for the people for whom you are performing.

- In musical theater, when auditioning for a specific show, you will most likely be auditioning for the production staff, including the director, music director and choreographer. If you are hoping to be considered for a specific role, it is common to come dressed as that character, so that the production staff can get a visual image of how you might look if they cast you.

It seems a shame that audition decisions can be affected by nonmusical factors including attire, but this *is* an important *reality*. So if you are interested in the gig, make the effort to clean up and dress up, then perform in such a way that they *have* to take you!

Beyond Your Control

For theatrical roles, keep in mind that there is usually one female and one male leading role. For a Broadway show audition, it is not uncommon that 500 people will audition for each lead role. That means 499 people come away disappointed. Therefore, the overwhelming odds are that you will *not* get cast in that role. So, what have you got to lose?!? Go for it! Give it your best shot and have fun in the process. If you do not get cast, try to figure out why. Use the audition as an educational experience and learn from it. See if it is possible to get some feedback that may be helpful to you in the future—so that you will be better, stronger, more experienced and more confident at your next audition.

For example, it is quite possible that you might be the most talented singer auditioning for a role but that your dance skills are limited, and the producers want to cast someone with great dance abilities. If you don't get cast, consider taking some dance lessons—and come back next time as a "new and improved" dancer. This kind of attitude will speak louder to a production staff than anything you can say. Or, they may be seeking a specific physical type, and, even though you may be the best singer *and* dancer who auditioned, if the role requires a 5-foot-3-inch performer and you are 5 feet 10 inches tall, you will not get cast in that role, even if you presented the best audition.

It is also important to remember that audition results can be highly subjective, hence you must subject yourself—and your performing abilities—to other people's opinions. And people's opinions (and taste) in music are as varied as the people themselves. What is the better dessert: chocolate cake or apple pie? Objectively, both are great desserts. Subjectively, chocolate cake is *so* much better—absolutely unequivocally, without a doubt—at least in this author's opinion!

What to Say/What *NOT* to Say

Remember: In most auditions you are being evaluated from the first minute people see you to the last minute you leave the room. Practice entering a room with a quick, lively and confident step and a smile on your face, and be ready to respond to anything. If they say "hello," then respond; if they don't, you don't have to say a word.

There is a well-known audition test where the panel asks you (as the person auditioning) to step up to a line on the floor, then state your first name and where you are from.

If you respond:

"Hi, I'm Steve Zegree and I'm from Kalamazoo, Michigan," you have already lost the gig—*even before you have the opportunity to perform!*

If you respond: "Steve from Kalamazoo and I'm really excited to have this audition opportunity," you have already lost the gig—*even before you sing your first note.*

If you walk right up to the audition table and shake the hand of the director, you have already lost the gig—*no matter how extraordinary your talent may be.*

The test is designed to see how well you listen and follow directions, because that is an important part of your relationship with the director, once you have been cast. Notice that this test has *nothing* to do with your musical abilities and, in some ways, is more important.

The most appropriate response to the question would be:

1) Step up to the line on the floor, not beyond it and not behind it.
2) Think before you speak, then
3) Smile and say: "Steve, Kalamazoo."
4) Smile and wait for your next direction.
   (Remember to keep breathing!)

When I am auditioning someone and hear potential in his or her musicianship, I will always ask a few seemingly innocuous questions that are ways for me to gather more information about and better evaluate that person. Those questions might include:

"Do you know who wrote that song?"

"Who is the lyricist?"

"What key do you sing that in?"

"That song was in Italian. Can you tell me what you are singing about?"

Answers to these questions can help determine the musical intellect of the person *and* how well the person auditioning expresses himself. I believe a serious musician should also know something about

> I believe a serious musician should also know something about the repertoire he or she is singing, starting with the composer and lyricist.

the repertoire he or she is singing, starting with the composer and lyricist. If the person auditioning says she has no idea what key she sings in, or what she is singing about, I suggest, "Next time someone asks you that question, you should!"

Should I happen to encounter that person a day or two after the audition, I will ask the same questions again and see if she has done any research. If she now has answers to my questions, this tells me that the student is motivated, curious and anxious to learn. If she does not, it is perhaps a signal that the student does not really care about the audition results or the gig, or more importantly, about *her* own self-improvement. I would be less inclined to include that student in my program or cast her in a show.

Sometimes when people get nervous or excited, they tend to talk more than they usually do (or should). Please be aware of what you are saying and how you say it. Avoid excess verbiage! And don't try to present yourself as smarter, hipper or more sophisticated than you really are. Oftentimes I am put off by a student who acts like a know-it-all when in fact he really doesn't know much at all.

I will always remember the time a talented first-year student (the politically correct way to refer to a freshman!) came into my studio, clearly wanting to impress me with his witty, hip, urbane and sophisticated demeanor. All was going his way until he coolly put his hand on the wall and inadvertently turned off all the lights in the room. Imagine his embarrassment! I could hardly contain my laughter.

Be humble. If you do not know the answer to a question, simply say, "I don't know, *but I will find out*"—and then look it up immediately thereafter. No one expects you to know all that there is to know—that's why you have teachers! If you knew it all, I would be out of a job—so it is very important to me that you do *not* know it all!

Be honest and be true to who you are. Answer all questions succinctly and don't offer WTMI (Way Too Much Information).

Read as much as possible about all aspects of the audition and gig prior to your audition so that you are well informed. If you have a question, make sure that the answer cannot be found in the audition pack or in printed material that you could have obtained prior to the audition. A poorly researched question would be another tip to the audition panel that you are not as motivated or thorough in your preparation as other candidates are.

Sometimes you will receive instant comments and input from members of the audition panel. How you respond to questions and comments may influence your audition result. Above all, use active listening skills. Be present. Maintain eye contact with whoever is talking to you. Do your best to understand and comprehend what the panelists are saying. Think before you speak.

If the panel offers specific suggestions for improvement, smile and say "thank you." *Do not* make excuses or in any way sound defensive or argumentative. If you do not understand a question or comment, then you may politely ask for an explanation or further elaboration.

You may be cut off before the end of your prepared selection. This should not necessarily be interpreted as a negative, so don't respond with a negative reaction. Keep smiling and wait for the next direction. In many auditions I hear a great talent and I know after just a few seconds of singing and/or playing that I want to consider this person at the next round or at callbacks. In the interest of time, I will cut off the performance, thank the musician, and excuse him or her from the room. The student may leave feeling dejected and rejected, when in fact he or she is leaving as one of the top contenders for the gig.

> Keep smiling and wait for the next direction.

When you hear the famous line "That will be all, thank you," you may respond with a smile, say "thank you" and quickly depart.

Relating to Your Accompanists

One of the most important aspects of an audition can be the instant musical and personal relationship you establish with an accompanist. I'm writing this from my perspective as a pianist and one who has had the privilege of collaborating and performing with musicians in the classical, jazz, musical theater and pop fields ranging from professional recording artists, opera and Broadway performers, national tours of Broadway musicals and international jazz artists to elementary school children—and virtually everything and everyone in between!

Our first order of business is to consider substituting the term "accompanist" with "collaborative pianist." It *sounds* better and, more importantly, is a much more accurate description of the function of the pianist. The term accompanist, when used by some people, can have the connotation of delegating the collaborative pianist to second-class status— and, believe me, when you are developing a musical association with another person, it is in *your* best interest to want the pianist to be (at least) an equal partner in your music-making.

The Pianist (and/or trio). Here is an important question for you to ponder: How well do you want your collaborative pianist to perform, especially in an audition? Your pianist's attitude toward you will be influenced by *your* attitude toward the pianist, especially at your initial meeting. If you treat the pianist like a "hired hand" and with disrespect, he or she will most likely not try quite as hard for you.

In every audition:

- Approach your collaborative musicians with respect and a professional attitude.
- Have a well-marked, clear and concise lead sheet or accompaniment sheet music. Make sure you know in advance whether lead sheets are acceptable.
- Try to minimize the total number of pages and make the page turns easy and in appropriate places.
- If you need to give an explanation, make it concise and to the point. The ability to communicate (displaying your musical intelligence) with your collaborating musicians will instantly give you more cred-ibility. Describing the style of your selections, accurately and confi-dently counting off the tempo, and using standard musical terms such as "head," "bridge," "turnaround" or "tag" will gain the respect of your collaborators
- Know and use the appropriate vernacular vocabulary. In jazz and popular music these terms can include intro, bridge, I-vi-ii-V7, turn-around, head, feel and groove, and specific grooves like samba, bossa nova, ballad, rubato and medium swing.
- Be confident of your preferred tempo and be able to count off the pianist or rhythm section *in your tempo*. It is completely permissible to bring a metronome to your audition in order to guarantee the correct tempo.

- *Do not assume* that your pianist can instantly transpose any accompaniment (be it classical, jazz, musical theater or pop). Bring your music in the key that you want to sing it in, along with all appropriate edits and cuts clearly marked in the score.

- Present yourself professionally, as a smart musician and not as a rhythmically challenged singer with little or no *musical* intellect.

- Know the key for every song you sing or perform. Know the composer, when he or she lived, the lyricist, and, if the song is in a foreign language, know the translation—the *actual, literal* translation, not necessarily the one in English that is provided under the original text. A good example of a bad translation is the original Latin text for "Ave Maria," which I have seen translated to an English text that has absolutely nothing to do with the Hail Mary prayer, and therefore most likely does not represent the original thoughts of the composer. So, find an accurate translation, and know what you are singing about at all times, then allow your face and physical attitude to reflect the text.

- After your audition, the pianist is oftentimes consulted as to how *you* presented yourself to *him or her.* How well prepared were you? What did your score look like? What was your attitude? Were you competent and friendly, or disorganized and disrespectful? Even if your performance was stellar, if you get a bad review from the staff accompanist, then you will *not* get the gig. Remember, the jury panel also wants to know what you are like to work with, behind the scenes and offstage. Are you cooperative, and can you follow directions?

Keep in mind that quite possibly you are being evaluated at all times, and not always by the people that you think are the only ones making the decisions.

Sound Crew

Knowledge and use of microphones is a crucial and indispensable component of contemporary music, and your ability to work with a microphone can be a great asset in an audition. Know and develop good mic technique. Learn how to be consistent, so that the people at the soundboard can deliver the best possible sound to your audience. I am a strong advocate of the "mouth to the metal" microphone technique, to achieve the best sound control.

Remember:

- Hold the shaft of the mic—not the ball, as many pop artists are inclined to do—at a 45-degree angle down from the mouth and face.

- Hold the mic in your hand; or put the mic on a stand, thereby making it easier to maintain a consistent distance from the mic.

- Never point the mic at a monitor or main speaker, as this is a frequent source of feedback.

- Learn how to confidently remove a microphone from a mic clip and then how to confidently replace it.

- Be nice to and respectful of the sound, light and stage crew. You could possess the best voice and the best costume in the world, but if the sound crew doesn't turn on your microphone and the follow-spot operator "accidentally" forgets to hit you with the follow spot—no one will ever hear or see you!

ESSENTIAL WRITTEN MATERIALS— OTHER THAN MUSIC!

A very important part of the audition process takes place *prior* to your actual audition—the completion of a written audition form. If possible, fill out all forms in advance. Take your time; think before you write; be neat, precise, accurate and honest; write legibly; use spell-check; *and proofread everything that you write or type*! Make sure that your spelling, grammar and syntax are all correct. You can create a terrific initial impression if you express yourself well—not only in your speaking, but also in your writing. It is quite likely that you will also be evaluated on the style, content and presentation of your written materials, including your audition forms.

If given the opportunity, consider writing something that may be different from (and more memorable than) most others who have a typical resumé. If there are ways that you can be unique in a positive way, or otherwise distinguish yourself, do so! Remember to always exhibit good taste, and try not to attract negative or excess attention to yourself.

You may bring letters of recommendation, a resumé and other supporting materials to an audition. If you choose to do so, please be reasonably certain as to the contents of your letter of recommendation, and that your reference is saying only positive things about you, both as a person and as a talent.

Resumés

It is quite likely that a student will not have developed an extensive professional resumé by his or her senior year in high school. Even if that is the case, create a simple, one-page form that includes your personal contact information, a brief statement of professional goals and aspirations, educational background and any professional accomplishments, roles, awards, honors or outstanding performance opportunities that you have achieved, as well as the names and contact information of two to three people who are willing to serve as references for you.

Above all, when writing your resumé, be honest and accurate. Present the facts and *do not* exaggerate. For example, if, as a sophomore in high school you sang in nonauditioned festival choir of 1,000 students that was rehearsed by a well-known professional conductor, do not write "Sang under _(name)_ ", because that would imply that you had a personal, professional experience with that musician, and that the conductor would most likely remember you and be able to offer an opinion about you if asked.

> Keep in mind that you are being evaluated by everyone, all the time!

If a prospective employer and/or music schools are interested in you, they *will* contact your references—*and* quite possibly contact people who may *not* be on your resumé, but who they know might offer more information about you, your musical and performance abilities, and your personal attributes. Believe me, these contacts occur frequently. How do I know? Because *I* do it on a regular basis!

So, again, it begs the question: What do you want others (your friends, teachers, employers, and even acquaintances whom you don't know well or associate with on a regular basis, but who have the opportunity to evaluate you and develop an opinion about you and your work) to say about you? Keep in mind that you are being evaluated by everyone, all the time!

In addition to your resumé, you can create a separate repertoire list that includes all of the advanced musical material that you have learned, memorized and performed, or the roles you have played. You might highlight the pieces that are in your current repertoire (and that you are willing and able to perform) with an asterisk.

Letters of Recommendation

Very often auditions and applications require as many as three letters of recommendation. As obvious as this may sound, make sure your references will say positive things about you before you ask them to write a letter of support.

The most common sources of letters are private and school music teachers, favorite classroom teachers, guidance counselors and advisers, civic and community leaders, and employers. Be courteous and give your reference sufficient time to write prior to the due date. Be certain that the people you ask to write on your behalf know you well enough to be able to offer *specific* positive information in their letter.

Please realize that the people who read your letter see hundreds of letters of recommendation, and most of them basically say the same thing: "She is an outstanding person, talented, etc." So try to find ways that the letter-writer might say things a bit differently about you—ways that might distinguish you from the others. Ask your reference to make the letter personal to the people at the institution where you are applying; i.e., "I believe Lisa will make a great student at____ because…," then relate a specific reason, or, "Out of the thousands of students I have taught, Justin ranks in the top 1 percent because of his musical intelligence, sight-reading ability, keyboard skills, personal attributes, maturity and great attitude." A statement like that will cause people to sit up and pay attention, especially if the source is a person with an excellent reputation. While of course you cannot tell a reference *what* to write, you might give your reference a copy of your resumé or a listing of salient points or positive attributes.

Of course, a great letter of recommendation can be helpful, but it is still up to the person auditioning to prove the letter-writer correct and to demonstrate all of those abilities with confidence, excellence and artistry.

THE PYRAMID

As a student develops and matures, the competition for auditions tends to get more challenging, and the talent level rises too. The best performers who come out of middle school music programs matriculate to high school, where they then compete against other new and outstanding former middle school students, *plus* other returning high school students who may be three or four years older (and more physically and mentally mature and experienced).

> As a student develops and matures, the competition for auditions tends to get more challenging, and the talent level rises too.

The competition increases as students prepare for a college audition. For example, at Western Michigan University in a typical audition year, nearly 200 singers audition for acceptance into the School of Music as voice majors, whether in performance, education, jazz, composition or music therapy. Most of these singers are talented, and most typically played leading roles in their high school musicals, and were the outstanding soloists in concert performances. Unfortunately for the majority of students who audition, the School of Music admits only 28 new voice students each year. Therefore, as a candidate, what can you bring to this audition that will distinguish you in a positive way from the others?

And, if you are fortunate to be among those admitted, as a first-year college student you are competing for roles and ensemble placement against other undergraduate students who may be three to four years older (and wiser and more experienced and more mature!) than you, not to mention graduate students who may also be in the program, and they are even older and *more* experienced! This is perhaps a good time for you to decide whether you prefer being the proverbial "big fish in the little pond," or vice versa, or whether you hope to find the perfect combination of both: i.e., a school where you would be challenged and inspired by those who may be older and more experienced, yet where you *would* have the opportunity to audition for and perform in the top ensembles and productions, from day one. I think finding this balance is a wonderful compromise, as you can then be challenged and inspired by the more experienced performer, and learn from him or her, and then pledge to yourself: "I want to be just like ____ when I'm a senior"!

The following section discusses specific types of auditions as well as guidelines for what to expect and how to successfully prepare yourself for your audition. This information is intended for students and parents, as well as for teachers who may serve in an important advisory capacity. It may be used as a reference guide for your intended major.

HOW TO PREPARE FOR A COLLEGE MUSIC AUDITION

One of the most daunting tasks facing high school music students is the prospect of selecting the colleges and universities where they will submit applications and then subsequently audition for admission and acceptance as a college music major. What follows is a discussion of the process, including a timetable, the procedures a student should follow, and tips for preparing an audition that will *"wow."*

Why Music?
The first and most important question to ask yourself is: Why do you want to major in music in college?

Music is a *very* challenging major, typically much more demanding and requiring more discipline than most other academic majors. Quite often high school students have no way of knowing or even anticipating the demands placed on the college music major.

Pianists are expected to practice an average of two to four hours a day, *every* day—and this is typically more than they averaged in high school. Singers are required to learn and memorize songs and practice daily on their repertoire and vocal technique. And everyone is required to develop keyboard skills. You cannot avoid this, and you will not graduate until you achieve piano proficiency. So, start now and get used to practicing daily.

Many people decide to audition to be a music major in college because band or choir or orchestra was the most fun class in high school and because they enjoyed participating in the high school musicals and stage productions. These are not really good reasons to select music as a major in college. I tell prospective students: "You do not pick music—music picks *you!*" So, choose music as a major only if you *have* to do it and you cannot imagine doing anything else.

Major or Minor?

When I talk to students who are considering possible majors in college, I advise them: If you love anything else as much as you love music, do *that*—because the music major requires a special set of skills and abilities. You can always keep music as a vital and important part of your life by participating in vocal and instrumental ensembles in college, or in church choir, community theater, or community bands, choirs and orchestras. You might also consider *minoring* in music. If this is the case, choose a college that accepts and includes non-music majors in their ensembles.

I can recall many instances when non-music majors in one of my ensembles were in fact *better and more talented* than many of the participating music majors. In other words, the students *could* have easily majored in music (based on talent and ability), but instead chose to pursue another major in college, such as business, engineering or pre-med, because their career aspirations were different. These students are also often the most passionate and spirited ensemble members, since they are participating because they *love* to, not because they *have* to!

At some universities, non-music majors and music minors can register for regular music major classes or other general offerings such as jazz appreciation, the history of rock or live music appreciation classes. Check the catalog of course offerings and availabilities at the schools that you are considering.

Remember that once you are in college, you are allowed to *change* your major, to or from music, or you can become a music minor, or you can even *double* major in music and something else. You are not signing a contract for the rest of your life when you enter college and declare a major. It is quite common for students to change majors—even several times—in the course of their academic pursuits.

There are a multitude of career options, and there are no right or wrong choices. You should select a major that you really *want* to study and that *you* enjoy, and then work extremely hard in that major. Keep in mind that certain majors can lead to more lucrative jobs than others, and that typically jobs in music or the arts or education do not pay as well as jobs in the business world, in medicine or in law. Therefore you must also think about and consider what kind of lifestyle you might like, and how important that is to you. As I tell prospective students, fast-food restaurants are always hiring, so you can always find work! I encourage you to find the career that you love, and find a "job" at which you enjoy

> ... you have to have a great *Wow Factor* in order to compete for the best jobs or roles.

putting in many hours of "work." Remember that there are no guarantees in a performance degree (music or musical theater), so that is why you have to have a *great* **Wow Factor** in order to compete for the best jobs or roles.

Plan ahead

The junior year in high school is an excellent time for fact-finding and exploratory searches. Published guides contain excellent information about the college application process, as well as listings of colleges and universities, with specifics on size, location, offerings, curriculum and scholarships. For more specific information, visit the Web sites of the colleges that you are considering. Some factors that may help you in making an informed decision include:

- Size of the university
- Location of the university
- Size of the School of Music
- Choice of majors

Once you have narrowed down your list to three to five schools, I suggest making an unofficial visit to the campus on a regular class day (as opposed to during the summer) so that you can get an accurate impression of campus life. Even if you must make some sacrifices to take this trip, it is important to get a visceral feeling for the institution, and you can gather only so much virtual information from a Web site, e-mail communications and the advice of others. Especially if the campus is far away from your home, you need to know what it feels like to travel to the school and to know (in reality) how far you would be from your hometown, and if that is important to you.

If you plan in advance, you should be able to schedule a campus tour, plus meet with someone in music admissions, visit classes and ensemble rehearsals, and perhaps even meet with the prospective faculty in your area of interest.

Important Questions to Consider When Choosing a School

In addition to determining answers to the questions posed previously, honest, thoughtful and thorough answers to the following questions may help you in narrowing your choices, and also serve as a way to compare the schools you are considering. Remember: There is no "right" or wrong" answer to any of these questions. They are simply a guideline to assist you in determining what is important to *you* and therefore "right" for you.

Enrollment and Acceptance Rates

- How many people audition for the music program annually?
- How many are accepted?
- What is the number of undergraduate versus graduate-student enrollment? Does the school cater more to undergraduate or graduate students?

Faculty and Access

- Who is on the faculty and who would be your primary teacher(s)?
- How often would you have a private lesson?
- How much access to the faculty would you have on a regular basis?

Facilities

- What facilities exist? Rehearsal and performance spaces? Practice rooms? Technology? Computer labs? Recording studio? What is their condition?

Location and Size

- Is it an urban or rural campus located in a big city or small town?
- Is it a more "traditional" campus, with football stadium and marching band, and a wide variety of curricula, majors and extracurricular activities, or more of a unidimensional school such as a technical school or a music conservatory?

Reputation and Mastery

- What is the reputation of the college, and perhaps more importantly the reputation of the music/theater departments?
- What are the performance opportunities for you as a soloist?
- How do the ensembles sound? Have you heard the bands, choirs and orchestras, or attended a production? Would you be able to participate in those ensembles?
- Are there local, national and international travel and touring opportunities for ensembles and productions?
- Are there scheduled master classes and guest artist concerts and clinics, and what opportunity would you have to participate?

The Students

- What do you know about the other students in the program? Make sure you are aware of their musical abilities and personalities. These are the people that you will likely be surrounded by for the next few years—musically, intellectually and socially.

> These are the people that you will likely be surrounded by for the next few years—musically, intellectually and socially.

Progress Assessments

- What are the jury requirements? How often do the faculty listen to you perform in a jury? This important process allows faculty the opportunity to assess each student's progress and offer suggestions for improvements.

Placement After Graduation

- What is the graduate/placement rate?
- What are alumni doing in the professional music world? Ask for a list of specific players and singers and their accomplishments.

Your Preparation

The suggestions below indicate how you can best prepare during the high school years. The advice provided describes two things: first, an ideal set of knowledge and skills goals for college-level applicants; second, competencies needed by musicians as they practice the various aspects of the profession in college and beyond. In brief, you should prepare as much as you can as early as you can.

1) *Take Responsibility for Your Own Development*

Each musician brings a unique set of talents, aspirations, and abilities to an audition. The audition process encompasses your preparation, your presentation, your performance and your production. Although you are in school and probably studying with a private teacher, you are in control of the decisions you make on how you spend your "free" time. Your preparation should be multidimensional and not restricted to the mastering of your performance medium. Whatever you intend to do in music, practice it as much as possible. This applies not only to your instrument and/or voice, but also to other types of musical work. For example, composers should practice composing, prospective teachers should try to observe and gain teaching experiences under appropriate supervision, those interested in music scholarship or criticism should practice writing and speaking on musical topics, and those interested in music therapy should shadow a professional therapist in order to get a realistic impression of the profession. Several factors will determine your acceptance to an undergraduate music program, but *you* are responsible for your choices about how you use your time to prepare for your future.

2) *Master Your Performance Ability*

Performance ability is essential for all musicians. You should be an outstanding performer on at least one instrument or with your voice, regardless of whether you intend to have a performance career. Keyboard skills are essential for all music majors. Students with well-developed keyboard skills have a head start as music majors. Membership in large and small ensembles develops different kinds of musical skills. Developing ensemble skills comes primarily through practice, participation and performance.

3) *Understand Theory and Train Your Ears*

Be able to read both treble and bass clefs and know all key signatures, interval qualities, triad qualities, the major and minor scales, and how to write basic notation. Knowledge of musical terms and usage is important. Train your ear by taking courses or studies in musicianship that include sight-singing, ear-training, sight-reading, rhythmic and harmonic dictation, and so forth. Developing the ear is a lifetime job. The earlier this work is started, the better.

4) Listen, Listen, Listen

You need to be familiar with far more music than that which you perform. Be familiar with as much music from as many historical periods and cultural sources as possible. Ask your teachers to recommend a listening list for you that covers the various solo, small- and large-ensemble repertoire in your performance area. Make sure that you have heard the major works of all types in the particular area of music that interests you. If possible, follow the score as you listen.

> Developing the ear is a lifetime job. The earlier this work is started, the better.

5) Learn How Music Works

Take opportunities to learn the basics of musical structure, including studies in such areas as form, harmony, counterpoint, composition and improvisation. Like so many other aspects of music, this knowledge will continue to develop throughout your lifetime. Those who get started early have an advantage. Work with your music teachers, enroll in an AP music course if one is available in your high school, take classes at your community music school, and otherwise explore opportunities to gain initial acquaintance with this material.

6) Become a Proficient Sight Reader

For many students, one of the least favorite and most dreaded audition requirements is a sight-reading test. Remember: *Sight-reading is a skill, not a talent!* One does not have to have amazing musical abilities to have great sight-reading abilities. It simply comes down to *how much* you read. Owning great reading skills is a guaranteed **Wow Factor** in virtually *any* audition, but especially for college music schools. It is also *imperative* for future professional gigs (road shows and Broadway tours with one rehearsal), commercials and jingles and studio sessions with no rehearsals. In recording studio sessions you are *expected* to get it right in the first read-through, and then perform/ record it the second time through. And if you do not have the reading skills, don't even *think* about taking the gig, because you will not work for those people again.

I have found a wonderful analogy to compare sight-reading skills to reading the English language. You were not born either speaking or reading English. You most likely learned to speak the language first (even before school and studying grammar) simply by listening and imitating. You may have also learned reading fundamentals prior to attending kindergarten. However, in school you were taught to read, then were given books and asked to read every day. This daily reading habit has probably continued throughout your life, whether your reading now consists of academic books, magazines, the newspaper, Internet searches, or even a novel for pleasure—most likely a day does not pass that you don't spend at least a few minutes reading.

> Remember: Sight-reading is a skill, not a talent!

Can you imagine how well-developed your music reading abilities would be if you spent even one-half the time that you spend reading English, reading music?

What's more, there are 26 letters in the English alphabet, and only 12 different notes in the chromatic scale! So learning to read music is in fact much less complicated than reading English. Imagine how accomplished you could be with just a bit of effort and regular practice.

I will often give a new student an excerpt of printed literature to read out loud to me—from any source, a book, magazine, whatever I can get my hands on, as long as I know the student has not seen the words before. I ask the student to read out loud, and almost invariably he or she "sight-reads" the words perfectly, and I even comprehend what is said! The same standard must hold true for musical sight-reading—make it great the first time.

Tips on practicing sight-reading

- Practice sight–reading for five minutes every day. Notice I did not suggest 15 minutes or two hours a day—just five minutes!

- Find examples of new music that you don't know. These can be found in sight-reading method books, but also, for example, in Bach chorales. Read the soprano line first, then the alto, then tenor, then bass. Men should be able to read both treble and bass clef.

- Look at the music first and notice as much as you can, from the most obvious—notes, rhythms, key signature and time signature—to intervallic relationships, and try to anticipate big interval leaps.

- Try to use your *musical* intellect. Is there a key signature? If so, what key is it in? Look at the first and last notes for clues. Remember: the melody could be in major *or* minor!

- Is the composer's name printed anywhere? Bach will most likely have a different sound (and note expectations) than Bartok!

- Find secondary information: tempo indicators (allegro versus largo and metronome markings), articulation (phrasing, accents, staccato versus legato), and dynamics, including crescendos and decrescendos.

- If you are a singer, ask for a starting pitch. If you are asked what you would like to hear to get started, ask for the starting specific pitch, plus perhaps a triad in the key of the piece (if you know it!). This, of course, calls into question your knowledge of basic music theory (all key signatures, time signatures, note values, etc.), as this is something that you need to have—and, if you want to be a music major in college, this is *basic* information that will be required—so you might as well get started on it now! Again, it will help if you develop functional keyboard skills—including playing scales in all 12 keys, chord patterns, and be able to play and harmonize a simple melody (like "Happy Birthday") using I, IV and V chords.

- Start and then keep your eyes moving to the right. Establish a tempo and keep it constant. If you are in 4/4 time, put 4 beats in a measure and then play or sing the downbeat of the next bar at the appropriate time. Do not stop and/or try to correct yourself. Keep going, even if you think you are not doing well. The point of sight-reading is to do your best and get as much of the music right the first time through.

> Keep going, even if you think you are not doing well.

7) Learn to Speak and Write English Fluently and Effectively

As a musician, you will communicate in music, but you will also rely heavily on your ability to communicate in words. Many music-related activities—from rehearsals to teaching, to writing grant proposals, to negotiating, to promoting your musical interests—rely on fluent English skills. Focus attention on learning to speak and write effectively. If English is your second language, you will most likely have to pass a reading and writing proficiency exam prior to your admission into the college or university of your choice.

8) Study Foreign Languages

Musicians practice their art internationally. You are likely to perform music with texts in foreign languages, and to work with musicians from all over the world. Significant musical writings are in foreign languages. If you seek advanced degrees in music, reading fluency in one or more foreign languages is often required. Since foreign languages are difficult for many people, you should begin acquiring knowledge and skills in at least one foreign language as early as possible. Consult with your music teacher about which languages are best for you.

9) Get a Comprehensive High School Education

Music both influences and is influenced by other fields of study: the humanities, mathematics, the sciences, the social sciences, and the other arts—architecture, dance, film, literature, drama and the visual arts. For entrance into college-level study, you are encouraged to gain a basic overview of ancient and modern history, the basic thought processes and procedures of math and science, and familiarity with works in as many of the other arts disciplines as possible.

The best musicians continue to learn throughout their lives. They are constantly studying and thinking, always connecting what they know about music with their knowledge of other fields. Since you never know the direction your career will take, it is wise to spend your high school years gaining the basic ability to understand and work in a variety of fields beyond music. Keep music at the center of your efforts, but take every opportunity to gain the kind of knowledge and skills in other areas that will support both formal studies at the college level and your music career beyond.

After graduation

After you graduate from college, you have myriad career options (depending on your major and your earned degree), including:

Music Education. Teach at the elementary, middle school and/or high school level.

Music Therapy. After an internship, find a multitude of opportunities in the therapy profession, including working with developmentally disabled children and adults, neonatal to hospice and everyone in-between.

Musical Theater. Locate yourself in a professional situation that has numerous audition opportunities and hope that your hard work will have the big payoff!

Music Performance. Depending on your discipline (vocal, instrumental, classical or jazz), the typical options include applying to graduate schools to continue musical growth and development (earning a master's degree and possibly a doctorate), or locating in a place where you can audition, perform, set up a teaching studio and offer private lessons, or any combination of all of the above.

Music Business. A combination of the study of music and business, including arts management. In any case, it is advisable for a student in any of the fields listed above to acquire as much knowledge as possible about the business of music, including negotiating contracts, professional expectations, publishing, recording, fees, taxes, etc.

Other career paths in music include **Composition and Arranging, Conducting, Musicology, Recording and Studio Work, Film, Television and Multimedia applications**, and last but certainly not least, **Teaching at the College Level**, although this usually requires earning a master's degree, minimally, and most likely a doctorate.

HOW TO PREPARE FOR A MUSICAL THEATER AUDITION

An audition for acceptance into a college musical theater program, theme park, cruise ship or Broadway production is usually separate and distinct from a pure music audition; however, the preparation procedures and the processes are usually quite similar. Preparation for admission into a college musical theater program (with the intention of majoring in musical theater) should begin years before the audition date. A prospective musical theater student will be evaluated primarily on his or her ability to sing, act and dance. As in the college music audition, other factors may be included in the final decision process, including academic transcripts and test scores, keyboard and music theory skills, resumé and experience, preparation, professionalism and attitude.

A prospective musical theater student will be evaluated primarily on his or her ability to sing, act and dance.

Vocal Audition: 16 bars

Typically you will be asked to prepare only 16 measures of two contrasting (in rhythm, mood, character, and style) selections from standard Broadway literature. Most songs are longer than 16 measures, therefore it is important that you find the *best* 16 bars for your voice in each song. You will most likely be required to work with a collaborative pianist provided. Typically, singing *a cappella*, with a prerecorded accompaniment or with your own accompanist will not be permitted. Therefore you must have written accompaniments (no lead sheets), clearly marked and in the correct key. Make sure the score is clean and easy to read. Mounting the music in a three-ring binder may make page turns easier for the accompanist. Do not expect the accompanist to transpose your pieces.

Monologue: Acting!

You should be prepared to deliver one or two memorized solo monologues, usually one minute in length. Your selections should be age-appropriate and avoid dialects. Try to find material that you can understand and relate to. Be prepared to discuss and answer questions regarding your selected material, including the source of your monologue. Monologues that include some comedy, action and physicality are always welcomed, but above all, *demonstrate good taste.*

The Dance

Your dance audition will most likely consist of a combination from a Broadway musical that you will be taught on the spot, therefore there is no way to prepare for your specific audition. However, years of ballet, jazz and tap lessons will undoubtedly give you the technique and experience that will help you succeed and "*wow.*" If you are interested in musical theater as a major in college and have never had any formal dance training, start now!

You should bring "standard" dance attire to your audition. Make sure that your clothes are comfortable and allow for ease of movement.

Women should bring leotards, tights, dance skirts, leg warmers, and character or jazz shoes or ballet slippers.

Men should have tights, jazz pants or shorts, T-shirts, dance belt, and ballet or jazz shoes.

Heavy sweatpants and sweatshirts, tennis shoes and/or bare feet are not encouraged and may not be acceptable.

What The Panel Is Looking For

In a musical theater audition, the panel is typically evaluating two aspects of the performer:

1) Who you are

2) What you can do

In the first category, they will want to see your personality, how you present yourself, your appearance, your strengths, your passion and desire, and your commitment to the arts.

The second category will evaluate your musical, acting and dance skills, your physical presence, your talent, your intellect and your emotional range.

A number of technical elements will be evaluated.

Voice: Pitch, range, rhythmic sense, vocal quality and health, articulation, diction, style.

Physical: Posture, use of hands and arms, poise, freedom and ease of movement, energy, commitment. In addition, you will be evaluated on how quickly you learn and how well you execute the dance combination.

Communication: How do you relate to the audience? Can you identify with the subject of your song and/or monologue? Do you understand the text? Can you demonstrate emotional range and share those feelings with the evaluators?

Tips

- Arrive early.
- Be prepared to wait. Bring a water bottle, snacks and things to occupy your time (books, iPod) while others are auditioning. Use your free time to get settled and focused before you walk into your audition.
- Make sure you thoroughly warm up your voice and your body prior to your vocal and dance audition.
- Audition with confidence, enthusiasm and positive energy! Be polite and remember to use good manners.
- Be yourself, and be supportive of others.
- Dress conservatively. Class, elegance, professionalism and comfort win over trashy and trendy.
- Practice your vocal solos and monologues in advance of your audition on stages and in rooms of different sizes.

- Some of the moves in the dance combination may provide a challenge for you. Remember to keep trying and never give up. Sometimes energy, facial expression, enthusiasm and attitude can compensate for a lack of technical dance skills.

- When selecting your audition repertoire, keep in mind that a "good song" is not necessarily a good song for *you*. Remember, it's *you* who are auditioning, not the song!

- Perform your musical selections and monologues for teachers and coaches prior to your audition, and get honest, objective input.

- Even though auditions can be stressful and nerve-racking, they don't *have* to be.

- View your audition as a wonderful opportunity to perform and share your talents and abilities with a new (albeit small) audience. Have fun and enjoy the experience.

- Remember that an important part of your audition is how you handle yourself when you're not the center of attention. Don't be loud distracting or attract unnecessary attention unto yourself.

- Directors and the audition panel want to see you succeed and do your best. They want to see you act naturally—and remember, acting naturally in an audition is a craft. It takes lots of practice and hard work to act naturally!

- You will likely not win every audition you enter, no matter how good you are. Remember, you didn't have the part or make the cast to begin with, so you have lost nothing. Don't take it personally. There will be more auditions in your future.

> It takes lots of practice and hard work to act naturally!

FOR EVERYONE—MEET YOUR DEADLINES!

Once you have decided on the schools where you will apply, know all important dates and deadlines, and submit your application materials well before those deadlines. I suggest organizing a separate audition file for each college and maintaining a special "deadline" calendar to make sure you submit all applications for admissions, auditions and scholarships in a timely fashion.

Keep in mind that most colleges and universities require *two separate applications*: one for general admission to the university (based on your academic record) and another that is your audition for acceptance into the music program. Regarding your academic achievements, I encourage you to earn the best possible grades in all of your academic classes and tests in high school, as this is the objective criteria upon which universities base their admission decisions. Your grades are part of your permanent record, and they can—and will—be used as a factor in determining your admission status (and possible academic scholarships!). Your grades can also be interpreted as an indication of your academic discipline and your work ethic. It would be disappointing to be admitted to an excellent music program based on your audition, and then to be denied admission to that university based on your academic record. The moral of this lecture: Earn good grades!

Most schools have designated "New Student Audition Days" for potential incoming music students, and I suggest attending one of those dates for a live audition if possible. You will most likely be sent more printed materials than you care to read. Nonetheless, I encourage you to read everything carefully, especially with a consideration for specific audition requirements, expectations and deadlines.

If you are unable to make an on-site audition, you will most likely need to record a CD or DVD of your audition material. Here are some points to consider:

- Make sure the quality of the recording is high (professional grade from a studio would be ideal).

- Make sure that your recording contains an honest and accurate representation of you and your abilities; i.e., don't use edits or studio tricks to create a product that you cannot re-create in a live setting.

- Don't exaggerate or inflate the truth on your resumé—it will only get you in trouble!

- If you are performing on DVD, practice a spoken intro, such as "Hi, my name is _____ and the first piece I will be performing is _____ by _____." Write your introduction and memorize your lines until you can deliver them naturally.

- Make sure you know the proper pronunciation of all titles and composers' names!

- Look directly into the camera and smile. This is your "first impression" opportunity on video, and you will be judged not only by your musicianship, but also by your appearance and your ability to express yourself verbally.

- Make sure you check and play your recording for audio and video quality before sending it in.

THE BOTTOM LINE: WHAT WILL IT COST?

The fact is, higher education comes at a price. Colleges and universities are becoming more and more dependent upon generating income from tuition as a primary funding source. Prospective students and parents should explore any and all options for financial aid and scholarships before making a final decision on which school to attend. Here are some of my thoughts on finances and higher education:

- First, plan ahead. Meet all deadlines for applications, as this may affect your eligibility for scholarship consideration.

- Thoroughly research all possible sources for financial assistance. The university may offer academic scholarships based on grades and test scores. These can be independent of and in addition to any music or fine arts talent-based scholarships. *Earn good grades!*

- Parents and students should fill out a Free Application for Federal Student Aid (FAFSA) form. This will help determine if you qualify for student loans or work-study programs.

- Investigate any scholarships that are offered in your hometown and sponsored by civic organizations, including community foundations, music clubs, or service organizations like Rotary or Kiwanis.

- If you are a nonresident applying to a state school, see if there are programs to lower the non-resident tuition fees.

After you have been notified of your acceptance at the institutions of your choice, determine the annual cost of attending. Your total expenses will include tuition, room and board, books, fees, supplies, travel and personal expenses. Every college and university has a different rate for tuition and expenses. Subtract any and all sources of financial aid and you will then have an idea of your annual expenses.

Make sure you determine the bottom line: What is your final cost per year?

Here is a scenario:

School "A" offers you a $20,000 annual scholarship, and you are quite flattered and excited.

School "B" offers you a $1,000 annual scholarship, and you think: "In comparison, they must not like me or want me very much."

There may be more to consider than the size of your award. In this case, School "A" costs $50,000 a year to attend, so, after your large scholarship your net cost (bottom line) is still $30,000. School "B" costs $10,000 a year to attend, so your net cost is only $9,000. Additionally, School "B" has a better reputation, a stronger faculty, and a higher rate of student alumni successes. If everything else is equal, which school would you select? Of course, School "B"! Even though the scholarship was not as big, the bottom line is that the school accepted you as a student and you will probably get a better education for *less* money at School "B."

Dollars and Sense

The final determination as to where you pursue your higher education should be based on several factors, and not be limited only to cost. At some point you will need to make a decision based on *all* of that input, plus your own impressions of the program and the school.

If you have done your homework and answered the "Important Questions to Consider" listed earlier in this chapter, then you might have a clearer idea of the best school for you. Remember that some of the more important factors include location and size of the school, depth and reputation of the department, faculty and access to the faculty, performance, rehearsal and practice facilities, technology, quality of ensembles, touring and performance opportunities.

One more essential ingredient that may help influence your decision is to find opportunities to meet other students currently enrolled in the school. When prospective students visit my campus, I like to introduce them to my students, and then I leave the room. I encourage the prospective students to ask questions such as, "What do you like about the school? What *don't* you like? Are you glad you are here and are your professional aspirations being met? Why or why not?" I find that current students will give honest answers, and their responses can be extremely enlightening to a prospective student. Also try to get an accurate impression of these students. Are they nice? Did they have an "attitude," or are there any negatives? Chances are these are the people you will be spending time with in a year—so choose wisely.

There is no substitute for meeting people "live" and in person. You will definitely develop an opinion or "vibe" about the schools that you are considering after your visit, meeting people and finding the answers to my questions. You should listen carefully to your inner voice and "vibe." Your parents and teachers may try to influence you in a specific direction or toward a certain campus or professor. I'm sure that their motivations are honest, sincere and valid, and that they have good reasons for their opinions. But the fact remains, the ultimate decision should be *yours* and not theirs. Your mentors and loved ones can all agree that you should go to School X and study with Professor Y, but if, for any reason, you do not feel a spark or a connection, then it is possible that school is not the right one for *you*, despite the best intentions and advice of others. Remember there are no "rights" or "wrongs" about this decision. You may simply have to trust your "vibe"!

Finally, remember that when you make your decision and commit to attending a school, you are really committing to only one semester, not four years of study. Although I hope your decision is the right one for you, if at any time you feel as though you are not happy or not

> The college experience is a special time in your life where growth, change, new experiences and opportunities all occur simultaneously.

challenged, you are allowed to change your mind. The college experience is a special time in your life where growth, change, new experiences and opportunities all occur simultaneously. If the major you selected is no longer the right one for you, change it. If the university is not what you had envisioned, transfer to another school. Most importantly, enjoy every minute of your college career. Work hard, have fun, and of course, keep developing your individual *Wow Factor!*

IN CONCLUSION

Are auditions:

a) Daunting?

b) Nerve-racking?

c) Exasperating?

d) Frustrating?

e) Fun?

f) Necessary?

g) Scary?

h) Stressful?

i) Difficult?

     j) Suspenseful?

     k) Educational?

     l) Required?

     m) All of the above?

The correct answer: Yes and/or no to any and all of the above! It all depends on your attitude, preparation, talents, abilities, timing and perhaps a little bit of luck. What is important for you to understand is that if you have an interest in performing, the audition is *inevitable and unavoidable*. And the sooner you understand and comprehend this crucial fact, the sooner you will be able to determine what you truly want and how hard you are willing to work to attain it. Remember, the more you do it, the easier it becomes, so get out there and "*wow*" them!

CHAPTER FOUR

IFs, ANDs OR BUTs—
AND RULES TO LIVE BY

"Be personable, positive and enthusiastic. In many situations, the abilities of those auditioning might not be markedly different, and it comes down to this: Which person seems to be the most enjoyable to work with?"
—*Gary Fry*

"Honesty and sincerity cannot be manufactured— audiences pick up on fakes very quickly." —*Diana Spradling*

● ● ●

In many ways, I believe this chapter offers some of the most essential ideas on how to "*wow*" the people with whom you would like to associate. These concepts have a very specific application to the professional music world and can be applied to all aspects of your life, regardless of your age or profession.

I am convinced that teaching music is only a small part of my professional life. I am truly fortunate to perform as a pianist, to write music that people sing and play, and to receive invitations to appear as a guest conductor and clinician throughout the world. Although all three of my earned college degrees are in music performance—not music education—I have been passionate about teaching and education throughout my career. Essentially, I think of what I do as teaching people *through* music, rather than simply teaching people music.

It is crucial for a professional musician to develop certain basic musical skills, abilities and competencies, and to have a cadre of facts, knowledge and statistics immediately at hand.

Those competencies include:

- the technical ability to sing or play an instrument at a high level of accomplishment.
- an understanding and functional/practical knowledge of basic music theory.
- functional keyboard abilities.
- an understanding and knowledge of the history and traditions of the musician's preferred sphere of musical activity, be it choral, instrumental, vocal, classical, jazz, musical theater, composition, arranging, music therapy, or even pop and rock.

Of course, these skills take years of disciplined study and practice to develop, but, at their core, they simply represent technical skills and factual knowledge. With a bit of discipline, hard work and effort, virtually *anyone* can develop those skills over time. As a matter of fact, we will now take a giant leap of faith and *assume* that you have already developed your technical skills and abilities. For example, as a pianist, you can play scales and arpeggios in all keys, you are a fluent sight reader, you have developed your abilities to musically collaborate and improvise, you can harmonize and transpose, and you have a wide, varied and expansive repertoire of memorized pieces. Congratulations! This is quite an impressive accomplishment that represents years of study and practice.

But do these skills and abilities alone qualify you for the gig? Or are other **Wow Factors** necessary and vital to guarantee your success? I think another entire set of skills is an essential part of your total package. And these other factors have *nothing* to do with music, and *everything* to do with your employability. I am referring to the *personal* skills that you must develop to accompany your musical talents and to increase *your* individual **Wow Factor.**

One of the biggest compliments that can be bestowed upon a child is that he or she "plays well with others." This, of course, means that the child's socialization skills are developing well and are appropriate for the age group. I like this phrase because it can serve as a wonderful metaphor when used to describe a musician. It applies to musical skills (a play on the word "play") as well as personal and social skills. A person with "*wow*" must "play well" musically, and also (and more importantly) "play well" personally. Quite simply, it is crucial that you develop a set of personal skills that will match (or even exceed) your musical skills.

As students, teachers, colleagues, friends, employers, employees, children and parents, we are continually being evaluated and judged on our actions, reactions, interactions, decisions, competencies, attitudes and abilities. Whether we like it or not, we each develop a professional and personal reputation based on the judgments and opinions of others. Therefore, an important question that you must ask yourself is: "What do I want other people to say about me?" It is essential to project a positive persona that communicates well—both written and verbally. While it is impossible to please everyone, it is a worthy goal to attempt to earn other people's respect through your *actions*, in

> ...it is crucial that you develop a set of personal skills that will match (or even exceed) your musical skills.

addition to your words. We have all heard that talk is cheap and that actions speak much louder than words, and this is certainly true in developing your reputation.

Ifs, Ands and Buts

As a professor of music (and one who teaches primarily college students), I have learned that I must keep things simple! Therefore, for the sake of this discussion, we will divide the world into three groups of people: *Ifs*, *Ands* and *Buts*. Your objective, as a performer and as a human being, is to be referred to as an *And* and not an *If* nor a *But*. Keep reminding yourself: "What am I going to do?" and "How am I going to act?" The words "act" and "do" are action verbs; therefore, they require some sort of action. I hope all of your actions, reactions to and interactions with other people will be positive, thereby causing people to think of you as an *And*.

What are *Ands*? *Ands* are people who are accomplished, in every sense of the word. As musicians, they have worked long and tirelessly and with a sense of discipline to develop the necessary skills and abilities to "play well with others," and to function professionally in all of the areas of music and arenas of performance in which they hope to participate.

Once they have achieved a level of musical competence that allows them to compete favorably for gigs and in auditions and interviews, a variety of other components will help determine whether they are the people that others would like to "play with."

For example, an accomplished singer would have a varied repertoire of songs that demonstrate a wide variety of styles and tempos. With a repertoire that includes jazz, pop, or Broadway standards, the singer should

1) memorize the original melody and lyrics of every song, and sing each with proper technique, appropriate style and good intonation.

2) know the composer and lyricist, when the song was composed and for what event.

3) know his or her preferred key.

4) have clearly written and legible charts or lead sheets in the preferred key that can be given to other musicians.

5) know the form of the tune and be able to explain to collaborative musicians exactly how the arrangement goes.

6) be able to "count off" or confidently indicate to the accompanist the preferred tempo.

7) memorize the chord changes of the song, thereby reinforcing the singer's knowledge of harmonic structure.

8) be able to accompany oneself at the piano, even if only with a basic chordal accompaniment.

9) know basic music theory, including all keys and key signatures.

10) have well-developed, functional keyboard skills.

Having command of, or "owning," the above **10 (Vocal) Musical Commandments** will place most singers in an elite category of competence that will cause employers, producers, directors, and other collaborative musicians to *want* to have a musical association with you. And that, of course, should be one of your primary goals. Your other primary goal is to be thought of as an ***And***! When other people talk about you, what will they say? If you have earned the ***Wow Factor***, people will praise your technical and musical accomplishments. They will talk about and admire your total ownership of the 10 commandments (above). *And* there are all of the other, equally important add-ons (or ***Ands***). These have *nothing* to do with music, and *everything* to do with your employability and professional success. Therefore you would like for them to say, "She totally owns the 10 commandments…

1) "***And*** she's always on time.

2) "***And*** she is so much fun to work with.

3) "***And*** she has such a terrific attitude.

4) "***And*** she's a real 'pro' in every sense of the word.

5) "***And*** she's so reliable and responsible.

6) "*And* she's thoughtful and considerate.

7) "*And* she's so helpful and cooperative, a real team player.

8) "*And* she's also great when we are not rehearsing, like at mealtime.

9) "*And* she is always so grateful and gracious.

10) "*And* she is mature."

These are just a few examples of the things others should be saying about you. What are some other *Ands* that can be added to your list? Can you think of anyone you know who is an *And*? Being known as an *And* is something that we should all strive for, and is a crucial ingredient to the *Wow Factor* recipe.

What is an *If*? An *If* is someone who may be best described as a work in progress. He or she may have developed a good work ethic and may live by several of the commandments but has not yet reached the exalted status of a complete *And*. Sometimes *Ifs* are inclined to make excuses, such as:

1) "*If* only you had heard me sing this in the practice room yesterday—I nailed it.

2) "*If* only I could wear my favorite outfit.

3) "*If* I didn't have to wake up so early."

Or, what others might be saying:

1) "*If* only he would pitch in and help move equipment at the end of the gig.

2) "*If* only he had a few more memorized songs in his repertoire.

3) "*If* only he was more comfortable meeting and greeting new people."

The good news is that being an *If* is not a hopeless cause. *If* you are able to determine what your *If* behaviors are, you can make an effort to correct or alleviate them, and turn them into *Ands*!

What is a *But*? A *But* is essentially the personal polar opposite of an *And*. A *But* is a person who may have successfully earned and achieved the 10 Musical Commandments, however, "but" is the word that an observer would use as a qualifier when describing that person. For example: "He totally owns the 10 Commandments,

1) "*But* he's always late for rehearsal.

2) "*But* he never practices the music we are working on.

3) "*But* he talks negatively about others behind their backs.

4) "*But* he's always whining and complaining.

5) "*But* he has a problem with personal hygiene.

6) "*But* his personality is so dark.

7) "*But* he simply has a bad attitude about everything.

8) "*But* he's selfish.

9) "*But* he acts like a know-it-all.

10) "*But* he thinks he is better than everyone else."

You may be the best singer or instrumentalist in your city, but if you have one or more **Buts** attached to your name, I can assure you that prospective employers will seek out the second-best singer in the city who has the reputation of being an **And**—and the **And** will get the gig. Simply put, don't be a **But**.

Old-Fashioned Rules to Live By

Like the great American standard song "I'm Old Fashioned" (music and lyrics by Jerome Kern and Johnny Mercer), I proudly hold on to "old school" values that I believe are vitally important to teach and instill in my students. To my way of thinking, these values are obvious and essential, yet I am continually amazed at how often they are lacking or totally missing as a basic skill set among some students. Once embraced, these values can go a long way toward increasing your *Wow Factor*.

These values include:

1) Showing respect for elders in both language and gesture. By virtue of their age, experience and relationship to you, your parents, grandparents, employers and community leaders deserve your respect, at least until/unless they behave in a manner that is not worthy of respect.

2.) Showing respect for teachers and professors. Naturally, students will like some teachers better than others, and relate to some better than others, but by definition, the teacher has educational concepts to offer. It is the "job" of the students to show up for class, to do all homework assignments to the best of their abilities and to ensure that the work is turned in on time (or early!).

Even in the subjects you don't care for, you as a student should always do your best. If a class is required and if you do not earn a passing grade, it is a certainty that you will take that course *again*. So an important question to ask yourself is, "How many times do I want to take this course?" I would hope that the answer to this question is "one." You should choose to give your best effort, *especially* if it is a subject that is not a favorite. So, if the class (or subject matter or teacher) is one that you dislike for whatever reason, then it should be your *obligation* to *work really hard* in that class, do well and earn a great grade.

By doing so, you will teach yourself an important life lesson. There *will* be times in other areas of your life when you will not feel like completing a task, but you will still have the *obligation* to do it, whether you like it or not. In this way, you learn about the importance of responsibility and maturity, and prove to yourself that you *can* be successful, even when you might not *feel* like it. And, who knows, maybe you will end up *liking* the subject matter and discovering a new area of interest—thus ultimately benefiting even more than you might have previously imagined.

3.) Using appropriate speech and good grammar. Perhaps this is a pet peeve of mine, but I think a student needs to use two types of speech. One is the street speech or "slang" used to communicate with friends in an informal, social way. However, the other is the more formal speech that must be used when communicating with adults, teachers and professionals—especially in an interview situation, when first impressions *do* matter. There is no substitute for articulate, coherent speech and an ability to communicate effectively, clearly and concisely. I can assure you that it creates a wonderful and positive impression.

> There is no substitute for articulate, coherent speech and an ability to communicate effectively, clearly and concisely.

Here are some of my speech pattern pet peeves and personal prejudices:

Never begin a sentence (especially in response to a question) with the word (or sound) "um" or "uh." Think before you speak, and choose your words well. If you consciously observe people's speech patterns, you may be surprised at how many are guilty of this unnecessary habit. I am on a crusade to eliminate "excess verbiage"—for the teacher or director in rehearsal, and for the student's style of verbal communication. Further examples of excess verbiage found in everyday speech include "you know"—typically needlessly interjected in mid-sentence—and the ubiquitous "and he was like" instead of "and he *said*." I like the word "like," particularly when it is used in its appropriate context. Formal speech uses words like "awesome" only occasionally, and only in the original concept of the word—just like "like"!

4) Using good manners. Be polite, cordial and thoughtful, and always remember to say "please" and "thank you."

5) Avoiding gossip. When talking about or referring to someone else, please consider speaking "on the record" (a term used by journalists meaning that you are personally accountable for everything you say and are willing to be recorded, quoted and credited with whatever you have said). I make it my personal and professional policy to be "on the record" whenever I speak about or refer to another person, whether that person can hear what I am saying at the time or not. When talking about another person, I would be comfortable having that person hear exactly what I am saying, exactly as I am expressing it. If you resort to "trash talking" and "backstabbing" (i.e., speaking negatively about someone in an effort to demean, slander or impugn that person's stature or reputation), the odds are that your words will come back to haunt you and that you will regret having needlessly spoken negatively of another person. A good mantra, when referring to another person, is simply to be willing to say only what you would say directly to that person's face.

Also, make sure your facial expressions and *tone* of voice accurately reflect what you are trying to communicate. For example, if you combine a compliment such as "I really like your hair" with peculiar facial expression and/or odd tone of voice, you can give a mixed signal to the person you are addressing. The person may think you are insincere and/or sarcastic, or will have no idea *what* to think.

Either way, you are not successfully communicating your intent. If that spoken line was transcribed and subsequently read out loud objectively, it would state: Steve said, "I really like your hair." Therefore, one could assume it was meant to be a compliment. However, the facial expression and tone of voice caused the exact *opposite* to be communicated.

6) "A" as in....
I am often asked what qualities, abilities or qualifications I am seeking when holding auditions, whether they be for Gold Company, festival choirs or soloists. In response, I turn the tables on the questioners and ask what qualities *they think* I am seeking in an audition. The responses I receive typically include a great voice, sight-reading abilities, music theory knowledge, scat singing experience and keyboard skills.

While all of these ultimately may have some bearing on the selection of the person auditioning, most people are surprised to hear which specific quality is at the *top* of my list. In alphabetical order: A … as in … *Attitude*. By far, my number one audition attribute and most important skill is an excellent attitude. The other factors listed earlier are also important and will ultimately determine the results of an audition, *when combined* with the attitude factor. Everything else (including musical deficiencies) can be remedied if the person auditioning has an excellent attitude toward learning, cooperating, working hard and playing well with others.

> By far, my number one audition attribute and most important skill is an excellent attitude.

7) Keeping an open mind. This is a phrase that is so easy for me to write, and yet a concept that is so difficult for some people to embrace. By being open and receptive to new input, suggestions, thoughts and ideas, you place yourself in the position of embracing change. And, whether you like it or not, whether you care to admit it or not, time moves on, and things *do* change. Technological advancements and the Internet have brought the entire planet closer together and indeed have created a global village. We are now accustomed to instant feedback and communication to and from anyone, at virtually any place on the planet. With the assistance of two computers, we can have spoken conversations and a live video image, in real time from any two locations—anywhere—for *free*! This technology was considered science fiction just a few years ago.

Maintaining an open mind and being receptive to new input is important for both students *and* teachers (and for more "mature" people who may have a tendency to be set in their ways, or patterns and methods of teaching). I am not suggesting that you change the core educational values and philosophies that represent the cornerstone of your program, for those most likely are timeless. I will steadfastly hold on to the "old-fashioned" values I mentioned earlier in this chapter. It is important, however, to perceive and accept the unavoidable changes in society, technology and perhaps even audience tastes. These changes are vital and necessary, and by not accepting them you would most likely create an undesirable chasm between your students, your audiences and you.

It is equally important to impart to your students the concept of keeping an open mind. First, they are too young and, quite simply, don't know enough to *not* be receptive to new thoughts and input. Second, it is your *job* to fill their minds with new input and fresh information, and to inspire them to achieve and accomplish that which they did not think possible. And it is their *role* to accept the gift of the knowledge, wisdom and experience that you impart.

I have a fond memory of a former student who sang in Gold Company. This student loved singing vocal jazz literature but *hated* learning and performing the choreography that accompanied one or two of the pieces in our repertoire. (Although I consider Gold Company to be a vocal jazz ensemble, we typically include a small amount of choreography in a performance.) This undergraduate would question me as to *why* we had to learn choreography and dance, especially since this was a vocal jazz program. My response (as it is part of my educational philosophy) was that I want my students not only to be aware of but also to *experience* all of the aspects of live performance. You never know when some of these skills and experiences may be called upon or be useful in the future. As an 18-year-old first-year college student, he was a vocal jazz "snob." He lived for and loved the sounds and harmonies that are typical of the idiom. He had a passion for the arrangements of Gene Puerling, and he cherished the freedom associated with solo interpretations and the musical and technical challenges presented by scat singing.

He was not a gifted dancer and clearly did not enjoy any time spent in rehearsal that revolved around a discussion of "jazz hands." However, he trusted my judgment, kept an open mind and opened himself up to new input. Cut to a few years later: The same student gave more than 2,000 performances in the role of Tom Collins in *Rent* on Broadway, and his only choreography experience prior to his *Rent* audition was in Gold Company—which he said he was able to draw upon, and which helped him tremendously at his audition. Furthermore, if someone (a soothsayer, for example) had told him (while he was an undergraduate, vocal-jazz-loving student) that in the not-too-distant future he would have a leading role in a Broadway musical production, he would have laughed and said, "No way!" At the time, I, too, probably would have thought that career path to be implausible (or at the very least a "stretch")

> Never say never, and never rule out a possibility.

for that particular student, but my experiences with students have repeatedly proved: Never say never, and never rule out a possibility.

I have observed scenarios like this one numerous times. Sometimes (especially after a student has left college), concepts like "real life" and "having to pay the rent" manifest themselves, and I am always amazed at what my former students will consider as plausible career options—that only a few months before (in their utopian college world) they might have scoffed at!

The moral of this story: If my student had not been receptive to new input in his formative years, he most likely would not have benefited from some incredible and memorable performing opportunities and experiences in his professional life.

An aside to teachers: In my university, students have the opportunity to fill out professor evaluation forms for every course that is taught. These evaluations are done anonymously and the professor does not see the results until after final grades are submitted, thereby allowing students the freedom to express themselves without thoughts of recrimination. I am always interested in the results of my student evaluations, as they provide an excellent insight into how I am perceived, and they serve as a source for direct feedback. As a result, they provide an opportunity for my own self-improvement. Although this system is certainly not empirical nor without its flaws, it can serve as a direct reflection on how various aspects of your teaching is perceived. What interests me most are the student's written comments (as opposed to numerical answers), as herein lies the opportunity for the teacher's growth and development. It would be easy to embrace all of the positive comments and dismiss the negative. After all, the negative comments were most likely written by the unmotivated student, or the one with behavioral "issues," or worse. I take the negative comments to heart and reflect on them, and ask myself what I might have said or done differently to connect with that dissatisfied or disenfranchised student. Perhaps the answer to that question is "nothing," but, quite possibly, there might have been several ways to establish a better connection with that "lost lamb."

As an educator, I constantly seek ways to improve my teaching and to be more effective and efficient in the classroom. Also, I take my responsibility as professor quite seriously. Of course, the job of music teacher requires equal parts musician, psychologist, cheerleader, mathematician, historian, stage manager, mediator, community organizer, travel consultant, equipment schlepper and fundraiser. As a communicator, my goal is to reach each and every student that I encounter. Sometimes this is impossible, but I will go down trying.

Remember, the old adage says, "You can bring the horse to water, but you can't make it drink"—but I think it's worth repeating that I prefer to bring the horse to water, then figure out how to make it thirsty!

8) Working hard on the first gig. It is often very easy for a student of mine to get the "first gig." I am always happy to receive calls and letters asking me to recommend current or former students for various positions in the professional world. I am also quite proud of my former students who make their living as musicians or professionals working in the world of music, doing what they love doing, *and they are being paid for it!* They are employed as jazz musicians; recording artists; Broadway performers and theater technicians; recording studio engineers and producers; professional audio technicians; vocalists and instrumentalists touring with recording artists, making jingles and recording music for major motion pictures; and, last but certainly not least, music educators at the elementary, middle school, high school and university levels. I may be able to help them secure an initial interview based on my recommendation, but from that point on, the burden of proof rests on their shoulders. It is *their* responsibility to be hired, or to be offered a return engagement. The proof of their success comes in several forms, and they will be evaluated in ways we have already identified. Did the person come prepared? Was she musically competent? Did he arrive on time? (Five minutes early is already 10 minutes late!)

> ...when a teacher makes a recommendation, the student's behavior then becomes a reflection on the teacher's reputation.

A follow-up phone call that I *never* want to receive is the one asking me, "What were you thinking when you suggested _____ for this gig??? She was terrible..." followed by a litany of the reasons why... all having to do with **buts**. It would be difficult for me to mask my disappointment in a student who so egregiously violated all of the **Wow Factors** she had been taught. Upon further reflection, I would question how I might have failed as a teacher to get such fundamental points across to my students. Also, it is important for a student to know and understand that when a teacher makes a recommendation, the student's behavior then becomes a reflection on the teacher's reputation. There is never a reason to create the "Inverse **Wow Factor**."

9) Being humble. Apologize if you are late—*especially* if *you* made the appointment. Call ahead. Always leave a voicemail message in advance of your tardiness. The exact time of your call will be documented, thereby raising your responsibility factor, assuming you call in advance. This may reflect a certain "old school" attitude, but do not rely on texting or Email to notify people that you will be late for a rehearsal or appointment—make the effort to call and leave a voice message.

10) No excuses. The world is full of people who want to make excuses for their behavior, as opposed to taking full responsibility for their actions. Here are a few of my favorite "excuses":

You should have heard it in the practice room a few minutes ago.

I could do it yesterday.

My nice clothes are in the laundry.

I didn't have time to take a shower today.

I woke up late.

I couldn't find the book.

If only I had worn my lucky ring.

There was lots of traffic.

I ran out of gas.

My alarm didn't go off.

The Blame Game is Lame. It is OK (and necessary) for you to take responsibility for the things you do that are great, and especially (more so) for the things that aren't so great, even though it is very hard to admit our shortcomings. The good news is that deficiencies can be overcome. All it takes is 3D—desire, discipline and dedication. I realize that once we reach a certain age, it becomes increasingly difficult to admit the things we do not do well, and perhaps more importantly, resolve to make those things better.

Just because I have earned degrees in music and developed some abilities as a pianist or conductor does not mean that I should be able to play, for example, the violin. If I decided that I wanted to learn to play the violin, I would have to start practicing the instrument just like anyone else, whether it be a 3-year-old child taking the Suzuki method or a fifth-grade student enrolling in a school string program. Most importantly, I must accept and realize that I will not be very good initially. No, I will be pretty *bad* at the start; the sounds that emanate from the instrument will probably not be too pleasant… and that is OK! It is all part of the process that *everyone* has to go through in order to achieve success.

11) No smoking. Warning: Cigarette smoking is harmful to you and those around you, and I am about to get on my soapbox.

People who smoke are a distinct minority, and statistics indicate that the number of smokers is decreasing. More and more cities (domestically and internationally) and states are banning smoking in the workplace, including in bars and restaurants. The reason for this is simple: Smoking is bad for you. It is bad for your body, and through secondhand smoke, it poses a health risk to the people around you.

So, why would a person ever get started with such a miserable, despicable habit? Perhaps in an attempt to think you are "cool" or "mature"? Think again! Anyone who tries to inhale smoke the first time is usually greeted with an unpleasant, physical reaction of choking, gagging and coughing. That intense, involuntary reaction should be your first clue that your *body* is saying, "This is *not* a good thing you are doing to me…please *stop it…now.*" But, if you choose not to listen to your body, and continue to poison yourself, you run the risk of developing a physical dependency on nicotine, a highly addictive drug. Of course, once you are addicted, the addiction makes quitting that much more difficult. So, the moral of this story: *DON'T START!*

My reasons for being on a soapbox here are twofold:

A. Smoking cigarettes is a self-destructive habit. Objectively speaking, and from a perspective of good health, it has no redeeming positive qualities. It is bad for you. It causes disease and shortens your life, and is also bad for the people around you. It makes you, your hair, your clothes and your breath smell bad.

B. Many professionals would rather not work with or hire people who smoke, for myriad reasons. Therefore, it is in your best interest as an aspiring professional to never even get started with such a filthy, nasty and stinky habit. Make your health a high priority. The healthier you are, the better you feel. The better you feel, the better you present yourself and the more desirable and marketable you are, and as a result you increase your chances of establishing **The Wow Factor** and for collaborating with others.

12) Writing thank-you notes! Another "old-fashioned" means of communication is something that is now commonly referred to as "snail mail." Today, even if a person has to wait overnight to have a "real" package or letter in an envelope sent via traditional carrier (as opposed to the Internet), it is considered a "snail's pace." Nonetheless I believe there is *no substitute* for a handwritten letter (on a note card or stationery with letterhead) thanking someone who has done something nice for you, or extended you a favor, given you a recommendation, or hired you, or even inspired you. Not only is it good manners, courteous and appropriate to acknowledge someone's generosity, it is also a good business policy and a way to "*wow*" that person. If you get hired to a new job, or put on a gig for the first time, follow the performance with a note to the new boss or leader. Thank the person for hiring you, say how much you appreciated and enjoyed having the opportunity, and indicate that you hope he or she will consider you for future jobs or performances. In addition, if you were recommended for this job, it is important to thank the people who recommended you, assuring them that all went well, that you showed up on time, and that the boss was pleased with your performance *and* impressed by your attitude and professionalism. Teachers: Remind your students to include thank-you notes and pens when packing for a road trip or tour.

I suppose that, if forced, I must admit e-mail, text messages and even having "friends" on certain social Web sites can be acceptable forms of communicating, but nothing can replace the extra effort that goes into handwriting your thoughts, as well as the joy one can attain from affixing a postage stamp to an envelope.

> ... nothing can replace the extra effort that goes into handwriting your thoughts, as well as the joy one can attain from affixing a postage stamp to an envelope.

FAQs

In my travels I have encountered students, teachers and audiences in a wide variety of performance and educational settings. Geographically these have been on five continents, in large cities and small, from concert halls to banquet rooms, and for huge crowds as well as audiences where there have been more people on stage than in the house. In all situations, I am interested in interacting with people, mostly for my own experience, education and edification—to learn about the area, the people's likes and dislikes, what they think, how they think and why they think that way, and what is important and of value to them. The more I travel, the more I realize that people essentially are the same everywhere. There may be differences in political systems, religions and spiritual beliefs, languages and social customs, but in many ways those are less important than the foundations of humanity that unify us all. A smile and an extended hand transcend any language or political belief. And music is perhaps the greatest unifier of all. After I ask my many questions, I continue this good dialogue by taking questions from the audience, be they music students, teachers or the general public.

What follows are a few questions I am often asked, followed by my responses. Perhaps if I am fortunate to see you at some point "down the road" you can think of a question or two not answered here!

What is the secret "shortcut" to get to be good?

It seems that there is a prevailing attitude among students today to find the "end around"—a way to circumnavigate the learning process so that they can more quickly reach their goals. Perhaps this attitude is societal, with advancing technology, and Internet access and instant information from virtually any location on the planet. My belief is that this "fast track" is commonplace for people born after about 1990. Those who hail from a generation before might remember ancient societal artifacts such as the aforementioned snail mail, typewriters, dial telephones, and very expensive long-distance telephone calls.

Quite simply, the secret shortcut to get to be good is hard work. And—

> ...the secret shortcut to get to be good is hard work.

unfortunately for those who might be averse to hard work—there is no substitute.

How long does it take to get to be real good?

How long do you want to take before you are good? If your goal involves musical practice for one year, and you practice every *other* day, then your goal will take you two years to achieve. If it involves one hour of practice each day, and you practice for 30 minutes, it will take you twice as long. Do the math. How long do *you* want to take? I can guarantee that there are people who will not only put in the *minimum* time, but they will be working even longer and harder, because they are *hungry* to be real good *sooner*. And those people (ultimately) are the ones you will be competing with. So how well do you want to compete with them?

Why do we have to work this hard?

If you are serious about your own growth, development and self-improvement, then get used to it—for any *smaller* effort will result in a less-than-stellar final product. Hopefully hard work does not necessarily have to be unpleasant. It can be a joy to work hard and give 110 percent effort at all times.

What do I need to do to get a "C" in this class?

If I am asked this question by a student at the beginning of the school year, I typically suggest that the student either immediately drop this class (as I am not particularly interested in teaching a student whose highest aspirations are to earn a "C" in the class—although, as we have learned—it is possible for a person like this to eventually become president of the United States!) or re-evaluate his or her motivation. Even if this is a class that does not particularly interest the student (but is required), a very important lesson can still be taught. There are many times in school—and later in real life—when you will have a class (or perhaps a job) that might not be your personal favorite (or perhaps the teacher is not your favorite) but the class is an obligation nonetheless. You have a choice as to how to react. The easy way would be to express no interest, have a bad attitude, have bad attendance, put little effort into the homework assignments, and, as a result, earn a barely passing grade (at best) and/or fail the class (at worst). The harder (and, in my opinion, much *better* and *smarter* choice) would be to give your best effort to all aspects of the specific situation, even if you don't like it. The byproducts can be beneficial. First, if you keep an open mind, you may discover that the course material actually is something that you enjoy, and that your newly gained knowledge is something that can benefit you in your future professional endeavors. Second, you may discover that the "bad" teacher is, in fact, an excellent one. Perhaps the teacher's methodology causes the student to have to think more independently, or to be more self-reliant and resourceful—something that many students initially resist. Students tend to like to be spoon-fed. And why not? It certainly worked well when we were babies! A teacher who causes students to achieve greater personal and intellectual growth and independence is a true gift to that student. Unfortunately, sometimes this is a lesson that the student does not learn (or appreciate) until long after the actual class experience.

Finally, earning a great grade in a class that is not your favorite (but is nonetheless required) will teach you about discipline and focus, especially when you *don't* particularly feel like doing it. And this is one of the most important values a student (and aspiring professional) can learn. I have found that some of the most important and profound growth and development can come at times when I force myself (or, in an ensemble setting, when the ensemble is asked to work harder) to practice or study, *especially* when I don't feel like it, or if it is not fun.

From an ensemble member: "Can I solo in this song?"

While I advocate giving people new educational opportunities, it is important for a student to want these opportunities for the right reasons. I suggest to students that they learn, practice and *memorize* any potential solo on their own time, *outside* of the rehearsal. Then if they would like to try it out, they can do so in a rehearsal, but I expect them to perform with a certain degree of confidence due to the effort they have put into the learning process. I will almost never program a soloist in a concert setting without having heard the singer try it out and then sing it more than once (for consistency and confidence) in rehearsal.

Good training

It seems as though sports metaphors and analogies are used in everyday speech to help describe aspects of our lives that have little to do with that sport, or the original or literal intention or use of the phrase. Consider phrases such as:

> He hit a home run with that one (an **And**).
> She dropped the ball (a **But**).
> He's a real heavyweight (**And**)...
>> or...
> a lightweight (**But**).
> That was a slam-dunk (**And**).
> You've got to go the distance.

This last metaphor is something that I have used in both my professional and personal lives. Although it originates from the world of professional boxing, I use it as both a literal and metaphorical inspiration when training to run a marathon. Completing a distance of 40 kilometers (26.2 miles!) is not a task that can be accomplished without a significant commitment of time, effort and energy. It can also include pain and discomfort in the process. Why then do "sane" people choose to pursue this goal? Although I cannot answer that question for others, I chose to undertake this quest for the following reasons:

1) I like challenges and this was a big one.

2) There are obvious health benefits: I knew that as a result of the training I would be in very good physical condition.

3) I could eat whatever I wanted, whenever I wanted to, without fear of gaining excess and unneeded weight!

4) It is an accomplishment that must be *earned*.

5) After successful completion, there is a sense of accomplishment and a tangible result that no one can take away from you.

6) This was a solo project and I did not have to (nor could I) rely on nor was I dependent upon anyone else for motivation or support.

7) It serves as a metaphor for the quest or journey of any serious musician. The musical path is a long road, and the journey will present challenges to body, mind and spirit. But dogged determination and

discipline will manifest themselves with truly earned rewards, and the benefits will come as a result of extreme effort, for which there is no substitute.

Taking this athletic analogy one step further, a determined athlete's life revolves around practice and training. Can you imagine a serious, world-class runner who would decide to take a week or two off from practice just before an important race? Of course not! Even the mere thought is ludicrous. Similarly, a serious musician cannot afford to take a week or two away from practice, especially before an important recital, audition or concert.

Therefore, in order to successfully accomplish a lofty goal, one needs to make a commitment to a regular, focused, and disciplined practice routine over an extended period of time. This concept is easy to say and think about, but is more difficult to make a reality. This is why only a small minority of people who initially set a goal to run a marathon successfully complete the race. This is also why only a small minority of the people who start a doctoral degree actually complete it, and why the people who are able to make their living in music are a small minority compared with those who love and participate in musical activities as an avocation.

Running (or any other similar, regular physical activity) is an excellent analogy or metaphor for musical practice, hard work, discipline, desire, dedication, having

> The musical path is a long road, and the journey will present challenges to body, mind and spirit.

goals and objectives, and especially *having* to do something, even when you don't feel like it. Are you passionate about something? If so, if you *have* to do music, if you cannot imagine *not* doing music, if it is a driving force in your life… then you must know this feeling!

For me, to have to give up running would be like giving up music—which would be like giving up on living. Running (as an individual event) is a metaphor for the loneliness of (solitary) practice. Music practice—like running—involves focus and endurance. Like music, running also can include talent (for those world-class runners who win Olympic gold medals). But talent alone will not ultimately win the race, nor will it achieve the musical goal, as talent **must** be combined with hard work. A less talented performer who has a stronger and better-developed work ethic will ultimately prevail. Think of the famous fable of the tortoise and the hare. In running, one must constantly remind (and push) the body to cover the requisite distance, in a certain amount of time (or less). Whatever goals you choose to establish

But talent alone will not ultimately win the race, nor will it achieve the musical goal, as talent *must* be combined with hard work.

are self-imposed; therefore, the only person you are competing against is yourself! This is an excellent parallel to achieving the goal of how much music to learn in a day, or how many pages to sight-read, or how much to practice improvisation, or learning a role or even developing new dance steps!

If only we could exist in a professional and personal world where there were significantly more **Ands** than **Buts**, I believe our lives and the ones we affect would be greatly enhanced. Remember: *You* decide how you want to act and what you say. If you are a teacher, you can have a profoundly positive influence on your students in these areas. If you can successfully master the qualities included in **Ands**, instill them in those around you, and eliminate the **Ifs** and **Buts**, they will be eternally grateful, and their chances for achieving successes and the **Wow Factor** will be greatly enhanced. And those whom you have influenced will be eternally grateful for the gift that you have bestowed upon them.

CHAPTER FIVE

DON'T GO TO YOUR FACE
Putting the Polish on Your Performance

*"If we could all learn to rehearse in performance mode,
I think we might accomplish more polished and fulfilling performances."*
—Hilary Apfelstadt

*"Practice, practice and know the material very well.
Look like you are having FUN!"* **—Don Shelton**

● ● ●

It has been said that a performance group has 20 to 30 seconds to create an initial impression on an audience. Think about it. As an audience member, what are you thinking about and reacting to just before the start of a concert? Here are some of the initial questions I ask, factors I observe and evaluations I make:

1) What is the performance venue? Theater, restaurant, gym, cafetorium, church, etc.—each space can present unique challenges in terms of sonic quality and visuals.

2) Who are the typical audience members? Students? If so, what ages? Adults? (What ages?) Parents, teachers, complete strangers who may or may not know anything about the performers or the program?

3) What does the stage look like? Pulled curtain? Choral risers? Platforms and different levels? Is there a set? If so, how is it constructed? Is it effective? Is the stage neat or needlessly cluttered? Are instruments on the stage? Is there a pit? If so, is it neat? Sloppy?

4) Lighting? Is there special lighting? Follow spots? Any special rigging or light trees? Colored or "special" lights or lighting effects? (gobos, strobe, UV, etc.)

5) Is there a printed program?

6) Is there a PA system? If so, how many microphones and what kind? Where are the main speakers? Are there monitor speakers?

7) Was admission charged? How much? Where and how did I get my ticket?

8) Is there an air of excitement and anticipation?

Once the actual concert and music commences, there is a crucial period where audience members typically make an entire second round of evaluations based on initial reactions to the music and what is transpiring from the stage. Here are some things that most people tend to evaluate (whether consciously or not) in the first few seconds of a concert: (Keep in mind that although these are objective observations, the audience members react subjectively and formulate instant opinions based on what they see, hear and feel.)

1) Who is performing?

2) What are they wearing? Are the outfits flattering and attractive?

3) How did the performers enter the stage?

4) How do they look? Happy? Excited? Energized? None of the above?

5) What does the music sound like? (Blended and in tune?)

6) How is the overall volume and balance?

7) Are there any props or extramusical devices?

8) How well do the collaborative instrumentalists play?

Here is an important point for you to consider: Most people react to visual stimuli first. I tell my students that people listen with their eyes. I realize that sounds like a contradiction of the senses, but in fact, as people listen to music, they are also influenced by their visual input. Therefore, whether you like it or not, whether you value it or not, or whether it is an area of interest or competence to you or not, the fact remains that your audiences *will* be judging you and your group on appearance, wardrobe, makeup, hairstyle, and many other factors … *none of which* has anything to do with the music. I realize that this can seem at best trivial and at worst unfair; however,

...people listen with their eyes.

attention to this important aspect of your performance will greatly enhance your *Wow Factor*.

Don't Go to Your Face

I am not exactly sure where or when the phrase "Don't go to your face" entered my consciousness and became an entrenched and integral part of my educational philosophy. The phrase has entered legendary status with my students, and I know that it is one with which I will always be identified.

What, exactly, is the meaning of this ever-popular phrase? Quite simply, during a performance and while on stage, keep your hands to your sides (or where they are required to be) and, *no matter what*, discipline yourself, resist temptation and avoid putting your hands anywhere near your face. "Going to your face" serves as a huge distraction, and, perhaps more importantly, is a sign of lack of discipline. Here is a caveat: I realize that this value of mine borders on "pet peeve" status and that it may not be nearly as important to you in the training of your students and ensembles. If it is not, I would ask that you consider the following:

When a choral group performs on stage (regardless of size, formation, attire and repertoire), the singers can be seen by audience members from their initial entrance (either from backstage or through the audience) until they leave the stage and are safely out of audience view. It is important to realize and impart to your performers that they are in the view of the audience (and *all* members of the audience, which may include a wide area of seats, with depth and possibly a balcony, and even occasionally behind the stage as is common in many symphonic halls) at *all* times when they are on stage. This involves all of the times when they are *not* performing, including, the entrance from backstage to where they perform, the time during audience applause, the time (for singers) during instrumental introductions, interludes and solos, and the time during any spoken word, such as the ensemble director addressing the audience. Although most attention will be focused on the solo speaker, it simply involves the undisciplined actions of one person adjusting a strand of hair, or scratching an ear or nose, and the audience is distracted and diverted from the soloist to the person who

> It is important to realize and impart to your performers that they are in the view of the audience ... at *all* times when they are on stage.

is needlessly moving. This rule applies to all performers for the entire time they are on the stage, including immediately after bows, when hands tend to go to the face. Also, stage conditions such as excessive facial perspiration or stray hairs can cause a performer to be tempted to go to the face, but to paraphrase a famous athletic shoe slogan: "Just DON'T do it!"

How to Talk to Audiences

The concept of addressing an audience from the stage seems so simple in theory, but for many people this task presents a challenge of significant proportions. The result of a survey indicated that, other than death, a person's greatest fear in life is speaking in front of an audience. Indeed, there is something daunting about a microphone and "live" people anticipating our pearls of wisdom that can reduce a usually competent speaker to a blithering idiot. This type of speaking is an acquired ability, and if it does not come naturally to you, or if the prospect causes you to become nervous, then as a result, your speech will sound at best unnatural and, at worst, ineffective or unintelligible.

Here are my thoughts and suggestions on how to improve your speaking abilities:

1.) **Know Your Audience.** Do your best to learn as much as possible about your audience before your performance. If you are aware of their demographics and ages, consider altering what you say or how you say it. Try to *anticipate* every aspect of your audience and their musical tastes. Be flexible and adapt to your environment.

2.) **Prepare!** Write your spoken lines in advance, practice and rehearse them (as if they are lines in a play) so they sound natural. This essentially becomes acting, and you become a character in your own play. Your character is charged with appearing cool, calm, collected and confident when addressing an audience. Practice your pacing, cadence, timing and enunciation. Record yourself using both audio and videotape. The playback may be (initially) painful to you, but remember, the camera never lies! It is through the study of video that you can notice common physical manifestations such as blotchy complexion, perspiration, nervous ticks, excess verbiage or distracting gestures. Practice in front of other real people and ask for their honest input, reactions and feedback. Having a "live" audience in practice may also cause symptoms including nervousness and anxiety that might not exist when you practice alone.

3.) **Avoid Excess Verbiage!** *Never* say "um," "uh," "like," "you know" and "OK." OK?

4.) **Don't Talk Too Much.** Remember, the concert is not about *you* and your talking— it's about the music. Spread out your talks so they do not seem as long. There is probably no need to talk before and after every piece of music on the program. Plan exactly where and when you will speak and have a *reason* for talking. Ask yourself: Do I *need* to talk here? Does my speech advance or improve the program, or is it superfluous and unnecessary?

5.) **Watch Your Timing.** Use your speech time as a stage device if needed to make transitions from one position to the next, or if the performers need a short break after performing a physically exhausting or technically demanding piece, or costume change, or if the band needs to make transitions to other instruments. Know how long each of your speeches is in *real time*, and time yourself every time you practice so that you achieve consistency. Also, if other performers are depending on your speech for their own transitions, they will gain confidence in accomplishing their own tasks.

6.) **Talk to the Audience in *Their* Language.** Do your best to relate to and connect with your audience. Whenever I am in another country, I make a point to learn a phrase in the native language of my audience. By saying a foreign phrase to an international audience, you can immediately help bridge a natural gap. In addition, when performing at a locale other than your hometown, try to make connections or references to people and places that are local to wherever you are.

7.) **Be Careful in Using Jokes or Humor.** Indeed, people like humor— but make sure whatever you plan to say is funny to people other than *you*! Test your material in advance to see if you achieve the desired result. Make sure that your humor will be appreciated and understood by a general audience. Make sure you are politically correct, and avoid any "inside" jokes where some people will feel left out. Be prepared for *any* audience reaction; they may laugh at your jokes, or they may not. Be prepared to respond accordingly. That is one of the beauties of "live" theater.

8.) **Do Your Homework and Research Thoroughly**. Do not repeat what is already in a printed program that has been distributed to the audience. Activities such as these must be relegated to the Department of Redundancy Department.

9.) **Stay on Task and on Script** unless you are an experienced improviser. This takes discipline, but do not succumb to the temptation to go off script.

10.) **Coach Anyone/Everyone Who will Speak.** The previous nine points apply to anyone and everyone in your program who speaks to the audience. If you assign lines to students or other inexperienced speakers, make sure they gain the necessary confidence so that their speaking style will appear to be smooth, seamless and effortless, and that *what* they say is easily understood.

GOLD COMPANY PERFORMANCE RULES AND POLICIES

Throughout my years of teaching and directing Gold Company, I have sought to develop, adapt and refine *Wow Factors* that, when applied to the individual performers as well as to the entire ensemble, help to elevate the performance to a higher standard of professionalism. As a result, there exist performance rules and policies that have become standard performance practices for Gold Company. What follows is a list of those rules and policies that will help ensure that the high standards by which this ensemble is known are maintained and enhanced. Although some of the items may seem simple and commonplace, it is important that every member of the ensemble understands the importance of and adheres to these standards.

- STAMINA (mental and physical). Most individuals or groups are capable of starting a performance with positive energy, focus and a great attitude. But it is equally or perhaps more important to finish a performance even more strongly than you began. Once again we can use an athletic analogy. The footrace is almost always won by the runner who has some reserve left for a final push or sprint at the end of the race. Physical and mental stamina must be learned and practiced by knowing how to control and pace yourself throughout the entire performance. As a performer, you have to find the fine balance between having some reserve left for the end of the performance (and possible encores) and yet feeling as though you have given your all when leaving the stage.

- ENERGY. I am a firm believer of the power of physical and mental energy in performance. Energy can transcend and be applied to all styles, genres, tempos and idioms. Most audiences respond favorably to a performer or group who is energized and fully committed to the performance. For singers, breath is the fuel, and proper breath management is needed to give an energized performance. The higher your energy level, the more efficient your body. The more efficient your body, the better you feel

> I am a firm believer of the power of physical and mental energy in performance.

and the more you will use your talent to produce outstanding results.

- **PERFORMANCE ENERGY** must be maintained from the minute you walk on stage from the beginning through the end of your performance—including your stage exit. Practice knowing how your facial muscles feel when you say "yes" and exude a positive, pleasant look.

- **DON'T GO TO YOUR FACE.** If you have an uncontrollable itch … If there is perspiration on your nose … If you bump your teeth on the microphone … resist the temptation to react. Simply follow the title of the Paul McCartney song … "Let It Be."

- **FOCUS ON THE ACTION.** If someone is singing a solo, have the entire ensemble turn their bodies to face the soloist. As performers, it is our responsibility to cause the audience to see and hear what *we* would like for them to see and hear. I refer to this as "audience manipulation." By pointing out (through focus and physical gesture) who is singing or playing a solo, you also assist the audience visually and therefore enhance their listening experience.

- **MOVE WITH A PURPOSE.** Whether you are on or (perhaps more importantly) offstage, know where you are supposed to be, and know the quickest and most efficient way to get there. If you have a solo that is downstage center and you must travel to the solo microphone, know exactly how long it takes for you to get there. You should arrive in enough time to calmly gather your thoughts prior to your solo, and yet not arrive too soon, so as to avoid feeling awkward while the rest of the ensemble is singing. The same thinking applies when you are moving to a new position on stage. Make your walking pace faster than your "normal" leisurely pace, and, when you exit the stage, *keep walking: Do not stop,* even if you are off stage and out of the sight line of the audience. If you are part of a large ensemble, remember that people leaving the stage are still behind you. One of the most unpleasant stage experiences is getting caught in backed-up traffic because the line in front of you slowed down or stopped, because of the sluggish departure of the people who already exited the stage. The exit must be rehearsed, so that the first people in every row know exactly how far and how fast to keep walking until everyone behind them has cleared the stage quickly and efficiently.

- **BOWS.** A performer must be prepared to acknowledge audience applause. I believe that failure to do so is both disrespectful and rude. Soloists should take a small bow after their solos, as the audience most likely will want to show appreciation; this is quite common in live concerts, especially in jazz. However it is also common in musical theater and even in opera, where the audience will interrupt the flow of the show and break into applause after a great solo or aria. One exception to this solo bow rule is during the performance of an *a cappella* ballad. A soloist should discourage audience applause in the middle of a tender ballad, as that can be quite disruptive. Upon completing the solo, the soloist should simply turn around and return to his or her position, without any acknowledgment to the audience. The soloist can take a well-deserved solo bow at the conclusion of the ballad. Always be ready for a group bow (without hesitation). Like all other aspects of your presentation, bows must be practiced. It can be quite impressive when an ensemble presents a unified bow. It is a sign of professionalism.

- **SOLOS** should be performed on the solo microphones at downstage center (unless otherwise instructed). In Gold Company, all soloists approach the solo microphones at center stage by entering and exiting through the center of the ensemble, then returning to their position on stage.

- **FRAGRANCE.** Never wear fragrances (such as perfumes, colognes, body lotions, scented hair spray, etc.) during performances. The individual scents, when combined with heat, perspiration and one another, can create a funky atmosphere (literally)—and I don't mean funky in the "rhythmic" sense of the word! Some individuals are allergic to perfumes and other scents, and the chemical reactions can be toxic. In addition, a successful vocal performance is predicated on successful breath management. Therefore, it is in your best interest to keep the air on stage a "fragrance-free" zone. Remember to use an effective deodorant or antiperspirant. Stage lights, stress, nerves and the energy of live performance can combine to contribute to increased perspiration.

- **HYGIENE/APPEARANCE.** Always look good, neat and clean. Good personal hygiene is a requirement, not an option. Hair is always worn back and off the face (at least halfway above the forehead) for performances. This will allow stage lights to better show your face, plus ensure that your eyes will be visible to the audience. Your eyes are your most important expressive facial feature. Remember: Personal hygiene is your friend. Wash your face and brush your teeth!

> Your eyes are your most important expressive facial feature.

- **PERFORMANCE CLOTHES** must always be neat, clean and pressed, and shoes must be polished. Outfits may be coordinated, from "one size fits all" (choir robes), to the men wearing the same suit or tux and the women the same dress, to individual outfits that are either color coordinated or reflective of a specific style or era. If possible, accessorizing can add a great deal of class and pizzazz to your "look." This can include (but is not limited to) matching shoes and earrings or necklaces for the ladies, and identical shoes and/or ties for the men.

- **KNOW YOUR GROUP STAGE POSITIONS.** Always know how to get to your position quickly, quietly and efficiently. Gold Company has two basic stage positions: 1) "vocal jazz," with women in sections (SA) in the front row and men in sections (TB) in the back row, and 2) mixed couples where group members are arbitrarily placed in couples. This means some people will switch rows and others will change positions and microphone places within the same row.

- **GOLD COMPANY STAGE PLOT**

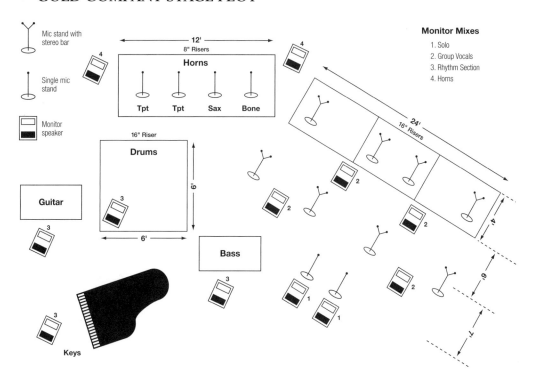

- **ANTICIPATE** and think about the set lists for every performance, bows, grooves, the necessary attitude for each piece performed, stage changes, costume changes, instrument changes, pitches, solos, entrances and exits. Be mentally present at all times. Function in the immediate present and the immediate future, and never think about and dwell in the past (until after the concert). What has taken place cannot be changed—for better or for worse.

- **BE FLEXIBLE.** Unexpected things can and do happen in live performance. Do not panic, but simply adjust if, for example, a microphone is not working, a mistake is made, or any number of things happen that could ordinarily distract from your concentration. If you are aware that the microphone you are supposed to use for a solo is not functioning properly, reach for or walk to another mic, or share one with another performer. If you make a mistake, "Let It Be." Obviously we hope to avoid mistakes in concert, but should something happen, do your best to disguise your mistake from the audience, as opposed to drawing attention to it through an inappropriate physical reaction or negative facial expression.

- **KNOW YOUR INSTRUMENT.** Be responsible for preparing your body and instrument for rehearsals and performances. Whether you realize it or not, everyone has physical limitations. **Your performance success can often be predicated upon the amount of sleep and rest you get.** Use common sense. Do not stay up until 3 a.m. and think that you will perform well at a 10 a.m. school assembly. That behavioral choice would be irresponsible, immature and not in your best interest or that of your ensemble. I would be remiss if I did not mention that (especially in younger students) in spite of how you may think you feel, **you are probably more tired than you *think* you are.**

- **OTB ("On the Bus").** Never say anything negative about anyone or anything when at a performance site. (Actually, this rule applies anytime!) You never know who is listening and who is observing you at a distance. Always say "thank you," and display mature behavior and good manners. Your attitude should always be "yes," and you must be respectful of your audience and your hosts. Even if you just walked off stage after giving what you thought was your worst performance in your life, do not reveal your thoughts or emotions to anyone *until* you are safely "on the bus"—meaning that you have departed from the performance site and are among only friends and fellow students or cast members. At that point you are free to discuss any and all aspects (both positive and negative) of the performance.

Generally, people do not like to be surrounded by negativity. Plus, if a group is sponsoring and hosting a performance by your ensemble, its members are probably quite excited to have you in their town, at their school or in their auditorium. You can enhance your personal reputation and that of your ensemble and school by being gracious throughout your entire visit. Should someone come and congratulate you on your performance, simply smile, accept the compliment and say "thank you." Even if you *know* that the performance was not up to your usual standard or that the ensemble was subpar, *do not* express those thoughts to your host. Also, should audience members come up to you and say, "That was the best concert I ever heard in my whole life!"—please don't respond by contradicting them or, worse yet, offering an excuse such as "Oh no it wasn't" or "You should hear us when we're good" or "Tonight we really sucked." This is not what excited audience members want (or need) to hear. If they tell you they just heard a great concert, then that is their opinion, and, even if you do not agree, it is not professional nor appropriate for you to try to change their opinion.

> You can enhance your personal reputation and that of your ensemble and school by being gracious throughout your entire visit.

- **NEVER** applaud for soloists or yourselves. Although you should enjoy the individual performances and solos that are given by your fellow cast and ensemble members, let the applause emanate from the audience members. If you enjoyed musical moments or solos from people in your ensemble, make a point to tell them—*after* the performance!

- **ALWAYS** respect someone else's "home," whether it be an auditorium, a church, a school or an actual residence. See to it that the "home" (including dressing rooms and backstage areas) looks cleaner when you depart than when you arrived. This can be achieved by assigning a cleanup crew to go through all spaces to make sure that all surfaces are cleaned and trash is thrown away. Leaving a venue clean will also leave a lasting positive impression. In addition, if you have been invited to spend a night with a host family, and their hospitality included providing a place to sleep and some food, it should be required to write a thank-you note. You can either leave this on the pillow in the bedroom (if you plan in advance and bring note cards with you), or you can find their snail-mailing address and send a brief note thanking them for their hospitality and generosity. I guarantee your *Wow Factor* will rise dramatically by making this small gesture.

- **DEAD STAGE TIME** must be avoided, and you must make every effort to do so. An important *Wow Factor* is programming and pacing. Dead stage time is the period of awkward silence that can occur between numbers, after the applause is completed and before the next piece begins. If you are achieving success in "audience manipulation" then you will keep their attention captured at all times. However, if you give your audience the time and opportunity to think about other things and look at their watches, you will have lost them. It is your goal to keep the audience's interest. Make your musical and stage transitions fast and efficient. Give new pitches quickly and quietly, and anticipate and rehearse your transitions so that your program has a natural flow that keeps your audience mentally engaged and musically involved in your performance.

- **STAY ON THE MIC.** Your sound crew can work only with the sonic information that goes into the microphones. When holding the mic, make sure your hand is below the ball of the mic. Do not let your movements cause you to move away from the center of the mic while you sing. Between songs, move away from the mic unless there is a fast transition or an extended solo, or unless the director is addressing the audience. Of course you will not comment on the joke you have heard 20 times!

- **SOUND EQUIPMENT.** Our PA system and sound equipment are valuable and all this equipment is a crucial part of our presentation. Preserve and protect it by handling it with care. Every person in the ensemble will have a specific assignment that will assist in the setup and strike processes. Load in and load out should be fast and efficient. No one eats until *all* the work is done. Greet family members and guests *after* your assigned task is successfully completed and the sound system is in its appropriate place. If you have completed your task and others are still working, ask if you can assist them. Have fun in this important process, but stay focused and do not get distracted!

- **CONFIDENT** (but not cocky) stage presence is always in order. Smile and engage the audience. Know where your audience is sitting, and do your best to make eye contact with all sections of the audience throughout the performance. If people are sitting in a balcony, remember to occasionally look up. If there is a wide spread to the audience seating, remember to glance left and right. Make a point to try to look at everyone in the audience at least once in every performance. If direct eye contact makes you uncomfortable, then give the illusion of looking at the audience, but focus your eyes just over the people's heads.

- **FRESH.** Every performance should be fresh and new, as if it were the first—no matter how many times you perform the same material. We often rehearse and practice for months on repertoire that we perform only once in a major concert or recital. I think it is a blessing when a soloist or ensemble has the opportunity to perform the same program multiple times. Repeated performances have several benefits. First, the program quality will improve and performer confidence will increase with repetition. Second, after rehearsing for so long, it is a great reward to have the opportunity to present the music more than once. Third, there is an excellent educational opportunity for the performer to learn to maintain quality, standards and consistency in performance. Finally, if the performer is fortunate to have the opportunity to perform a program many times (a Broadway production typically gives eight performances each week), then the performer must find a way to give his or her best effort for every performance. It is your obligation to do so, especially if the audience is paying to see the performance.

> Every performance should be fresh and new, as if it were the first— no matter how many times you perform the same material.

Yul Brynner was a legendary film and stage actor, perhaps best known for his role as the King in the movie version of Rodgers and Hammerstein's *The King and I*. However, he also appeared as the King in the original Broadway production and on national tours. In fact, he performed the role of the King 4,626 times in his career. That is the equivalent of performing the role every day for over 12½ years.

A jazz concert, by definition, includes improvisation as an important and essential ingredient in the overall success of the performance. The same ensemble can perform the same repertoire night after night, but each time it will sound different, because each player's note choices change. When I perform classical music, my goal is to do my best to faithfully and consistently recreate the intentions and directives of the composer. The score is my source and I do my best to seek original, unedited editions. There should be little variety from performance to performance. If you were to ask me to re-create a jazz performance that I just gave, even immediately after the piece ended, I would not be able to re-create exactly what I played, especially if the performance included several choruses of improvisation. I would have already forgotten what I played and exactly how and when I played it. Conversely, I would aspire and hope to play a selection of classical repertoire exactly the same way twice in a row, ideally playing all of the original notes, harmonies, dynamics, articulations and other expressions as close to the composer's intent as possible.

Similarly, a role in a musical theater or theme park production has very little room (if any) for variety once the show has been rehearsed, choreographed and staged. Therefore it is the responsibility of the performers to keep it fresh and find a way to "*wow*" the audience in each and every performance. Even though *your* performance does not change much from show to show, your audience does! Can you imagine if Yul Brynner had grown bored of his role as the King and had started to "phone it in" after just a few performances? I can assure you that he would never have achieved 100 performances, let alone thousands.

- **STAGE SET.** Everything must be clean, neat and *consistent*. All cables must be wrapped properly (you will be instructed in the proper way to wrap a cable, so that it can be maintained and preserved), and all mic and speaker cables will be taped down to the floor (this helps ensure performer and audience safety, plus is much more visually pleasing). Everything must look good and neat at the soundboard in the audience. The band setup must also be specific, neat and clean. Get all extra junk (equipment, cases, etc.) out of the way backstage—and also out of the way where people walk backstage. Appreciate and thank your stage and technical crew—ultimately they control the show. You could be the best-sounding and -performing group on the planet,

Smile, enjoy, be grateful and humble, and send "yes" energy.

but if the music that you are creating on stage does not come out of the main speakers correctly, it doesn't matter, because your audience will not perceive the music in the manner that you intend.

- **ENJOY** every minute. Say "**YES**" every minute. Be **THANKFUL** that you have the opportunity and are able to do what so many others would love to do. Smile, enjoy, be grateful and humble, and send "yes" energy.

The points discussed in this chapter may seem at times to be rather trivial and/or mired in minutiae. However, I believe it is *precisely* in these points where the difference can be found between a plebian and a polished performance. When you consider adding these simple directives to your rehearsals and practice, the result will translate into a significant upgrade of your ***Wow Factor***.

"Don't go to your face" requires a discipline and professional commitment that is difficult to achieve and is not common among amateur ensembles and solo performers. Although it may not be *crucial* to the presentation of a concert, it serves a wonderful educational purpose, and, as a result, helps elevate and raise the status of your performances from ordinary to "*wow*."

CHAPTER SIX

HOW TO EDUCATE AND ENTERTAIN

"As a director, it's a good idea to memorize the score, establish mutually respectful contact with the performers, and get right to work."
—Ward Swingle

*"**The Wow Factor** must exist in the leader/teacher/conductor's imagination before it will be brought to fruition in a performance."*
—Eph Ehly

● ● ●

Is it possible to create that perfect world in which both education and entertainment can peacefully coexist? Or are these two terms oxymoronic and contradictory? I have colleagues who believe there is no place for entertainment in education, and vice versa. Although I value their opinions, I respectfully, yet vociferously, disagree with this point of view. In fact, I think finding a way to both educate and entertain is an essential ingredient that can be found at the core of **The Wow Factor.**

As music educators and performers, how can we combine the highest standards of musical interpretation, technique, scholarship and artistic expression into *both* an inspiring educational experience as well as a memorable, *"wow-entertaining"* performance experience for our students *as well as* for our audiences?

In this chapter we will explore how to develop an educational philosophy and then combine and incorporate your philosophy with elements that can serve to educate, stimulate and inspire your students and your audiences.

CREATING AN EDUCATIONAL PHILOSOPHY

I believe it is crucial for all educators to develop a personal educational philosophy. This should serve as the fundamental essence of *why* you teach, and it should be at the core of why you chose music education as a career.

You must determine what it is that you want to teach, then devise an efficient and consistent method to accomplish it. Although fashions and styles constantly change, your educational *philosophy* can remain constant. You may have to adapt your *methodology* to incorporate changing trends or new technologies, but your underlying principles should remain steadfast.

> You must determine what it is that you want to teach, then devise an efficient and consistent method to accomplish it.

How does one develop one's own educational philosophy? As is so often the case in the music world, there is no right or wrong answer. I have found that many teachers teach the way that they were taught. This is not necessarily a negative, but is simply a natural result of one's education. For example, many teachers of voice teach what they learned from their voice teachers, who taught what they learned from *their* voice teachers, and on and on. Therefore without constant examination and re-evaluation, it is possible that some of the "truisms" that we teach and preach may be sadly out of date, and that our "current" information may be at best woefully out of touch and at worst inappropriate.

I contend that it is wise to glean, adopt and employ some of the best and most effective teaching philosophies and methodologies of your former teachers, professors and mentors, *and* apply those to your own, personal and unique teaching philosophy and methodology. It has been said that too many teachers spend too much time teaching *their own* past, as opposed to *their students'* future. If teachers are not open to new information or change, then their teaching styles and the knowledge they disseminate can become quite antiquated.

Here are some thoughts on ways to develop your own teaching philosophy and to help determine what is important to you and what you would like your students to learn from you:

1) **Artistic standards.** Know what high quality is and how to achieve it, and be able to communicate that to your students and your audiences.

2) **Personal standards.** Life skills (in addition to or in conjunction with the teaching of music) that can be applied to all aspects of your students' lives include discipline, responsibility, reliability, punctuality,

maturity, compassion, sensitivity, cooperation, self-control, consistency, selflessness and stamina.

3) **Music selection.** What can be taught through your choices of music? Some possibilities are text, technique, history, languages, culture, mathematics, theory, phrasing, dynamics, expression and emotions.

4) **Work ethic.** Nothing worthwhile in life comes easy, or without a price, or without some effort!

I have developed a very specific teaching philosophy that has grown and improved over time. Essentially, my intention is to train and inspire students to achieve their musical best and to develop their personal and professional social skills and abilities, thus helping them become well-rounded, responsible and positive citizens of the world.

Although an in-depth description of my personal teaching philosophy and methodologies would be too lengthy to detail in this book, some of these include:

- Achieving the highest musical and artistic standards for individual students and ensembles.
- Teaching keyboard and music theory competencies, and developing an ear.
- Challenging students—mentally, musically, personally and physically.
- Causing students to experience things first-hand, oftentimes *outside* of the classroom.
- Preparing students for "the real world."
- High personal expectations. (No excuses, punctuality, respect, good manners, play well with others.)
- Efficient use of time (in both work and play).
- Knowing how to practice.
- Strong work ethic.
- Maintaining a positive attitude.
- Developing confidence through competence.
- Developing consistency.
- Developing 3D: Desire, Discipline and Dedication.
- Personal responsibility and maturity.
- Developing versatility, flexibility and adaptability.

- Developing a healthy self-esteem.
- Developing an understanding of the Business of Music.

I inform my students that there is a *reason* for *everything* that I teach, and they are always welcome to ask *why* we do things the way we do them. I will always have an answer as to the "why." The students do not necessarily have to agree with my answer, but at least they know that there is thought behind it, and that nothing taught is either capricious or taken for granted. It is important to clearly articulate and justify your teaching philosophy—to parents, students, prospective students and your higher administration.

CREATING AN EDUCATIONAL ENTERTAINMENT EXPERIENCE

Programming

Programming is one of the most important tools that you have to create an entertaining (and educational) performance. I make no apologies for considering entertainment value when creating programs, regardless of style. Ultimately you are responsible for what your students and ensembles perform, so it is up to you to determine the how and why of your repertoire selections. We will discuss programming from both a macro and micro perspective. Here are some points to ponder as you select your program:

1) **Who is your audience?** What are their demographics? I typically program different repertoire for a "mature" audience as opposed to an assembly performance for high school or middle school students.

2) **Styles.** Keep your audience guessing, and keep them entertained through the variety of repertoire you select. You might select repertoire from traditional styles that include swing, ballad, Latin, classical, gospel, rock, spiritual, Broadway, pop and world music, but it is also good to include other genres such as novelty tunes for comic relief, songs in the style of a specific historical period such as 1940s Big Band era, 1960s Beatles, or even disco—which could cover both an era *and* comic relief!

3) **Tempo.** General audiences respond to variety and contrasts, and changing tempos is a great way to hold your audiences' attention. Without significant contrasts in grooves and tempos, audiences will gradually develop ear fatigue, and you run the risk of losing their interest.

4) **Key relationships.** Know the initial and final keys of your repertoire. Try to avoid too much real time in the same key, especially on successive pieces. Ear fatigue can also develop from an overexposure to the same tonal center.

5) **Accompaniment forces.** You can easily achieve sonic variety by changing accompaniment forces. Consider programming ensemble pieces that are *a cappella*, with just piano accompaniment, or with rhythm section, or with horns. Perhaps you can add strings, or pieces that call for just brass accompaniment, or percussion ensemble, or even harp! If you have a fine instrumental ensemble that is a part of your ensemble, consider featuring them as a band without any vocals. A solo singer can find creative ways to change accompaniment forces, even within the same song. For example, a jazz or Broadway song in AABA form could begin with voice and only string bass accompaniment for the first two A's; add drum set at the bridge; and finally bring in piano at the start of the last A. The song could conclude the way it began, but in reverse order, so that just voice and bass are heard at the end.

6) **Real time.** Have you ever attended a concert that was simply too long? Perhaps one—or five—too many pieces? If I had a dollar for every time this has happened to me, I could have bestowed several significant endowments upon numerous charitable organizations! An essential element to assembling a successful program is being aware of exactly how long each piece of music lasts in real time. The only way to achieve this is to time your performance (several times, with a stopwatch) to establish consistency. Also, know the length of all spoken lines and non-musical activities. This is especially important if you are sharing a program with others and have been asked to give a concert of a specific duration. Out of respect for the other performers and as a professional courtesy, make sure you stay within your allotted time. There are few things worse for an audience than to sit through a performance by a self-indulgent group or soloist that lacks any concept of real time—thereby leaving that audience with a feeling of "too much."

> There are few things worse for an audience than to sit through a performance by a self-indulgent group or soloist that lacks any concept of real time—thereby leaving that audience with a feeling of "too much."

7) **Imagination and creativity. (Think outside the Bachs!)** Often choral conductors have been taught a programming "formula" that they then adopt, and either through force of habit, or lack of imagination, never abandon. Although there is nothing wrong with beginning a choral concert with a piece from the Renaissance era and concluding with a spiritual, I encourage you to try new programming possibilities and create a nontraditional program. What if your concert *opened* with a spiritual, or with a non-traditional or avant-garde piece? That would certainly get your audience's attention! You could then follow that opener with a selection from the Renaissance era, especially if that would return your audience to their "comfort zone."

Another approach to creative programming is a themed concert. Themes can include subject matter as broad as "love" to a more specific area such as "Music From The Americas." You will find a wide variety of programming possibilities, even within what might appear to be a limited subject. Yet one more example could explore the setting of a specific text such as "Ave Maria," where you will discover a historical and compositional range for the setting of that text that spans more than 500 years. Don't be afraid to try to break away from tradition and create new and innovative ways to program your traditional literature. What have you got to lose? If the audience does not respond favorably and get excited and energized, you can always go back to doing it the old way; those traditions will still be there!

8) **Vocal/tonal approach.** One of my favorite aspects of the human voice is its tonal flexibility. You can alter the sound of your solo voice or vocal ensemble to achieve tonal and stylistic variety from one song to the next. Choral techniques such as the use of vibrato are important tools in determining the appropriate sound for certain repertoire. It has been empirically proven that minimizing vibrato is not harmful to the voice, and a senza-vibrato sound may be the appropriate choice for repertoire from the Renaissance or perhaps even for vocal jazz. Likewise, a fuller texture using more vibrato would probably be a good choice on a gospel selection. A choral group has the potential to sound like four or five different ensembles, even though the personnel does not change, and I encourage you to explore those possibilities with your singers.

9) **Segues and transitions**. One of my personal pet peeves as an audience member is excessive dead stage space, whether that is the

amount of real time taken to get the performers on and off the stage or the actual time taken between performed selections. Just as you practice and rehearse the music you perform, you must also plan

> Talk to the audience only when necessary, and use that time to give the performers an opportunity to prepare, mentally and physically, for the next selection on the program.

and rehearse how to quickly and efficiently get from one piece to the next. A bit of forethought and prior planning can alleviate or eliminate excessive stage space, thereby enhancing your audiences' listening experience. Here are some simple suggestions as to how this can easily be achieved:

- When your ensemble enters and exits the stage, have them do so in two simultaneous lines from each side of the stage. Make sure your performers step lively and move with a purpose.

- If you must reposition ensemble members between selections, do so during the audience applause—so that when the applause has finished, the ensemble is in place and ready to begin the next selection.

- As a director, you may quicken the pace of the concert by starting the introduction to the next song during the audience applause.

- Talk to the audience only when necessary, and use that time to give the performers an opportunity to prepare, mentally and physically, for the next selection on the program.

10) **Adaptations.** I owe a debt of gratitude to Fred Waring for showing me many of the teaching philosophies I continue to use to this day. For six decades, Mr. Waring and his vocal and instrumental group, The Pennsylvanians, sold millions of records and popularized choral music throughout the world. As a pianist for the Waring Workshops, I gained first-hand insights and perspectives on the factors that contributed to his long professional success. Mr. Waring was fond of telling choral directors, "You paid for the music, now do what you want with it" (with the exception of making illegal photocopies, of course!). Once you have purchased the appropriate number of scores, you can consider adapting the music to suit the needs of your ensemble, as

long as artistic integrity is maintained. Here are some suggestions as to how this can be achieved:

- There can be much repetition in popular (and classical) music. Consider eliminating second and third verses, especially if the musical content is exactly the same as the first verse. This will also reduce the real time of your concert and offer you the opportunity to program more material, thereby giving you greater options for increased variety.

- Medleys are a great way to hold an audience's interest. You may create a "theme" medley such as songs about the weather, or songs with colors in their title, or songs about cities, states or countries (thereby increasing your students' and audience's awareness of geography!), or a tribute to an era, style, artist or group.

THE VISUALS

Many audiences listen with their eyes. The previous sentence is not a misprint. Whether it is right or wrong, or important to you or not, the fact remains that the visual aspects of your performance deserve as much forethought and attention as the purely musical ones. As I mentioned in Chapter 5, I start evaluating a performance from the moment I approach the venue. Here again are some of the points I initially evaluate:

- Who is in the audience? What are their ages and demographics? What is their mood and attitude prior to the concert? Is there anticipation, curiosity and energy, or resignation?

- What is the condition of the stage set? Is it neat and clean? Does it look professional? Are microphone and speaker cables wrapped and taped to the floor, or do they resemble a large dish of spaghetti?

- Is the stage sufficiently and appropriately lit?

- Are there any other "special effects" or potential surprises that I can spot?

- Is there prerecorded music playing in the house prior to the concert? If so, what is it?

- Is there a printed program? What is the content? Is it comprehensive and professional?

Note that all of the evaluations listed above occur *prior* to the start of the actual performance. Remember, it has been said that once the performance commences, a performer or ensemble has between 20 and 30 seconds to "capture" an audience. Therefore, because you only have one chance to make a first impression, it is extremely important to consider what you want your initial musical and visual impression to be. Typically, the following sequence takes place at the start of a concert: The houselights dim, then fade to black. The audience becomes silent in anticipation of the music. Your most important decision is *how* you would like the silence to be broken and *what* you would like your audience to see first.

As always, there is really no right or wrong way to start a concert: You have myriad options. For example, is there a main curtain? Would you like to have the performers behind that curtain, or choose not to use it? Should you enter from backstage, or elsewhere in the auditorium? Whatever you choose, realize that the audience will use those initial few seconds to make instant evaluations that impact their impression and opinion of the entire concert. Therefore your *Wow Factors* must be in place from the outset. Here are some of the initial evaluations your audience will be making:

> ...your **Wow Factors** must be in place from the outset.

- What are the performers wearing? Are their outfits or costumes clean, neat, and flattering for all performers?
- Do the performers look as though they are genuinely happy to be sharing their music with the audience?
- Do they appear to be mentally and physically engaged in the performance?
- Is there a commitment of energy?
- Do the performers demonstrate a sense of pride and confidence?
- Are they disciplined?
- Do the performers exhibit a sense of personal hygiene?

It is important to remind all performers that they are onstage and that an audience is viewing them. It is safe to assume that at any point in a program, *someone* in the audience is able to see *every* performer on the stage. Therefore, while onstage, it is inappropriate for performers to "go to their face," i.e., fix their hair, adjust their costumes, or scratch themselves, even though they may have a big itch! I believe that real professionalism and true discipline can be demonstrated when performers can train themselves to refrain from the temptation to "go to their face"!

Costuming. I am constantly amazed after a concert when audience members tell me how much they enjoyed the performance: "Your group *looked* just great, and they are so much fun to *watch*." I am tempted to respond saying, "Did you *hear* any of the *music?*"—but of course that could be considered insulting, so I refrain. Perhaps those people came to the concert expecting to hear great music but were even more surprised by what they experienced with their eyes at the same time. I have found that most audiences will appreciate what you create visually as well as musically. In reality, some people are more responsive to and have a better-developed vocabulary for certain senses than others. For example, when I engage in a conversation, I can easily walk away remembering everything that person said and have no clue as to what clothes that person was wearing!

The fact is, audiences do make evaluations based on appearances, so it is in your best interest to find an outfit that represents, complements and flatters your group. This can sometimes pose a challenge, especially when you have a wide variety of body types and sizes. Although the "look" of your ensemble can vary, I think elegant and classy (as opposed to trendy) never go out of style. Here are some options for you to consider:

- Order the same outfit from a professional costume company. This way the ladies can wear the same dress—and even keep the same dress from year to year to retain consistency and reduce cost to others. The men can order a basic tuxedo from the same place, thereby ensuring consistency in the men's look.

- Men and women can wear a suit with jacket (and tie for the men). The jacket (and tie) can later be removed for variety and a more casual look.

- Set a color theme. Have people choose their own outfits while maintaining a specific color palette; for example, use only clothing that is black and white with red accents. Remember to check on each student's proposed selection prior to the concert in order to avoid a potentially awkward situation.

- Use intermission (or another appropriate time in your program when the singers are not onstage) to have your performers change or modify their outfits. The visual variety will appeal to your audience members who listen with their eyes.

Lighting and special effects. Although not a crucial aspect of a performance, lighting changes can greatly enhance a performance and increase visual variety. This variety can be achieved with relative simplicity and can include:

- Lowering the houselights (putting the audience in a darkened area) and raising the level of the stage lights, thereby bringing greater featured light on the performers.
- Judicious use of a follow spotlight to highlight soloists.
- Changing the overall level of stage lighting to reflect the mood or text of a song.
- Using different colored lights to achieve contrasts.
- Judicious use of special effects such as strobe or ultraviolet (black) light or mirror balls.

Staging. No law requires concert choirs to remain in one position on choral risers for the entire duration of a concert. Visual (and sonic) variety can be achieved by moving the singers in your ensemble into different positions. I enjoy eliminating the barrier that is often created between audience and performer. This can be achieved through spoken word as well as through the positioning and attitude of your singers. One of the hallmarks of an ensemble that I direct is the commitment of physical energy in performance. I like to "bring it" to the audience in terms of commitment of physical and musical energy, and when possible, locate the singers as close as possible to the audience. You can also consider having them sing from within the audience, or having them start a piece behind the audience and move through the audience to the stage.

> I like to "bring it" to the audience in terms of commitment of physical and musical energy,

Choralography and choreography. The subject of whether or not to dance when singing, and, if so, how much, is one that is sure to create a healthy debate. As you might imagine, I choose to take the high road and proffer that once again there is no right or wrong answer. It is up to you to determine how much or how little your groups or soloists move on stage, and this should be a direct reflection on your philosophy and priorities.

One way to determine the appropriateness of movement as a soloist or in an ensemble is to first consider the idiom or genre that you are performing. For example:

- A vocal soloist (whether singing classical, jazz or pop music) should develop an ability to create stage movements reflecting the text or style of the song. In a performance of a classical art song, the singer should reflect the character of the text through his or her facial expressions and gestures. This can be accomplished in subtle ways, and does not necessarily have to be "over the top." For example, the text of a love ballad can be greatly enhanced by raising your head and gazing beyond the audience, or lifting an arm and gesturing gently. Of course there are times when full-blown acting and "over the top" are appropriate—as long as artistic integrity and good taste are maintained. A jazz swing tune could feature a relaxed pose with the soloist snapping fingers on beats 2 and 4. Unfortunately, many of the current pop, rock, R&B, rap and hip-hop artists feature complex choreography and sophisticated dance moves, often "sung" to prerecorded vocal tracks, or using an automatic pitch tuner. Please don't ask me my opinion about this and the "educational" message that it sends to young singers. I want to keep this book G rated. ... OK, you twisted my arm! For starters, if you are a music educator, then you are a music professional with an earned degree in music. Your first responsibility is to teach music, and, unless you have another degree in dance, choreography should take a backseat. And it is your responsibility to give your students the musical tools and information they will need in order to achieve artistic excellence in live performance. Having them sing along with prerecorded tracks or using effects like auto-tuning are counterproductive to the entire educational process. Don't get me started!

- In a musical stage production, it is almost expected to have major choreographed numbers using principals and full chorus. We use classic or current Broadway shows as our benchmark.

- Concert choirs sometimes err on the side of a lifeless or expressionless stage presence. I find few things more boring. Singing is a physical activity and therefore requires physical energy. Without going overboard, individual choir members must be encouraged to engage their faces and bodies when singing. Choralography—the unified movement or gestures by a large number of singers, usually in a concert choir setting—can be an effective extramusical device on certain repertoire, especially those in the world, ethnic or contemporary music categories.

- Vocal jazz ensembles should be encouraged to move and groove, depending on the style of their specific repertoire. With Gold Company,

I encourage my students to develop their own free and natural movement style. Rest assured—we practice our "look" extensively so that when the ensemble is onstage the singers give the physical impression of being confident and relaxed. I do not allow individual singers to get out of control and draw undue attention to themselves.

- Show choirs, by definition, spend a large amount of rehearsal time developing a highly choreographed show or routine that typically includes three to four pieces of music and usually lasts 10 to 15 minutes. This same routine is then performed throughout the school year with little or no change or variety, with an emphasis placed on participating in show choir competitions. Although I love a great athletic competition, I have mixed feelings about the place for competitions among school music groups. Too often I have seen a negative message sent whereby Show Choir A "beats" Show Choir B. My preference would be to leave the competition to the football or basketball teams.

Remember, your music program and what you ultimately *teach* your students will be a direct reflection of your philosophy. When you periodically take time to reflect on your musical priorities and how you spend your rehearsal time, I would like to remind you that you are a *music* teacher first, and everything else, including choreography, should take a backseat.

> ... you are a *music* teacher first, and everything else, including choreography, should take a backseat.

Although I believe choreography and choralography to be an important part of a complete performance, in my case, I always insist that the *music* comes first. The reputation of Gold Company has been built on excellent singing, and, although my students also dance, I would be surprised if anyone listed choreography as their top reason for enjoying a performance by Gold Company.

Even though I am personally "choreographically challenged," I know that it is important for my students to at least marginally develop their abilities in this area, as it instills greater confidence in their stage presence, energizes both performer and audience, and develops a more versatile performer that will be better prepared to accept future professional performance opportunities that involve movement.

If you observe and analyze the stage presence of professional vocal groups such as The Manhattan Transfer, Take 6, The Real Group, The King's

Singers, The Swingle Singers, New York Voices and Chanticleer, you will find that they all address staging and choreography as an important part of their performance. This is a key point because all the aforementioned ensembles sing well and make excellent vocals their first priority and the focus of every performance. The addition of movement serves as a visual enhancement to the overall production. Again, I don't think anyone would associate these groups with their amazing dance moves, yet movement plays an important part of their presentation.

THAT'S THE TICKET

As a performer, you have an obligation to consider your audience, especially if they have paid for tickets. You are providing a service, whether it is pure entertainment or pure artistry, or, hopefully, a healthy combination of both. Try to figure out how to leave your audience with a sense of completion, fulfillment and satisfaction. You should feel as though you have prepared and consumed a *great* meal with perfect proportions (appetizer, salad, main course and, of course, a chocolate dessert) but that you are not *over*stuffed and feeling as though you have had too much.

A *"wow"* performance will include musical and physical variety (programming, movement, and possibly humor). The performance *has* to sustain an audience (in real time) whether it is a 15-minute or two-hour show. You want to transport your audience somewhere else and cause them to forget whatever their concerns were when they entered the auditorium, club or theater, even for a few minutes. Quite simply, this is your obligation.

Of course, all of the above *presumes* a program that is well-prepared, sung and played in tune, with confidence and with artistic integrity. I realize that, as you read this, you may be thinking, "*Wow*, Steve Zegree really thinks about every minute detail of every aspect of the performance." If so, you are correct! The professionalism in a performance and your ability to "*wow*" come from the music-making *plus* your commitment to all of the extramusical aspects of your performance. There is no substitute for attention to detail.

> The professionalism in a performance and your ability to "*wow*" come from the music-making *plus* your commitment to all of the extramusical aspects of your performance.

Yes, this may require a commitment of extra effort, energy, expense and time, but I hope you will find the result of your undertaking to be rewarding and satisfying, for your students, your audience and you!

I have had the good fortune, pleasure and honor of professionally and personally collaborating with the members of The Manhattan Transfer, in various different venues and mediums. In addition to being

> … an important part of *"wow"* is developing your ability to make each and every performance fresh, energetic and exciting.

personal friends, I am also a fan of The Transfer and very much appreciate all of their contributions toward raising artistic standards and expanding the repertoire of contemporary group vocals in the world of choral music education. Their repertoire is eclectic and includes a wide variety of styles. It can be technically challenging and sophisticated (for example, "Body and Soul" is as difficult to sing as virtually any piece in the choral repertoire), has high artistic standards and appeals to a jazz and musically "hip" audience, yet the singers have also figured out how to make their concerts entertaining and appealing to the general public. This general and popular appeal is created by several factors including musical integrity, commitment of physical energy in performance, costume changes, choreography and staging, lighting, humor and establishing a personal connection with the audience. It is not a coincidence that these are the same elements that can be found in a theatrical performance. These elements are also an integral part of many rock concerts, where sometimes the lighting, sets, staging, choreography, pyrotechnics and volume can serve to overshadow or compensate for the lack of great music-making!

Gold Company was recently honored to share the stage and perform with The Manhattan Transfer. During a rehearsal break my students had a Q and A session with the members of The Transfer. I have always been impressed by The Manhattan Transfer's passion for performance and commitment of energy "live" in concert. So, for the benefit of my students I made the following comment: "After all of your professional successes including numerous Grammy awards, touring and performing throughout the world, you don't *have* to give all of that energy and effort in concert anymore." The response from Tim Hauser was immediate, passionate and declamatory: "*Yes, we do!!* Even if we are performing 'Birdland' for the 5,000th time, we still have to make it seem as though it is as fresh as the first time. We owe that to our audience. It is a professional obligation that we take very seriously." I could see that Tim's response was both eye-opening and inspirational to several of my students, who realized that an important part of "*wow*" is developing your ability to make each and every performance fresh, energetic and exciting.

WHEN THINGS DON'T ALWAYS
GO THE WAY YOU INTENDED

As much as we rehearse, plan and practice, we cannot always control what transpires "in the moment" on stage, in a "live" performance. This, of course is one of the most exhilarating, joyful and terrifying aspects of performing. As educators, performers, directors and conductors we must learn how to recover from these sometimes challenging situations and use them as teaching moments.

I fondly remember a chance encounter I had with educator, author and motivational speaker Tim Lautzenheiser at a national music convention. Tim came up to me and said, "Steve, I owe you a lot of money..." Knowing Tim and his terrific sense of humor, I had no idea where he was going with that statement, and I'm sure my face reflected that. He continued, "I was in the audience at the Washington State music educators convention when you conducted the All-State Jazz Choir, and I watched you turn a potential disaster into a victory, and I've been telling that story ever since."

Of course I was keenly aware of the event to which Tim referred. It was the final performance of the All-State ensemble that included the finest high school jazz and choral singers in the state of Washington. Typically when I am invited to conduct an honor ensemble, I prefer to select repertoire that will challenge, educate and inspire the performers and hopefully do the same for—plus entertain—the audience. One of the pieces I programmed for this concert was the "Organ Fugue" by J.S. Bach, arranged for SATB *a cappella* vocal ensemble by Ward Swingle. Ward's arrangements typically present a challenge to the singer and ensemble (and conductor!), but I thought 2½ days of rehearsal time would be sufficient to teach that piece, in addition to the others on the program. Indeed, after two days of intense and focused rehearsal, the ensemble was well prepared to perform the "Organ Fugue" from memory, as well as all of the other repertoire on the program, and they demonstrated this fact several times in rehearsal and in the final dress rehearsal.

Let's fast-forward the story to the actual performance. The auditorium was packed with more than 1,500 excited people. The audience included performers' family members, teachers and other music professionals, fellow students and the general public, and an electric "buzz" filled the air prior to our taking the stage. The concert began with the ensemble performing beautifully and the audience responding with terrific support and enthusiasm. Then it was time for the Bach. The fugue began just as we had rehearsed and performed so well during our rehearsals. The four sections (SATB) each made their entrances on the subject theme at the appropriate time, and as their conductor I was feeling great and enjoying the performance. Then it happened. Maybe it was the placement of the piece in the program. Perhaps it was nerves, or a lack of focus. Maybe it was fatigue or quite simply a cognitive malfunction, but midway through the piece, one section made an early entrance—and this set off a chain of events that could best be described as a train wreck. In the period of a few seconds, the performance transformed from Bach to Schoenberg. The entire ensemble was confused and the sounds being made did not in any way resemble the original score or anything even remotely connected with the harmony of the Baroque era.

If you are a conductor, perhaps you too have encountered a moment like this. You may experience emotions that include panic, helplessness, frustration, embarrassment, shame or even incompetence. Or you can seize the moment and turn it into an opportunity to "*wow*." I made a split-second judgment call, gave the universal conductor's cutoff gesture and stopped the performance in mid-song. The silence in the room was deafening. I then turned to the audience and said, "This ensemble has worked tirelessly and with energy and passion for the past 2½ days, and they are completely capable of singing this piece well. So, if you don't mind, we are going to start the piece over and sing it again." There was supporting applause from the audience as I turned to the ensemble and asked for the starting pitch. I also gave the ensemble a look of confidence, focus

> ...you can seize the moment and turn it into an opportunity to "*wow*."

and urgency. Without saying a word, using my eyes, I told them, "You *know* you can sing this piece well, now let's show these people what you are *really* capable of."

What followed was not only remarkable and memorable for anyone in attendance, but it is also a moment in time that I will never forget. The ensemble performed the "Organ Fugue" better than they ever had in any rehearsal. It was clean, focused, spirited, accurate, confident, musical, in tune, intense, blended, balanced, virtuosic, exciting and fun. In other words, the ensemble (and the audience) experienced a "*wow*" moment. When the ensemble nailed the final chord (with the Picardy third!), the audience applause was deafening, and the ensemble received an extended standing ovation—in the *middle* of the program! Truly memorable.

I think there are several reasons that Tim was so moved by this event:

1) **Everyone makes mistakes.** If you are a human being, you have made mistakes. You were probably making mistakes before you were talking or even walking. Correcting previous mistakes and avoiding making the same mistake again is one of the best ways to educate. As a teacher, I can often anticipate a mistake that a student will most likely make, and even point that out in the process. However, sometimes the student must experience his or her own mistake in order to learn from it and grow. Especially if the mistake causes an unpleasant feeling, the student may make different decisions or modify behavior to avoid future unpleasantness. Even the greatest artists and musicians are capable of less-than-perfect performances.

   I was once in the audience for a performance by the legendary classical concert pianist Arthur Rubinstein. The maestro was at an advanced age when I heard him, yet he still played a full solo recital program. The opportunity to simply *hear* the great Rubinstein live was, by definition, a *"wow"* moment. Rubinstein programmed the *Ballade in G minor* by Chopin as the closing number in his program. The piece concludes with a virtuosic coda that finishes with a resounding G minor chord. Rubinstein's performance was awe-inspiring, right up until the final notes, when he played chords that included several notes that are not included in G minor harmony. Everyone in the audience knew that he had played some wrong notes, but nobody cared, and there was a spontaneous, simultaneous and extended standing ovation.

   > The issue is not *whether* you will make mistakes, but rather, *how* you will handle them.

   And the pianist … simply got up and bowed as if nothing out of the ordinary had happened. Indeed everyone, even the very best, makes mistakes. The issue is not *whether* you will make mistakes, but rather, *how* you will handle them.

2) **Make lemonade out of lemons.** I love this old saying. There are times in life (and in musical performance) that due to circumstances beyond your control you will be faced with a personal or musical situation that is less than desirable. Even though this experience may not be fun, you can rest assured that it *will* happen to you and/or your ensemble at some point. In a musical performance you have the choice of letting everyone know things are not going well (through physical reactions, facial expressions, spoken words, etc.)—or simply

accepting the fact that some things could be better, and let it flow like the water off the proverbial duck's behind.

3) **Create an educational opportunity/Carpe diem.** I believe that the desire to teach is inherent in human nature. People generally enjoy sharing what they know. This can be demonstrated to a young child through good parenting or good teaching, and these two things are often inseparable. An educational opportunity is even more effective when it is presented in a positive way. I will never forget when my son was in kindergarten and he had a classmate who expectorated on another student. The teacher could have reacted angrily and sternly shouted, "Tommy, DON'T SPIT on your classmates!!!" Instead, she calmly but firmly said, "Tommy, we keep our saliva in our mouths." Another "*wow*" moment. I was so impressed with that teacher's poise and presence of mind to create a wonderfully positive educational opportunity out of a less than pleasant situation. The situation with the Washington All-State instantly created several educational opportunities for the singers and the audience. Can you think of what some of them may have been? Among others, it taught the performers that with greater focus, determination and mental energy they were capable of achieving a level of performance that by far exceeded what would have occurred if the train wreck had never transpired.

So, we have determined that all performers (and conductors!) make mistakes. I realize that it is a natural reaction for a performer who makes a mistake to feel embarrassed or disappointed or even angry, but these emotions do not belong anywhere on the stage (unless they are an integral part of the text or character). Whatever the "mistake" may be, it probably will feel much bigger to the performer than to anyone else on stage or in the audience. Most audience members will be unaware of any minor errors—therefore the performers should never give the appearance that something is not as it should be on the stage.

TEACHING THROUGH WRITING

I am very fortunate to write and arrange choral music that has been published by several companies and sung and played by singers of all ages ranging from elementary school to senior citizens throughout the world. I say "fortunate" because writing and arranging music is something I do for *fun*, essentially as a hobby—a "busman's holiday" perhaps—but a hobby nonetheless. My primary profession (and passion) is being on the faculty at a major university's School of Music, and everything else in my professional musical life takes a secondary role and serves as a byproduct. In fact, if I were forced to choose between my career as an educator and my career as a performer (either as pianist or conductor), the answer would be simple. I am a committed educator and derive the greatest pleasure and joy from developing the abilities of my students and hopefully empowering and inspiring future generations of educators and performers. For me, there is no greater professional reward or satisfaction.

My reason for stating this is to point out that I do not depend on music writing to earn my living, therefore I do not consider statistics such as potential income and future sales when I write. Instead, I have just three criteria when deciding whether to write a new chart:

1) **Do I like the music?**
   "Like" is a matter of personal taste. Several factors may cause me to like a piece of music, including composer or lyricist, the text, harmonic and melodic content, rhythm, tempo and groove, emotional or personal connection, and historical context.

2) **Will I enjoy the creative process of writing and arranging?**
   Writing and arranging music involves a commitment of time, energy and creativity. Due to the fact that my "spare" or leisure time is somewhat limited, I need to decide how I might like to allocate that time. Therefore, if I choose to spend time writing music, I want to enjoy that time and use it as a creative outlet. The process should be fun, and there should be a sense of joy and satisfaction at the conclusion of the writing project.

3) **What will I be able to *teach* through this writing?**
   This question is the one that I take most seriously when writing new music. As a committed educator, I am always thinking of ways that I can include an "educational opportunity" or three in all of the music that I write for publication. My intention is that a director can use the music to "teach" and better educate his or her singers, regardless of age and experience.

What follows are a few of the musical and educational elements I consciously consider when beginning to write a new piece of music:

- **The level for which I am writing.** One thing I love to do is create musical and intellectual challenges for the singers, regardless of their age or experience. If I am writing for elementary school children, the degree of difficulty, harmonic sophistication and technical elements will obviously have to be much less demanding than something written for high school students. However, I have used the following musical devices in several two-part arrangements that still provide the director the opportunity to "teach" musical axioms: modulation, improvisation, mixed meters, musical forms, styles, quotes from classical compositions, historical aspects that may have influenced the composer or composition, and biographies of great composers and lyricists. You may also teach young students to become physically involved with the music with basic choralography, or one of my favorites: teaching inexperienced singers to snap their fingers on beats 2 and 4 on a medium swing tune. It sounds like a simple task, but try it! I'll bet you will find this undertaking to be more challenging than you might anticipate. In fact, this acquired skill may even present challenges to *experienced* singers, especially if they have little exposure to non-classical music.

First, make sure that *you* can master your ability to perform this seemingly simple task, then develop your ability to teach others! A couple of great standard songs you could use to practice your "snapping skills" are "I've Got the World on a String" by Harold Arlen and "Satin Doll" by Duke Ellington. Feel free to discover and learn about the Great American Songbook and the vast library of classic songs to which you can apply a medium swing feel.

> One thing I love to do is create musical and intellectual challenges for the singers, regardless of their age or experience.

- **Crafting the accompaniments.** I am quite particular about the piano accompaniments that I write. My training as a pianist allows me to write idiomatically for the instrument. I am also conscious of the style of the piece and craft the accompaniment accordingly. For example, if the arrangement is "jazzy" I will write an accompaniment that a classical pianist can read and learn accurately from the score, and as a result will *sound* like a jazz pianist, even without a background in jazz. This experience can serve as a catalyst for a young pianist to become more versatile and expand his or her musical horizons.

- **Text painting.** In the Renaissance era, it was common for a composer to make note choices that reflected the literal meaning of the words.

This device, called "text painting," can also be found in popular music today, and I certainly avail myself of the technique in my arrangements.

- **Intertwining music and history.** It is easy to connect a composer or an era to world history facts or important historical events or dates that occurred during that composer's lifetime. For example, both Franz Joseph Haydn and George Washington were born in 1732. Abraham Lincoln and Felix Mendelssohn share the same birth year—1809. If you want to connect great American composers to important literary or film personalities, consider the fact that Duke Ellington, Hoagy Carmichael, Ernest Hemingway, Alfred Hitchcock, Humphrey Bogart and James Cagney were all born in 1899, as was Al Capone! The makings of a great medley are undoubtedly in there somewhere!

- **Teaching geography through music.** It's a no-brainer: Students can learn about Austria through Mozart, France through Debussy and Russia through Tchaikovsky. Additionally, grooves can open wonderful doors to the culture and traditions of other countries. For example, we can learn about Brazil through the bossa nova and samba, and discover Cuba and Puerto Rico through mambo and salsa grooves!

- **Finding a fresh or nontraditional way to present old or traditional material.** This was successfully accomplished on the recording *Handel's Messiah: A Soulful Celebration*, whereby the recitatives, arias and choruses from the original composition were "updated" and performed by contemporary artists, in styles that range from pop to gospel. The gospel version of the *Hallelujah Chorus* is particularly memorable, and perhaps could even be controversial, but that opens the *wonderful* educational door for discussion, healthy dialogue, and comparisons and contrasts with the original.

- **Creating a challenge.** When I am writing for more advanced and mature groups (high school level and above), I enjoy educating by challenging the singers' aural capabilities. This is most commonly achieved through writing altered chords (including ♯9 or ♭9, ♯11 or ♭13) or adding or substituting nontraditional harmonies.

Natural Selection

With literally thousands of new choral publications released each and every year, the process of selecting educationally appropriate repertoire for your ensemble can be a daunting task. First, ask yourself these two questions:

1. What does the music teach?
2. What can I teach *through* the music?

Remember, your first responsibility as an educator is to *educate* your students! What you impart to them on a daily and annual basis will be a direct reflection on your personal educational philosophy and methodology. Hopefully this will include a wide variety of repertoire combined with experiences and opportunities that cannot typically be found in a more traditional academic classroom.

When selecting compositions from the standard classical repertoire, your obligation is to research the best or most critically acclaimed editions of the score. These can range from an urtext (original version, unedited) to an edition by a scholar or editor who is widely recognized as an expert on the composer or on the stylistic era that the composition represents.

When selecting new arrangements for your ensemble, you might first consider *who* arranged the music. I have found that arrangers, like composers, develop a "style" of writing, and that, for better or worse, it is difficult for them to break away from their writing style. This is why you can recognize a composition by Bach just by hearing it, even if you do not know the specific piece. Likewise, I can recognize a Gene Puerling chart upon initial hearing, even if I do not know the arrangement. The arranger will either be Puerling, or someone trying to write in his style. I daresay, after a closer examination, you will likely find common and unifying elements in my choral writing as well!

What follows is an objective list of criteria that may be helpful to directors when trying to decide what to program for your ensemble:

- Text. Is it appropriate? What does it teach?
- How/where does this piece fit within my total program?
- Degree of difficulty. The more challenging the piece, the more time that is required for rehearsal and preparation. How much total time do you have in your rehearsal process, and how can that time be divided?
- Accompaniment forces required and degree of difficulty of the accompaniment.
- Solo opportunities or requirements.
- Number of voice parts.
- Style.
- Range.

- Tessitura.
- Key.
- Tempo.
- Groove.
- Length (in measures and in real time).
- Choreography/choralography opportunities.
- Is it possible (appropriate) to modify and/or adapt the score to suit your needs?
- Are recordings available? (Original recordings, publishers' demo recording, etc.)
- Historical significance of the composition or arrangement?

INTELLECT AND EMOTION: THE SECRET BLEND

In addition to finding the coexistence of education and entertainment to create "*wow*" in your performances, you must add two more essential ingredients: intellect and emotion. These two elements are *not* mutually exclusive—intellect and emotion in performance can (and must) coexist. The intellect in your performance is a reflection of all of your accumulated formal education, training and knowledge. Typically this can include:

> ...intellect and emotion in performance can (and must) coexist.

- **Technique**. Through hard work and practice you must develop your technical abilities on your voice and/or instrument. At the most basic level this can mean vibrating a reed, buzzing a mouthpiece, drawing a bow over a string, or creating healthy vocal sounds. At more advanced levels, a well-developed technique will enable you to sing and/or play some of the most challenging and virtuosic pieces in the repertoire. For vocal ensembles and choir conductors, this means achieving requisite tenets of blend, balance, diction, appropriate tone and style. For specialized skills such as improvisation and scat singing, this involves years of practice and listening in order to develop competence and to master those abilities.

- **Research.** Although I do not want to sound too "academic" here, a healthy dose of research is an essential component of any "*wow*" performance. The term "research" does not necessarily have to refer to the formal study often associated with advanced graduate study, although that certainly qualifies as an important backdrop for many types of performances. Scholarly program notes that accompany a concert program are an excellent way to educate an audience and help their appreciation of your selected repertoire.

Research, however, can also serve as the culmination of years of less "official" study in specific areas. For example, the act of listening to music is one of the most important elements in the development of all musicians. When learning about the style and interpretation of classical music, it is a great idea to listen to any available prior recording and note similarities and differences. Reading the liner notes that accompany most recordings can also assist you in the accumulation of knowledge relating to the recording session, specific personnel, historical facts and figures, and insights from the producers and performers. In jazz and popular music, whether learning a specific song or studying a style, your research should include listening to every extant recording of that song for ideas on interpretation and inspiration for artistry.

Musicians who have done this important "homework" will often refer to the best-known or "classic" recordings associated with a genre. You need to be able to "hold your own" in these conversations, or if you are not aware of the repertoire, recordings or artists that are being discussed, take note and rectify that situation prior to your next meeting with those musicians! Doing this research and accumulating this knowledge base is an important part of your education and subsequently, your ability to educate others, while you entertain!

- **Repertoire.** This is one of the most important decisions you must make in determining what you choose to present to your audience. Regardless of style or idiom, there is more repertoire available to you than you will be able to prepare and perform in your lifetime. Therefore you need to develop a plan as to how you want to spend your practice, research and rehearsal time. What pieces, composers or arrangers are important to you? What do you want your students to know and experience? What are your *personal* preferences and how do those relate to the educational needs and goals of your students and audiences?

> Technique is simply the *vehicle* to arrive at your goal: musical expression.

- **Experience.** It is crucial that you understand that "intellect" described above is separate and distinct from achieving an aesthetic and beauty in your music and ultimately in your performances. One can experience the most technically virtuosic performance on the planet, but if it is not combined with musicianship, feeling, emotion or soul, then it is nothing more than a lot of fast notes. Technique is simply the *vehicle* to arrive at your goal: musical expression.

Typically, in our youth we tend to focus more on technical development than musical or artistic expression. Our goal, once we have achieved technical expertise, is to move beyond pure technique and discover the importance and joy of musical expression. In fact, one of the greatest compliments that can be bestowed upon young musicians is that they sing or play with a musical sensibility and maturity well beyond their chronological years. This is usually achieved either through inspired teaching and excellent mentorship, or through extraordinary talent and innate individual musicianship.

Herein lies one of life's greatest conundrums: Some things in life can be taught *only* through living and experiencing. Or, to quote George Bernard Shaw, "Youth is wasted on the young." For performers, conductors, directors and educators, with age comes experience, maturity and (hopefully) improvement of skills and abilities.

I must admit that earlier in my career I erred on the side of technique and virtuosity at the expense of emotion and expression in my music-making. This may have been a reflection on my youth, immaturity or ignorance, or a combination of all or none of the above! I was fortunate to have the extraordinary opportunity to study with and be mentored by Dr. Eph Ehly, who instilled in me (among many other important things) the understanding that technique alone does not ultimately impress or "*wow.*" Technique without emotion may be likened to junk food: It may temporarily fill you up, but in the end it is not satisfying—or nutritious!

You must arrive at greater artistry and increased emotional connection to the music in your own time and space. I tell my students that they cannot know and experience profound joy until they have experienced heartfelt sadness. Knowing sadness is not *fun* nor is it typically pleasant, and therefore hopefully can be minimized in one's life, but sadness is nonetheless an important emotion, and a part of the total palette. Once you have experienced a broader range of emotions, you will better relate to great texts and lyrics of songs. And you will be better able to discern between great and inspired recordings of soloists and

> You must arrive at greater artistry and increased emotional connection to the music in your own time and space.

ensembles as opposed to those that are simply commonplace. Most importantly, it is essential for you to embrace all of your accumulated life experiences as an artist and as an interpreter in order for you to develop the ability to teach your students to "feel" it—and then ultimately for your audiences to feel it too.

MAKE THEM THIRSTY

Most music-loving audiences also love harmony. Their tastes in harmony can vary from simple to complex, perhaps in a pattern analogous to the history of music, reflecting a line of ever-increasing harmonic sophistication. Initially, your students may also have limited tastes when it comes to appreciation for harmonic sophistication.

If you read some of the earlier chapters, you may remember that I like to put a new spin on the old saying about leading a horse to water, and I think it applies particularly well to educating both students and audiences: "You can lead the horse to water, then figure out how to make it thirsty." Of course, you can (and should) apply this "educational philosophy" to virtually any aspect of music education. We must learn to accept the students (and audiences) that we inherit, on *their* terms. Once they become your students, your challenge is to take them from where they are to where you would like for them to be, in terms of knowledge, sophistication, culture and standards. Your job is to find ways to excite, encourage, motivate, inspire, persuade, or cajole them into achieving and learning more than they could have possibly imagined.

Typically a student or students will come to you with good knowledge of current pop music as well as who and what is "hot" on the charts. It is quite likely they will know much more than you in that area. Your challenge is to *make them thirsty* and bring them to new levels of musical appreciation and sophistication. Start by asking your students what they are listening to on their iPods, and then listen to that music. If there is a lead vocal with background harmony vocals, you are in business!

You must find the "good" in pop music, and that is *not* an oxymoron! A logical step would be to introduce the students to some "historic" pop groups who used four-part harmony, such as Backstreet Boys, 98 Degrees, or Boys to Men. You may also point out the amazing lead vocal prowess of singers like Stevie Wonder and the extraordinary grooves and vocals of Earth, Wind and Fire. Once they develop an appreciation of the quality in those groups, your logical next step is to bring the students to the vocal and harmonic sophistication of professional vocal groups such as Take 6, The Singers Unlimited, The Manhattan Transfer, New York Voices or The Real Group, or even the more historic "boy bands" such as The Hi-Lo's! and The Four Freshmen.

And, if your students are fortunate enough to sing in an ensemble that rehearses and performs literature by groups such as these, they will be forever changed. Once they have had a taste of the joy of singing part of a harmonically sophisticated chord and the requisite effort that is necessary to create that sound, you will have made a tremendous educational achievement. From that point it is a relatively easy jump to the harmonies of Poulenc, Brahms, Mozart or Palestrina, as well as contemporary choral composers such as Eric Whitacre.

CREATIVE COLLABORATION

After you have developed your technical, musical and artistic abilities, and after you have achieved a certain degree of confidence through your experiences as a performer, you will have earned some of the "rewards" for all of your hard work and efforts. Sometimes these rewards can be subtle and recognized only by the performer(s) or perhaps a few knowledgeable or experienced audience members.

One of the greatest joys for performers (and audiences) is the spontaneity that can occur by being "in the moment." Vocal soloists must learn how to be creative yet controlled in their performances, and also how to react to and interact with all of their collaborative musicians. There can be a certain amount of risk-taking when performing live, but only the most experienced performers should have the courage to go to unchartered territory in concert!

One of the best examples of this courage is Bobby McFerrin, who has mastered all of the elements of "*wow*" to the degree that he is essentially fearless and completely free in performance. He enabled all other singers and also gave other performers "permission" to boldly go where no man (or woman!) has gone before, when he started giving solo, improvised vocal concerts. I was in the audience when Bobby performed a trio concert collaborating with the great jazz pianist Chick Corea and jazz drummer Jack

DeJohnette. Unbeknownst to the audience, prior to the concert the artists established just two rules that completely governed the performance:

1. The only rule before going onstage is that there were *no* restrictions, except that none of the trio could perform any music or songs that they already knew or had performed before.

2. There would be no talking to the audience and the performance would last for 90 minutes.

There was dancing by all three performers; there was vocal (spoken sound) improvisation. *Everyone* took a turn playing the piano, and completely unstructured freedom—sprinkled with unplanned fun at unpredictable moments—totally filled the hall for 90 minutes. As a result, an audience member who came expecting to hear "Don't Worry Be Happy" or "Spain" would possibly have been disappointed or perhaps perplexed by this performance. On the other hand, I was on the edge of my seat for 90 minutes straight. Immediately following the concert, the trio stayed onstage and proceeded to take questions from the audience. This was a *very* smart move on their part in that it helped give the audience opportunities to ask questions such as "What *was* that?!" It also helped to educate and elucidate the audience, thereby elevating their consciousness, knowledge and sophistication, and as a result making the entire experience more entertaining.

The spirit, spontaneity, energy, enthusiasm and supreme musicianship exhibited by these three extraordinary musicians combined to create something that I will never forget. It took courage, confidence and extreme competence, but Chick and Jack played with Miles Davis over 40 years ago, so there is a long musical history of collaboration between these players, and (perhaps most importantly), there is trust, without ego. There is no "right or wrong"—just the spirit of making music.

> There is no "right or wrong"—just the spirit of making music.

For several years I have had the privilege of playing piano in a jazz quartet that includes legendary drummer Billy Hart. Billy's resume and discography is a "Who's who" of the greatest jazz musicians on the planet. I know that I am not the same caliber of jazz pianist that Billy typically collaborates with, and I have no delusions of grandeur when we have the occasion to play together. I simply consider myself fortunate, and cherish the opportunity to have a professional and personal association with a master musician. A lesser person than Billy might approach this musical collaboration with indifference or worse yet, condescension. I have had experiences with both of these and believe me, it is no fun. Fortunately, because of who he is and how he chooses to live, Billy brings his very best "A game" to *any and every* performance, regardless of venue, time of day or identity or musical abilities of the collaborative musicians. Billy's passion and positive attitude are both infectious and inspirational—and completely professional.

When we perform together, Billy and I constantly maintain eye contact. He will often take his playing to very sophisticated rhythmic levels using musical devices such as metric modulations and displaced beats. As a performer, if I let my mind wander for even an instant, I will most likely lose track of where beat 1 is, even in a medium swing piece in 4/4 time. I truly enjoy being "pushed" by Billy and sometimes even have the courage to return the favor. When this happens, both Billy and I typically will play an accent on beat 1 following an eight-bar phrase. Three things can happen:

1. We arrive at the same time.
2. Billy plays slightly ahead of me.
3. I play slightly ahead of Billy.

Regardless of which of these three occurs at the downbeat of the new phrase, the audience will notice one thing: smiles on both Billy's face and mine. There is no "fault" for an early or late perception of where beat 1 is; no one is "right" or "wrong." It is simply great fun just going for it. Even though each player has his own thought and opinion about where beat 1 "should" be, the thinking is slightly apart, yet there is no blame or finger-pointing. That would not be in the spirit of creative collaboration. (By the way, when this happens, I automatically *assume* I am wrong!) This joy, spirit and energy is naturally communicated to the audience, and their listening experience and enjoyment will be enhanced.

IN CONCLUSION

Just as physicians are bound to the Hippocratic Oath when they commence their careers and assume the responsibility of practicing medicine, I think music educators and conductors should also be bound by an oath that holds them to the highest artistic standards and obligates them to make the musical and personal education of students and audiences their paramount objective.

Through the development of a personal educational philosophy and a skilled and experienced methodology, we must learn how to teach and inspire our students to achieve musical artistry and encounter peak performance experiences that by far exceed their expectations. As a natural byproduct, we will also "educate" our audiences through our students.

By creating a "thirst" in both our students and audiences, we will be able to elevate their standards, cause them to become better, brighter and more informed listeners, and develop their appreciation of true artistry, high quality and genuine artistic expression. The beauty of our commitment to education and entertainment is that we instill these philosophies, principles, techniques and musical gifts in our students and audiences through *our own* musical and artistic growth and personal development. Through this development and becoming known and respected for the highest and most rewarding standards of musical excellence, we establish expectations for ourselves, for our students and for the people for whom we perform. And, as a result we leave our students and audiences thirsty, which in turn creates a demand for even more artistic expression and high quality performances, thereby creating a wonderful circle of musical life.

> By creating a "thirst" in both our students and audiences, we will be able to elevate their standards, cause them to become better, brighter and more informed listeners, and develop their appreciation of true artistry, high quality and genuine artistic expression.

CHAPTER SEVEN

HOW TO WIN ON NBC's CLASH OF THE CHOIRS

"You've got to show the joy in what you do, and leave it all on the table. Don't hold back." —Nick Lachey

*"Open your soul and give of yourself, and then, and only then, will you even have a chance at achieving the **Wow Factor**." —Tim Noble*

• • •

How do "Flight of the Bumble Bee," Nick Lachey, rehearsing in winter coats, the importance of sight-reading, and a solid Midwest work ethic all combine to create ***The Wow Factor?***

Up to this point I have been sharing my educational philosophies, offering practical pointers on how to achieve greater success in rehearsal and performance, and, I hope, providing some new ideas and inspiration for your quest for musical artistry and personal excellence. What follows is a true story that serves as an example of how success and *"wow"* can be achieved when we put into practice all of the teaching theories discussed thus far.

I have been told—and I believe—that I am uniquely qualified to write this chapter, as I had the privilege of auditioning, arranging for and rehearsing the vocal ensemble that was selected as the winning choir on the inaugural season of NBC's *Clash of the Choirs*. The ensemble, formed in Cincinnati and named "Team Lachey," was led by Nick Lachey, singer and former member of the pop group 98 Degrees.

Based on conversations I have had throughout the country and on Web sites devoted to discussion and debate both during and after the broadcasts, I suspect there may be some readers who have formed rather strong opinions on the relative merits (or demerits!) of this television show. In this chapter I will address my experiences on the show, as well as offer insights and anecdotes about the development of the project and my involvement behind the scenes. Also, I will address some of the concerns that I have heard, with the hope that more healthy debate can ensue.

WHAT IS *CLASH OF THE CHOIRS?*

Clash of the Choirs was a television show that was broadcast live from New York City on NBC on four consecutive nights (Dec. 17-20, 2008). The show featured a competition among five auditioned choirs representing five cities led by five music celebrities. The premise, in a nutshell, is that the celebrities return to their respective hometowns to select a 20-voice mixed vocal ensemble auditioned from amateur singers (minimum age 18). The American viewers vote for their favorite choir each night after the broadcast (by phone or via computer), and the winning choir receives a $250,000 prize that is donated to a charity (previously selected by the celebrity) in the choir and celebrity's hometown.

> The premise, in a nutshell, is that the celebrities return to their respective hometowns to select a 20-voice mixed vocal ensemble auditioned from amateur singers.

The celebrities and their hometowns were:

Patti LaBelle	Philadelphia, Pennsylvania
Blake Shelton	Oklahoma City, Oklahoma
Michael Bolton	New Haven, Connecticut
Kelly Rowland (of Destiny's Child)	Houston, Texas
Nick Lachey	Cincinnati, Ohio

How I Got Involved

In mid-October of 2008, I was contacted by one of the producers from the show and invited to apply to be a "choirmaster"—one of five people selected to audition and rehearse the ensembles that would be led by the five celebrities. Admittedly, the producers knew very little about choirs and choral music, but they had done extensive research (through the Internet and personal recommendations) on people who might be appropriate choirmasters for this project. (I am still not sure whether to thank or curse colleagues who may have recommended me!) The producers were seeking choral directors with experience in pop music, as opposed to ones with essentially traditional concert choir training and experience. So there was a much smaller pool of qualified people with experience in contemporary choral styles, especially when the producers determined that the choirmasters could also arrange the choral music for their ensemble. At that time, they were asking the potential choirmasters to relocate to the city where the choir was based for three to four weeks prior to the show, in order to audition, select and rehearse the ensemble. Needless to say, this would be an impossible task for a full-time college professor, especially with just three to four weeks' advance notice. I declined, though I did offer my services as an unpaid consultant, just so the producers would get some input from a choral music specialist. When I learned that the broadcast dates were in mid-December—just eight weeks later—I *really* was skeptical, to say the least.

> When I learned that the broadcast dates were in mid-December— just eight weeks later—I *really* was skeptical, to say the least.

So for two weeks, I served almost daily as an "adviser" and really had no interest in being considered for a choirmaster position. I am fortunate to be gainfully employed in a job that I love, so I politely kept declining when asked. I did, however, recommend other potential candidates, including friends, colleagues and former students. It was eight weeks prior to the broadcast of the show, and the producers were not at liberty to announce who the celebrities were nor the specific cities involved. Though the producers had a good idea, the contracts were not yet signed—therefore they could not publicize the celebrities' names.

Unbeknownst to me, Nick Lachey was one of the five celebrities selected for the show. Nick was born and raised in Cincinnati and still maintains very close ties with the city. He attended the Cincinnati School for Creative and Performing Arts in high school and even sang in his high school vocal jazz ensemble! He stays in touch with his high school choir director, and when he asked her whom he should get for his choirmaster, she responded, "Steve Zegree."

The Interview

About two weeks after the initial contact, I received a phone call from the television producer, who told me that Nick Lachey wanted to speak with me—although she quickly added, "But you'll never get to speak with him.... We never have....We always have to go through a manager and we can never get to Nick himself. So you will probably get a message from his management asking you to call them and then see what kind of meeting can be set up after that." I thought, "Whatever…" When I got home later that same evening, I found a voicemail message on my home phone: "Hey Steve, it's Nick Lachey. Here's my cell and my home phone numbers; please give me a call." I knew that Nick wanted to interview me to be his choirmaster, but I was also equally interested in interviewing *him* to see if he was a person with whom I wanted to work. Because Nick had called and left me his personal contact information, I already knew that he was a "real" person and that I could bypass the "management." We connected in our first conversation, and by the end of that conversation I told him I would be willing to collaborate with him if the producers would accept my schedule and availability. And, although I told him I could not guarantee we would win on the show, I promised that we would have the best vocal group (perhaps a bit of uncharacteristic bravura or chutzpah on my part, but I believed it!). Nick and I passed each other's interviews, and we decided we would like to work together on this project. The television producers agreed to accept my schedule of available dates and times, so the deal was sealed.

Auditions

I flew to Cincinnati the first weekend of November and listened to auditions from more than 300 people in two days. I heard people representing all styles, all types and a wide variety of ages (from 18 to 72), experiences and abilities. Each person who auditioned was required to fill out extensive forms, include a bio, and answer numerous questions such as why he or she was auditioning.

In my perfect world, I wanted my 20-voice choir to be SATB balanced (5/5/5/5) and to be able to read music, at least minimally. I also wanted to include singers with choral and solo experience, who were versatile and could demonstrate vocal/tonal flexibility, and who looked comfortable when performing but would not be averse to learning staging or choreography. Knowing that this group would appear on national television, I could not ignore the visual aspect of the audition process. Just as in Gold Company auditions, I always look for singers with solid musical skills first—if we need them to dance, we'll teach them!

I always look for singers with solid musical skills first—if we need them to dance, we'll teach them!

I was joined by one of the executive producers of the television show during the auditions, all of which were videotaped. I was looking for the people I wanted to sing in the choir, and the producer was looking for backline stories or any potential "red flags." A fun anecdote: I had written several lines of sight-reading examples for the auditions, and when I heard a voice that I wanted to consider, I then asked that person to sight-read an example or two, and also asked if he or she knew the key. I could tell that the producer sitting next to me was becoming increasingly annoyed each time I asked someone to sight-read. Finally she said to me in an exasperated tone, "Steve, I have just come from auditions in Philadelphia, and I must say, Patti LaBelle did not have her singers do any of this." I simply smiled, thanked her for her patience, and continued with the auditions.

If a singer "passed" my audition, he or she was then interviewed by the production staff. Production choices never triumphed over musical choices (unless a situation or circumstance caused the production staff to eliminate a candidate for consideration). The staff did, however, make suggestions, such as, "If everything is equal, if possible we really like (name) if you can work with them." But I always had the final say.

My task after the initial round of auditions was to select 40 people to invite back the following weekend to sing for Nick Lachey, on camera. During the callbacks I was always sitting just off camera, listening to and evaluating all of the auditions with Nick. In response to comments I have received regarding my lack of "on camera" time, I knew that that was not a part of my function on this show. An analogy might be when a celebrity performs with a symphony orchestra. There is almost always a conductor/music director, but most people do not know who that person is, even though he or she is responsible for rehearsing the orchestra and running the show. (An aside: Recently I had the opportunity to conduct a symphony orchestra concert in Hong Kong that included movie actor Jackie Chan as guest vocalist. Jackie was absolutely delightful to work with, and in spite of his international renown and appeal, I found a certain satisfaction in knowing that he did not walk onstage until I gave the downbeat!)

Nick and I had the task of selecting the final 20 singers from 40 very capable candidates. I was glad that Nick often deferred to my opinions, knowing that I would be the person working most closely with these singers. As is so often the case in auditioning and selecting an ensemble, making final decisions can be an excruciating process. In the final judgment I was looking for people with wonderful voices, skilled musicianship, and great personalities and attitudes, and who would be fun to work with. Many of these factors are intangibles, so a decision is often made on nothing more than a "gut feeling." So we determined our 5/5/5/5 SATB ensemble with full vocal range and an excellent variety of singers ranging in age from 18 to 49—

all amateurs, with a variety of musical experiences. Our ensemble consisted of college students, church choir directors, stay-at-home moms, a nurse, social workers, a father and his daughter, a high school math teacher, a music therapist, a middle school choir director and two singers with perfect pitch! By evaluating personality and character (in addition to musicianship) in the audition process, we selected a group of wonderful and talented people—but make no mistake, they also were very determined to win this competition. Many had expressed a desire to bring a positive message to Cincinnati, which they felt had received some negative publicity in recent years. Plus another incentive was the $250,000 prize that would go to a terrific charity: Cincinnati Children's Hospital's neonatal care unit.

> In the final judgment I was looking for people with wonderful voices, skilled musicianship, and great personalities and attitudes, and who would be fun to work with.

On paper I really liked the musical potential and personality of our ensemble. Remember there was no emphasis on choreography and/or dancing or stage movement abilities in the auditions, but in the callback audition, Nick asked the people we were seriously considering if they were willing to "get down and have fun onstage." So the people who were selected had been given a clear message that there would be movement and choreography. However, let it be known that they were selected as *singers and musicians* first, and then they were taught how to move!

Selecting the Music

First and foremost, I insisted on having the responsibility of arranging the music for my choir. I also insisted on having the complete responsibility for the music that we sang. If the arrangements that we performed were terrible, at least I would know whom to blame! This undertaking meant writing eight new vocal arrangements in a period of about two weeks. My goal in writing the arrangements was to make the selections more "choral" in scope, as opposed to a large solo vehicle with some incidental background vocals. I also wanted each arrangement to have a musical twist or surprise, so that, even though the general public would recognize the song, the arrangement would not simply be a "cover" of the tune. Instead, we put our own unique style and statement on the music. I also wanted to include solo singing opportunities in our music, but I chose to use several soloists as opposed to one featured soloist, again to show our versatility, in terms of styles, genres and forces (solo vs. ensemble). With so many soloists, even if each person got a smaller solo, it still featured the *ensemble* over the soloist—something that I thought was important to emphasize. Again, all of these factors represent *choices* that a director makes on a daily basis. Each director is faced with choices regarding *every* aspect of the ensemble, from the most obvious— size, demographics, repertoire—to

> I also wanted each arrangement to have a musical twist or surprise, so that, even though the general public would recognize the song, the arrangement would not simply be a "cover" of the tune.

the less obvious—outfits, philosophies, rehearsal pace, rules and regulations. I believed that this approach and these choices might give our group an edge over the others.

All of the choral arrangements were required by the producers to be very close to 2:20 in length and could not exceed 2:30. Keep in mind that this music was going to be performed on "live" television, so all segments were timed as closely as possible. I was faced with the task of modifying the arrangements to make sure they fit within these specific time restrictions. Although this presented a challenge, it is not an uncommon request in professional music circles. Think how the music in radio and television commercials must be arranged to fit into a 30- or 60-second format. To make matters even more complicated, the producers came back later and asked if we could find a way to lose 10 to 15 seconds from each arrangement!

Selecting the specific repertoire for our ensemble was a complicated process on many levels. First I had to come to an agreement with Nick Lachey and his management team. Nick had some specific suggestions for songs that I thought were terrific. These included "Unwritten," "Friends in Low Places" and "Flight of the Bumble Bee." Yes, the suggestion of "Bumble Bee" came from Nick. He had sung it in his high school choir and loved the arrangement. When he asked if I could prepare that piece, I jumped at the opportunity!

Nick's management suggested selecting songs that were current and on the charts. I wanted to have a wider repertoire that would appeal to cross-generations and to as many people and musical tastes as possible, plus would show off the "choir" aspect of our choir. So there were some spirited conversations on this subject! In addition, all of our suggestions had to be approved by NBC and BBC Worldwide for availability and broadcast rights. The first song I requested was "Somewhere Over The Rainbow," but that was already secured by Patti LaBelle. (More about that later!)

Here are the pieces that we finally agreed on, with an explanation.

"Unwritten" (published by Hal Leonard #08202242)

Nick suggested this huge international pop hit by Natasha Bedingfield and I thought it was an excellent choice. The text is inspirational and the song had great exposure, including radio, television shows and commercials. I wanted to start the arrangement *a cappella* to feature the choral aspect of the performance. The piece begins with the women in three parts; soon the men join in. Then the rhythm section enters, followed by a solo. Even though the solo is only eight measures long, I chose to have two singers split the solo, each singing four bars. So already within the first eight bars there are a variety of forces and textures.

© 2004 EMI MUSIC PUBLISHING LTD., EMI BLACKWOOD MUSIC INC., GATOR BABY and WSRJ MUSIC
This arrangement © 2008 EMI MUSIC PUBLISHING LTD., EMI BLACKWOOD MUSIC INC., GATOR BABY and WSRJ MUSIC
All Rights for EMI MUSIC PUBLISHING LTD. in the U.S. and Canada Controlled and Administered by EMI BLACKWOOD MUSIC INC.
All Rights for GATOR BABY Controlled and Administered by EMI BLACKWOOD MUSIC INC.
All Rights Reserved   International Copyright Secured   Used by Permission

The entire ensemble sings the first chorus. My arrangement then modulates from the key of F to the key of G, and also has the band tacet, thereby featuring the chorus again in an *a cappella* section (with drum set providing rhythmic accompaniment). This also provided an excellent opportunity for the ensemble to engage the audience and to encourage them to clap along (on beats 2 and 4!).

The band re-enters on the next chorus, and with the addition of soloists riffing above the chorus, the piece rises to yet another level of energy, enthusiasm and excitement.

"Friends in Low Places"
(published by Hal Leonard #08202245)

This fun Garth Brooks hit song was another of Nick's choices. Nick had the idea to do something "different" in the middle of the song—to break it up and change the original concept (this is where the "arranger" gets to have fun!). My arrangement begins with a solo, and we had a young man in the choir who did an excellent cover of Garth Brooks. My concept was to feature the men in this arrangement, as I thought that other groups might not be able to do this. My arrangement featured a "breakdown" section that started with the basses singing a line quite low in their range, followed by the tenor section, and then adding the women's parts.

Copyright © 1990 by Universal Music - Careers and Sony/ATV Music Publishing LLC
This arrangement Copyright © 2008 by Universal Music - Careers and Sony/ATV Music Publishing LLC
All Rights on behalf of Sony/ATV Music Publishing LLC Administered by Sony/ATV Music Publishing LLC, 8 Music Square West, Nashville, TN 37203
International Copyright Secured   All Rights Reserved

The middle section of the piece goes into a double-time, quasi-gospel feel that in no way relates to or is part of the original song. This serves a couple of purposes. First, it demonstrates the versatility of the singers—thereby adding another style to their repertoire. Second, it is a yet another musical surprise (after the "breakdown" section) that the audience is not expecting—and therefore holds the audience's attention.

This section is followed by a modulation.

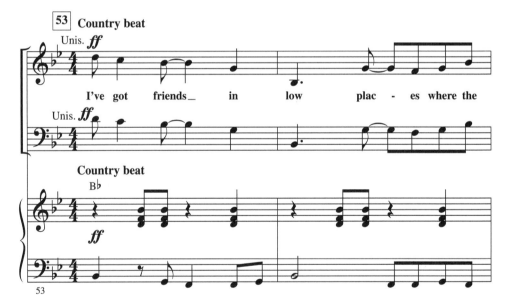

This device is something I learned from Barry Manilow. No, not directly! But in studying the lasting success of so many of his pop hits, I discovered they usually modulate around 75 percent of the way through the song. The modulation increases the energy, emotion and intensity of the song and essentially takes it to the "next level" in terms of sonic area and excitement. My goal in this arrangement was to show not only the tonal flexibility but also the vocal range of the choir, as well as their ability to "do it all," *and* to feature a solo singer from within the ensemble. When all of this is combined with an excited, energetic, joyous, fun and celebratory performance, the net result is *guaranteed* to "*wow*." "Friends" was also an excellent choice because it is a country song, so it would show the versatility of our ensemble and their ability to sing in a variety of genres and styles, and perhaps even "take it" to Blake Shelton, the country star, and *his* choir.

"Flight of the Bumble Bee"

From the first rehearsal, I thought Ward Swingle's arrangement of Rimsky-Korsakov's "Flight of the Bumble Bee" would be our "secret weapon," as I suspected no other group would even attempt a piece like that. Nick said, "Can you teach that?" and I said, "You bet!" But that was the least of our problems. When we pitched this piece to NBC, it was met with a combination of skepticism, doubt and curiosity. Some of the executives were intrigued, and others said it would never work, questioning how we could "pull off" an *a cappella* piece. Of course I had anticipated this reaction and had my answers prepared for the skeptics. I figured it was my job to show them that not only could we pull it off, but that quite possibly it would be a defining moment for the show.

Some of my justifications meant nothing to the network executives (with no background in choral music), but I felt strongly that a performance of "Bumble Bee" would add some "validity" to the television show, especially for my choral colleagues who were skeptical of the entire concept. I have prepared and conducted several of Ward Swingle's "classical" *a cappella* arrangements over the years, and they are universally appreciated by general audiences, so I was confident that a great performance of "Bumble Bee" would "*wow*" the audience. This Ward Swingle arrangement is virtuosic and presents extreme technical and musical challenges for the individual singer and for the ensemble. I also told the producers that this piece would provide a wonderful contrast to their other programming, that it would be unique, and that it, if performed well, could be a highlight from the entire week.

> From the first rehearsal, I thought Ward Swingle's arrangement of Rimsky-Korsakov's "Flight of the Bumble Bee" would be our "secret weapon"....

"What a Wonderful World"

I strongly pitched this song, and it was met with some resistance initially, but I was stubborn in my pursuit. In a poll at the end of the millennium, "What a Wonderful World" was voted one of the best songs of the 20th century, so I knew that it would be recognized and well received. In hindsight it was a *great* call in that the song, the beautiful singing and the text really won people over. This is a piece most often associated with American jazz icon Louis Armstrong and is most

> In hindsight it was a *great* call in that the song, the beautiful singing and the text really won people over.

often played at holiday season (even though it has a secular text that is not related to the season), and I also think of this song as cross-generational. Another consideration was the fact that the show was being broadcast Dec. 17-20, so the timing for the song and the message of the text could not have been better.

"Sing a Song"

This was a song that I pitched, and again my suggestion was initially met with resistance. I was viewed as "old school" in my musical tastes! Perhaps that is true, but Earth, Wind and Fire is universally acknowledged as one of the greatest and most influential funk bands in the history of pop music. My justification in wanting to program ""Sing a Song" was that there is an entire generation from the 1970s who know and love this music, plus my *current* college students know it and love it and still think it is "hip." So I really thought it would be wonderfully received. And again, the text is a winner! I was quite pleased that my idea was accepted, and I set out to arrange the piece. My arrangement included soloists, having the sopranos double the horn lines, an *a cappella* section, and, of course, a modulation, all in 2:20! My convictions about this song were substantiated at our first rehearsal with the orchestra on the set in New York City. In spite of the hectic and chaotic nature of rehearsals and preparations in the days prior to the show, upon hearing the introduction to "Sing A Song," the entire team of stage managers and crew stopped whatever they were doing and just listened and danced! It was a memorable moment—and at that point I knew that we had a winning arrangement even though it had yet to make its public debut.

"What's Left Of Me"

One of the biggest discussion points prior to the show was whether the celebrities would sing on the TV show. There was a great deal of posturing, and basically it came down to "I will if she will, but I won't if he won't." The general consensus was that it would be a good thing if each celebrity sang a song with his or her group. Of course the network and producers hoped the celebrities would agree to sing. Once the decision was made and they all agreed, Nick and I decided to perform "What's Left of Me," the hit song from Nick's album of the same name. We added background choral parts (not found on the original recording), and that made the collaboration with Nick fun and special.

"All I Want For Christmas"

Because the show was broadcast during the holiday season, each choir was required to learn and perform a seasonal song. We requested and were able to secure "All I Want For Christmas," and I based my arrangement and our performance on the popular recording by Mariah Carey. The song has a great beat and a fun spirit, with somewhat of a 1950s feel. This piece added contrast and variety to our ever-widening repertoire. The network and producers *thought* they could get the rights and clearance for us to perform this song, and even though they gave us their approval, there were no signed contracts granting us permission to perform this piece on national television. Nonetheless, I arranged and taught the song and we kept our fingers crossed. This was a risk I felt worth taking. We learned just three days prior to our performance that we had been granted the rights to perform that song.

Developing and Executing a Strategy

In assessing the conditions and circumstances of the television show, combined with the fact that the winning choir would be determined by votes from the viewing public, I realized that if everyone in Philadelphia voted for Patti LaBelle's choir and if everyone in Houston voted for Kelly Rowland's choir and if everyone in Cincinnati voted for Nick Lachey's choir, then we would not win, because both Houston and Philadelphia have a much larger population base than Cincinnati. I also figured that each celebrity would have an existing fan base, and that if all the fans voted for their favorite person, then those votes would essentially be a wash. So my goal was to appeal to the viewers across America who had no connection to any of the choirs or celebrities, and perhaps were fans of vocal music, or sang (or had sung) in their high school, college, community or church choir, so that if they voted objectively, then they would be voting for the best *choir*. I always kept in mind that the name of the show was *Clash of the Choirs*.

> ...my goal was to appeal to the viewers across America who had no connection to any of the choirs or celebrities....

In addition to having a wide variety of repertoire (in terms of grooves and eras) that would hopefully appeal to a wide variety of musical tastes, I also

> Our philosophy: Be nice to everyone; be supportive; and remember that we were from the Midwest, where a great work ethic can be found and also where people are genuinely nice and friendly.

wanted to demonstrate the *versatility* of our choir, in terms of styles and tonal flexibility.

I developed both a *vision* and a *philosophy* for our choir, and stuck to it, without ever having any second thoughts. Our vision: a balanced choral ensemble capable of singing technically and musically challenging literature in a variety of styles and genres. Our philosophy: Be nice to everyone; be supportive; and remember that we were from the Midwest, where a great work ethic can be found and also where people are genuinely nice and friendly. Our choir would *not* be tacky or petty or talk behind people's backs. We would be mature, responsible and professional, and also keep in mind that the final results of the show were completely beyond our control; i.e., we could be the best choir on the show, but if enough people didn't vote for us, we would not win! We also wanted to present a fun, excited and energetic stage presence. I chose to include solos in my arrangements but to feature several soloists on each song and to spread the solos out among different choir members so at least half of our singers had a solo. That way we could focus on featuring the choir, and also on featuring *many* of the people from within the choir.

Rehearsals

All of the choirs were treated equally and given the same opportunities. Each group was given a total of 40 hours of rehearsal time in its hometown prior to coming to New York City. This was mandated and monitored by the F.C.C. in order to keep conditions fair and equal. In order to qualify for inclusion in the group, all of the singers had to commit to being at all of the rehearsals, plus spend one full week in New York City. Some excellent people auditioned to be in the choir, but for various reasons including work or previously scheduled conflicts could not commit to the posted rehearsal schedule, so they were eliminated from consideration. Based on my schedule and availability, I chose to have 10 four-hour rehearsals for our group in Cincinnati. These rehearsals were held primarily on weekends and certain weekdays after 5 p.m. so that most choir members would not have conflicts with their work or school schedules. Our starting and ending time for each rehearsal was closely monitored, and we had to make a recording (progress report) at the end of every rehearsal and send it to the music directors of the show, so that they could monitor our progress as an ensemble, as well as offer thoughts and suggestions regarding the song selections or the repertoire or the arrangements. Fortunately I was never given any suggestions, which I took as a sign that we were on the right track. I chose not to mention any of this to the choir; we just kept working hard and practicing. We had a common goal: to achieve musical and performance excellence and to do so in a small amount of time. We did not know nor were we ever told anything about any of the other choirs, including what repertoire they were performing, so it allowed us to focus on our own development and not have to consider what other groups were (or were *not*) doing. If the discussion from our singers ever veered in that direction, I quickly squelched it, as I believe that type of discussion is both unproductive and moot—not to mention potentially negative—and I tend to emphasize accentuating the positive!

I was commuting by plane between Kalamazoo and Cincinnati for rehearsals, teaching full time at Western Michigan University, plus writing eight new choral arrangements for the choir. This usually kept me busy daily until 2 or 3 a.m., before starting over again a few hours later. It was a crazed lifestyle for a few weeks. However, there are occasions and opportunities in life where we learn that when a job needs to be done and someone asks "How long will it take?" or "How hard will I have to work?"—the only answer is "Whatever it takes." Some people (quick learners) will spend less real time rehearsing and practicing, and others might have to take four times more to achieve the same results. This practice does not make anyone better than anyone else by comparison—it is simply a matter of each individual learning to do "whatever it takes" to achieve the goal.

> …there are occasions and opportunities in life where we learn that when a job needs to be done and someone asks "How long will it take?" or "How hard will I have to work?"—the only answer is "Whatever it takes."

Shortly after auditions were completed and the results were announced, I assembled the group and said only two things when I was introduced as their director:

1) You have never worked as hard as you will in rehearsals with this ensemble.

2) Trust me.

Regarding #2 above: I realize that was a leap of faith for some of the singers, because they did not know me, had never worked with me and therefore had no reason to trust me (or my musical judgment) other than the fact that I had asked them to.

At our first rehearsal we started in immediately with "Bumble Bee," as I knew this was going to be a *huge* challenge and require the most rehearsal time. I always enjoy big musical challenges as a way to keep both the singers and me motivated and energized! I think most of the choir members were a bit overwhelmed by the pace and intensity of the rehearsal, but I did not let up. There was no time to waste, plus "Bumble Bee" established the tone and expectations for all future rehearsals.

I had also just finished arranging "Friends in Low Places," so we started on that selection as well. Remember that the original Garth Brooks recording is a country tune, but that our arrangement goes into a double–time gospel feel in the middle of the piece. The next day, prior to the start of the second rehearsal, one of the African-American singers in the group came to me and questioned my musical choices of both "Bumble Bee" and "Friends in Low Places." She said, "Steve, black people don't *do* country music," followed by, "You *know* that Kelly (Rowland) is gonna bring it." Indeed I thought that both Kelly *and* Patti LaBelle would have terrific groups. I laughed and reminded her of Point #2 ("trust me") and then secretly crossed my fingers that I was right—in terms of our repertoire selection and the arrangements.

Regarding the rehearsal process, I was in my element and had no doubts about pacing and a plan for the ensemble. After all, rehearsing choirs is what we do! Also, as a person fortunate enough to have had countless opportunities to serve as guest conductor in clinics and festivals where the primary task is to get a choir in great performance shape in a relatively small amount of time, I was very comfortable in this situation. I think it important that a director develop a philosophy for his or her ensemble, and then have a specific method to achieve that philosophy. You must establish rules and regulations, and focus on specific goals (be they educational, life lessons or performance), but also develop a *way* to achieve these goals, and hopefully as quickly and efficiently as possible. Finally, you must be able to effectively *communicate* your expectations and *inspire* your singers to achieve their highest level of creative and musical expression in performance.

One aspect that I have spent much time studying and developing is efficient use of time in rehearsal. (If you haven't read Chapter 2 yet,

> Finally, you must be able to effectively *communicate* your expectations and *inspire* your singers to achieve their highest level of creative and musical expression in performance.

it offers suggestions on "How to Practice and Rehearse for *The Wow Factor*.") My goal was to keep the rehearsal focused, disciplined (it always started and ended on time—to the minute), intense, all about the music with no extraneous drama, develop a healthy love and respect for each choir member, and perhaps most importantly, have fun! And, I believe that a combination of *all* of these factors is important (and necessary) for a successful choir rehearsal and ensemble.

Choreography

A professional choreographer whose resume included extensive Broadway and television credits came to each group's hometown for two days and choreographed several songs. He listened to us sing, observed our movement potential, and then developed and taught choreography that suited the abilities of our ensemble. We videotaped his rehearsal so that we could continue to polish the choreography after he departed. I continued to emphasize and review his choreography and staging in addition to rehearsing the choral music. Most of our rehearsals were in a dance studio at Xavier University

> And of course I had to constantly remind them, "Don't go to your face!"

with mirrors so that everyone could see themselves and work on their confidence and their "look." We divided the group and had them perform for each other and offer critiques. We worked on appropriate facial expressions in the mirror with different "looks" for different songs. We emphasized the thought that a camera could be focused on a close-up of your face at any time, and that image would be broadcast to the entire nation! We repeated our repertoire and "went for it" often several times in a row, to build stamina and also to work up a "sweat" so that the performers would get used to performing well, even if they were hot and sweaty. Lighting for television can typically be hot, so we tried to simulate those conditions. Once, after rehearsing "Sing a Song" three times in a row (including the energetic and aerobic choreography), with the choir panting and out of breath, we did it one more time—with our winter coats on—just to be in "condition" to do well regardless of the conditions. We were preparing for the heat, lighting, pressure and fatigue that would accompany us when performing "live" from New York City. In addition, while the singers were performing in rehearsal, I would run around the room as if I had a hand-held camera and get right in their faces, and require them to maintain their focus, keep smiling, keep performing—in spite of the cameras in their faces. And of course I had to constantly remind them, "Don't go to your face!"

Four days prior to our departure for New York City, when our repertoire was completely memorized and rounding into performance shape, we invited friends and family members into a dress rehearsal so that the ensemble could perform for a live audience. This helped the singers so that they could get used to cheers and applause, gain more confidence, and not be as nervous when in New York. In addition they needed to know and experience what it *felt* like to get pumped up and yet still maintain focus, not to oversing, and to still be able to perform in the way we had rehearsed. After this private performance, I knew the group was ready to represent Cincinnati in the Big Apple.

In NYC

The group flew to New York City on the Thursday evening prior to the week of the broadcast; rehearsals began on Friday morning and continued over the weekend. All travel expenses, accommodations and meals were covered by the show. Once we arrived in New York City, our goal for our choir was simply to perform all of the repertoire that we learned and rehearsed in Cincinnati on the "live" show in New York City. Whether we won or not was beyond our control, but at least if we sang our complete repertoire, that would mean that we "made it" into the final round and sang on every night of the show.

Each choir was assigned a "home room" that also served as a dressing room and rehearsal space. We were brought to the set and rehearsed each song several times each day. These daily rehearsals were for the director and crew to hear the group and see the choreography, determine camera angles, and hear who the soloists were and when and where they sang. There were four people whose job was to follow the musical score while we performed in rehearsal, and all this info went to the director, who then had final say on camera shots. There were 17 cameras in every possible location you might imagine. I had to get used to the concept of people with cameras following me (us) everywhere, and I also consciously did my best to stay off-camera most of the time, as I knew that this show was not about me. It was about the choir, the individual singers, the celebrities, and of course winning that huge charity prize for their hometown. On the other hand, I also humbly realized that in many ways the success of the entire show was predicated on the efforts and achievements of the music directors, the arrangements and how well their choirs were prepared and how well they performed.

The set was absolutely incredible. What made it so remarkable is that it was constructed in a 21,000-square-foot studio that only a week earlier had been used as Central Park for a major motion picture. The studio was completely empty on Monday, and by Friday the crew had built an entire set that included a large, movable stage, a loft for a 20-piece orchestra, state of the art lights, rigging and PA equipment, the 17 cameras, plus graduated theater seating that could accommodate a live audience of 300 people. Construction was going up around us during rehearsals, and final touches were still being put into place on Monday afternoon, the first day of the show.

After arriving in New York, in addition to being responsible for directing and rehearsing my own group, I was asked to rehearse and conduct an ensemble made up of 20 singers (a mixed quartet selected from each of the five choirs by their choirmaster). This ensemble would get to participate in a couple of special performance opportunities. From my choir, I selected a quartet of some of the best sight-readers in my ensemble—you see, music skills *are* important!!—as well as pitch-accurate singers. My tenor was a high school math teacher who had absolutely infallible perfect pitch. I tested him in many different settings on many different occasions and did my best to stump him, but his ear indeed was foolproof—so I knew he could always give the accurate pitch at any time in any place, without need of a pitch pipe or tuning fork, and with no other prior pitch reference. His ability was truly uncanny—and wonderful! I rehearsed this special group on a few *a cappella*

> For each 10- to 15-second musical segment that was ultimately shown on TV, we performed the selection about 20 times, each time with different camera angles and again for audio purposes.

selections of Christmas music. We were taken to Rockefeller Center at the heart of Manhattan and were videotaped singing in front of the famous Christmas tree. These segments were then used for 10- to 15-second teaser commercials such as "We Wish You A Merry Christmas," and as bumpers and intros coming out of a commercial break and back to the "live" broadcast.

An experience like this is when "fantasy" versus "reality" enters the picture. For each 10- to 15-second musical segment that was ultimately shown on TV, we performed the selection about 20 times, each time with different camera angles and again for audio purposes. This was done after dark so that the lit tree in Rockefeller Center was a perfect backdrop, and with the general public watching. They didn't know who we were, but with all of the cameras and lighting they *thought* we *must* be stars! Also, in the final segments for broadcast, the singers are all smiling and looking as if they are having fun. In reality it was *frigid* outside, the wind chill was near zero and it was *hard* work—though I must say, it *was* fun. I had the responsibility of conducting the ensemble, standing just off-camera!

On Monday of the broadcast, the same group of singers was asked to appear "live" on the NBC *Today* show, and Nick Lachey was the celebrity chosen to be interviewed. We woke up at the crack of dawn and again were taken to Rockefeller Center, where we rehearsed and did a sound check prior to the broadcast. The locale was the same: the outdoor area where "live" music events take place on the *Today* show. We shared a dressing room with the other guests that appeared that day, including Jordin Sparks and Gloria Estefan (and her band).

At the designated time, we were escorted to the outdoor area and placed on the risers (and again it was *really* cold). A large audience made up of the general public was waiting and screaming—perhaps at the hope of seeing Nick! Shortly after we were in our places (during a commercial break), Matt Lauer, Meredith Vieira, Al Roker and Nick Lachey all came out and took seats near the choir. Coming out of the commercial (again, this is live TV so there is no room for error) I was given a cue (a countdown from 10 seconds), and the singers all had their pitches and were warmed up, in place, smiling and ready. I conducted the ensemble and when the ensemble concluded the performance, the cameras went directly to the hosts and the interview with Nick, who dutifully plugged the show and also put in a good word for his Cincinnati choir!

I could not help but think how surreal those singers must have felt, in that just a few weeks earlier they had never even heard of *Clash of the Choirs*, let alone knew that they would be the beneficiaries of an all-expenses-paid trip to New York City. The story has an even happier ending for the 20 singers who were selected to appear on the *Today* show. Because they appeared on-camera, they all got paid for their appearance on the show. This was a "bonus," as they were not aware of this when they agreed to be a part of this special ensemble. One more thing—because I was conducting the choir *off-camera*, ask me if I got paid for *my* "appearance" on *Today*!

I generally never accept or decline musical opportunities based solely on whether or how much it pays, and I advise my students to do the same. I have always contended that what we musicians do comes because we *have* to do it—that we don't select

> I have always contended that what we musicians do comes because we *have* to do it—that we don't select music, but instead music selects *us*.

music, but instead music selects *us*. It is an added bonus when we can be paid for what we love to do and would probably do *anyway*! This story is a good example of that philosophy. So, no, I was not paid for my *Today* show appearance, nor did I expect to be!

Wardrobe

Each choir was assigned a team color. We were the silver choir, so our singers' clothes needed to have a silver theme. Everyone in the ensemble was fitted for two or three different outfits especially selected for our choir. The style theme was mix and match, and the wardrobe staff had racks and racks of clothing for everyone to try. Fitting 100 people (of all sizes and shapes)—and making them "camera ready" in three days—seemed to me an overwhelming task, but every ensemble looked terrific at show time, and everyone had a personal wardrobe that allowed them a different look each night. As a gift at the end of the show, all the singers got to keep *all* the clothes they wore on the show.

Hair styles and makeup were the responsibility of the individual singers. However, if the singers were performing a solo with the choir that night, they had their hair and makeup done professionally before the show. And I know they loved getting that special "star" treatment!

Strategy: What to perform on which night?

Nick and I went crazy trying to determine the best strategy of which of our songs to program on which night. Should we open with our best piece to (hopefully) ensure that our group would make it to the second day and not get voted off? But if you start with your strongest pieces, what if you make the finals and then don't have your best material and strongest songs left? Of course, there is no right or wrong answer to these questions, and, perhaps to our relief, the decision for the first night was made for us. The producers told us that our choir would be opening the first show (the first group to perform on the first night) with "Unwritten." My singers took this as a bad sign—that the voting audience would forget about us by the end of the two-hour show when it was time to call in and vote. As you might imagine, I had a different interpretation of the producers' decision. I thought the network wanted to do its best to grab the viewing audience from the onset of the show and "hook" them as viewers for the entire week. So I interpreted the decision to select Team Lachey as the first group as a *compliment*, and that (from their broadcast television perspective) the producers thought our version of "Unwritten" was strong, effective, exemplary and a great opener. I also assumed that they thought it was sung well and that the group looked great, too—and the fact that it was a very popular song may have also helped. Of course, no one from the production staff would ever tell us anything or give any insight into the "why" of their programming decisions.

THE BROADCASTS

Time flew very quickly from our initial rehearsal to the initial national broadcast. In just four weeks the ensemble had learned and memorized nine new choral pieces with staging and choreography. I could not have been more pleased with their efforts and their attitudes. I was confident of their ability to perform their entire repertoire with excitement, energy and enthusiasm and to present themselves professionally. I knew the ensemble was equally excited and nervous, but I also sensed that

> I knew the ensemble was equally excited and nervous, but I also sensed that they had developed an inner confidence as well.

they had developed an inner confidence as well. The time had come for us to "*wow*."

MONDAY

The First Night, two-hour broadcast: "Live" from New York City

Our days began typically with a 6:30 a.m. call to board charter buses from the hotel to the studio, and we did not return to the hotel until well after the show was broadcast at night. The daily routine included an extended rehearsal session on the set for each group, a choreography review, and a full dress rehearsal of that evening's show. In addition, unannounced videotaping sessions might occur at any time. These sessions were then edited and included in the backline story for broadcast that night or the following day. Needless to say, the days and nights were grueling for production, cast and crew. One lesson learned through participation in this show was to always be flexible, be adaptable, be able to cooperate and "play well" with others, as things were constantly changing. This especially applied to the television show producers, who also had their own production agenda and responsibilities, oftentimes involving the choirs or featured individuals from within each choir, shooting behind the scenes with the omnipresent cameras. From my perspective as choir director, these were counterproductive to the musical integrity of the ensemble, but, in the big picture, quite important to the ultimate success of the TV show. One example of being flexible was getting a call in the middle of an intense—and necessary—vocal rehearsal, that the choir needed to report to wardrobe—*immediately*—and even though I did not want to break up my rehearsal, I knew I had to do it, for the sake of the show.

Each night's live audience added greatly to the excitement of the show. The audience was seated one hour before show time and, as is the case in most live television shows, they were prepared, primed and pumped up, so it was always a thrill to perform for an energized and enthusiastic audience.

The first show opened with all choirs singing a version of James Brown's "Living In The U.S.A.," which each choir learned on short notice in New York City just two days before the broadcast. The opening segment was high energy, high tech and very slick. We then cut to a commercial break—and the stage crew had exactly four minutes to clear the stage of 100 singers and reconfigure the stage (and actually move set pieces) to accommodate the individual group performances. We were put in our places; then, after a few minutes of pre-roll video about the selection of our group, some stories about the audition process in Cincinnati, and the introduction of Nick Lachey, we opened with our performance of "Unwritten."

> One lesson learned through participation in this show was to always be flexible, be adaptable, be able to cooperate and "play well" with others, as things were constantly changing.

During the commercial break I was on the stage with the ensemble, assisting with the placement of the singers and offering words of encouragement to individuals and the entire group. I also thought it important to maintain a cool, calm, collected and confident exterior, as I thought this demeanor might be contagious and communicate to the singers a greater sense of confidence and inner peace. Once we were "on the air," I took my place offstage, just off-camera. I was absolutely confident in the performance abilities and potential of our ensemble. The singers were well-prepared and ready to perform. All that remained was for them to show America what they could do—and our choir went out there and *nailed* it. Their energy, enthusiasm, musicianship and love for performing were palpable. It looked and sounded great on the television broadcast and was even better "live" onstage. The live audience response was like a rock concert, and our performance set the stage (and performance level) for the other groups. And all of the other choirs rose to the occasion. Patti LaBelle's choir performed a gospel number that was terrific: high-energy and sung well. I thought her group was outstanding on that number, but in the back of my mind I wondered whether the group could sustain that level for the entire week. My mind kept returning to the knowledge of our diverse repertoire—and our "secret weapon."

It is interesting to note here that I received comments from several friends (including professional musicians) who had never previously watched a reality show, but were watching this one just to support me. They said they were hooked for the whole week within the first 15 minutes of the Monday broadcast. Needless to say, this is the intention of the show producers and directors who obviously know how to "*wow*" in this idiom. My job was to prepare and direct an ensemble that was capable of "*wowing*" the American viewing audience. Their job was to capture that audience, earn high viewer ratings and sell advertising. It's all a matter of perspective! There was a sense in the room early in the broadcast that they had found a successful, winning combination.

As educators and students of **The Wow Factor**, it is imperative that you objectively *study* the programs, artists, productions and ensembles that are successful and that you be analytical. Try to figure out *why* they are successful. What is the secret to their success?

The answer could be many things or many different combinations:

1) Hard work. Is their success earned and deserved?

2) Excellent management. Whenever I am involved in a major production, I like to surround myself with the best available personnel: performers, directors, producers, stage and technical crew, etc. I solicit their advice and also trust them to "do their thing" (lighting, sound) without giving them too much direction. Many times what they bring in their area of expertise far exceeds anything I am able to suggest, especially if it is not in an area of my personal expertise.

3) Looks.

4) Uniqueness.

5) Talent and skills.

6) Extramusical effects: lighting, staging, sets, props, costumes, sound.

7) Repertoire choices.

Get Out the Vote: I emailed everyone I knew in the music profession (all choir and band directors and friends) to notify them of my participation on the show. Because of my limited screen time, unless people knew in advance of my participation, they would most likely not know of my involvement in the show (unless they watched the final credits scrolling by at the end of each broadcast!). I asked them to consider voting for Team Lachey and to ask their students and their students' friends (and enemies!) to vote—early and often and every night!

As in political elections, the candidate is ultimately at the mercy of the voters, so it was crucial to ask people for their votes. The same philosophy applies to any performance that you give. If you do not inform people of the date, time and location, and also extend an invitation, do not expect to generate an audience. And generating an audience in most cases is ultimately crucial to your success. For example, if you have been hired

> If you do not inform people of the date, time and location, and also extend an invitation, do not expect to generate an audience.

to perform at a local restaurant or jazz club, you are being paid for your services. Therefore it is important that the club generate the necessary income to cover your performance fees. The income comes from patrons ordering food and drinks, and perhaps paying a cover charge. In any case, the commercial success of your performance is predicated on the amount of business the restaurant generates. Therefore it is in *your* best interest to generate business by getting as many people as possible to attend your concert. And I guarantee that if the restaurant or club does great business on a night that you perform, it will most assuredly invite you back. This is one of the best ways for you to develop a following, plus stay gainfully employed in the professional area that you love.

TUESDAY

Night Two, one-hour broadcast: Country Meets Gospel

All five choirs performed well on Monday night. All five were invited back for Tuesday, but one choir would be eliminated from the competition at the end of the night's broadcast as a result of Monday's national vote. Let the drama begin!

During the day, all five choirs were present at rehearsals. We practiced the elimination sequence, so the groups would know how to lose and the television show directors would have the sequence and process rehearsed. In order to rehearse the sequence during the day, the five choir directors randomly drew the names of all five choirs out of a hat, and the choir that was selected first would be the rehearsal "loser" that day. On Monday I selected Team Lachey out of the hat first, so we were the first group to be eliminated Tuesday "for rehearsal purposes only" (as the production staff kept reminding us). I viewed this as a terrific opportunity to tell my choir—

while we were alone in the dressing room!—that we were practicing losing "for rehearsal purposes only" so that we would never have to experience it "live" on the actual broadcast. Little did I know that I was a prophet in New York City!

In our daily rehearsals, the producers never let us know anything about the true voting results. I was amazed at how well the production team kept the final tabulations a secret from virtually everyone until the actual moment of the announcement. We rehearsed a different "loser" each day, so that when the real results were announced live during the actual broadcast, the reactions from singers were honest, authentic and in real time. It was actually fun for us to have the opportunity to "play act" being the losers. Although the "drama" of announcing an eliminated group was well-rehearsed, taking our turn as "losers" served as a good reminder of the importance of knowing how to lose with grace and a positive attitude.

It was decided by the producers that we would perform "Friends in Low Places" on Tuesday night. Keep in mind that the producers had to select pieces for all of the choirs and that they had to include variety and diversity in their programming. I was pleased with this decision and thought this was an excellent sequel to "Unwritten" because it is completely contrasting in style. It is a popular song, and one that is just plain fun to sing—not only for the performers but for the listeners too—as it is quite typical to have the audience sing along on the chorus of this song. I was confident of our ability to deliver a terrific performance, and once again Team Lachey did not disappoint. The crowd loved the breakdown section, especially hearing our bass section featured on the low notes—singing in "low places"! In fact, at the conclusion of the performance, the host of the show, Maria Menounos, kept making reference to the men in our ensemble. I was pleased because we were able to feature all of the sections of our balanced choir. Some of the other choirs had as many as 14 women and only six men.

With all choirs standing onstage near the conclusion of the broadcast—anxiously awaiting the results of America's voting—it was announced that Kelly Rowland's choir from Houston had been eliminated. I was quite surprised by this result and my singers were shocked, because, as previously mentioned, many in our group thought that Kelly's choir would still be in the running at the

> At that moment I knew that all bets were off and that we would have to step up our level of performance to an even higher level of professionalism if we were going to stay competitive.

end of the week. At that moment I knew that all bets were off and that we would have to step up our level of performance to an even higher level of professionalism if we were going to stay competitive. But most importantly, we knew that we had yet another day to sing!

WEDNESDAY

Night Three, two-hour broadcast: The Secret Weapon

This was going to be our most important performance night in that I thought that if we made the cut beyond this night, then we would have a good chance of making the finals. We had given excellent performances on Monday and Tuesday, and we knew that people were taking notice, in part due to the positive image we maintained off-camera and the energetic, polished and professional performances that we gave on-camera. The hours of relentless practice, drilling, repetition, confidence and drama-free team-building were all paying off. A second choir was eliminated from the competition near the beginning of the Wednesday broadcast, and the recipient of the unfortunate outcome was Michael Bolton's choir from New Haven, Connecticut.

The producers decided that on Wednesday night each remaining choir would perform three selections from their repertoire: their holiday song, the song with their celebrity, and a song of their choice. Our song of choice was our secret weapon. In the first two shows no group had sung an *a cappella* piece, and the degree of difficulty of most of the group selections was relatively low. The timing was perfect for "Flight of the Bumblebee."

As previously mentioned, there were mixed feelings from the executives at NBC and the show producers about "Bumble Bee." I felt as though I was on a crusade to convince the doubters that not only would it work, but that it had the potential to be a showstopper. Prior to getting the final approval to program this selection, some issues needed to be resolved before the naysayers' concerns would be put to rest:

1) The real performance time of the piece was only about 80 seconds, well short of the requisite 2:20.

2) How would the singers get their starting pitches and how would the piece begin?

3) How would they stay together and maintain a constant tempo on such a challenging piece, especially under the pressure of a live broadcast?

Having anticipated each of these concerns, I was ready with answers. The music directors knew that our ensemble was capable of performing the piece well because they had heard the recordings that we were required to make after each rehearsal in Cincinnati. As for the first two concerns above, the solution was simple. I just had to convince the executives that it would work. I proposed that the orchestra would begin "Bumble Bee" by playing the original Rimsky-Korsakov instrumental version "live." After about 20 seconds of playing, Nick would interrupt the conductor of the orchestra, stop the music, turn to the audience and say, "Even though we all know that 'Flight of the Bumble Bee' is usually played by instruments, because this is our secret weapon we'd like to sing it *a cappella*." In the meantime, the choir would be in place on the set ready to sing and they would get their starting pitches when the orchestra played the introduction (in the same key as the vocal arrangement). Plus remember our math teacher with the infallible perfect pitch—yet another secret weapon!

Finally there was the issue with Nick, who admittedly had little, if any, choral conducting experience, and he had the responsibility of keeping the group together on camera. So we gave Nick an in-ear monitor that allowed us to give him a click track at the exact tempo that we rehearsed.

The set-up worked perfectly and the performance by Team Lachey was truly astounding. Our "schtick" with Nick stopping the orchestra caught everyone off guard. The audience didn't quite know how to react to this maneuver, but they cheered and went along anyway! It was even a surprise to the family members of our singers who were a part of the audience in New York, who were not told of our "secret introduction." Afterward they told me they actually thought there was a *real* problem when Nick interrupted the conductor! Our plan worked to perfection! Nick did a great job of providing the ictus needed to keep the choir singing at a constant tempo. The audience gave an

> Our gamble and hard work combined to create a truly memorable "*wow*" moment.

extended standing ovation that was the loudest and longest applause for any piece by any group all week. Our gamble and hard work combined to create a truly memorable "*wow*" moment. In addition, by taking things "out of the box," Team Lachey had now morphed from what might have been initially described as an underdog choir to one that was recognized as a formidable force on the show. The audience could not pin a stylistic label on our ensemble and they now were eagerly awaiting our next performance.

The choir did a great job with "All I Want For Christmas." All five of our soloists sang well, and the arrangement (that included a section of half-time feel, and a modulation) was well-received. I was both pleased and proud of every one of our singers who sang a solo. Of course we rehearsed those solos until everyone was absolutely confident of their ability to not only sing the solo, but to do so with a confident smile, on camera, "live," and in front of a national audience. For a group of amateur singers, they were presenting themselves with true professionalism.

Our final piece on Wednesday night was the performance with our celebrity. "What's Left of Me" was a hit song of Nick's, and it was the perfect vehicle for him and the choir. Nick thought it was important that the solo part and the choir had an equal presence in the arrangement, so that was how I arranged the piece.

The preface to our performance is worth a mention here. As you may recall, initially I had requested "Somewhere Over The Rainbow" for our choir but was told that it was already promised to Patti LaBelle. "Over The Rainbow" has been one of Patti's "signature" songs for most of her career. Her performance of that song has been given "legendary" status and she lived up to that reputation on *Clash of the Choirs*. In addition to Patti's amazing voice and electric stage presence, this performance included her throwing aside

> During the commercial break, I could see that my ensemble seemed shell-shocked in the wake of Patti's performance, so I knew I had to rally the troops.

the microphone stand and kicking off her shoes. Someone could view these stage antics as "over the top," but I must say, standing just off-camera and only a few feet away from Ms. LaBelle's performance, I was *wowed*, as was everyone else who was present. We knew that Patti's choir would be formidable competition, and they did not disappoint. They were clearly the "favorite" in various Internet chat circles prior to the broadcast of the show, and they certainly acquitted themselves in their performances.

The show cut to a commercial break after Patti's stunning performance, and Team Lachey had the dubious honor of immediately following her act. During the commercial break, I could see that my ensemble seemed shell-shocked in the wake of Patti's performance, so I knew I had to rally the troops. I pulled them aside and told them what a wonderful *opportunity* this was! We were fortunate to *follow* Patti LaBelle's performance and to sing on national television with Nick Lachey, and if they performed as I knew they were capable, they would hopefully cause the audience to forget what they had just experienced. These words were just what the ensemble needed to hear at that time, as I could see they regained their focus, composure and confidence as they readied themselves for their performance.

Our ensemble and Nick took their places onstage, and their performance, though markedly different in style and tone from what had just preceded, was wonderful. And, in an inspired moment on-camera at the end of the performance, Nick Lachey kicked off his shoes. This spontaneous gesture from Nick was not meant to be disrespectful to Patti LaBelle—it was simply great fun. But it also helped to dispel the mystique of Patti's performance.

Our performance was followed by Blake Shelton with his choir. Because he wears cowboy boots, Blake could not easily kick off his shoes at the conclusion of his performance. Instead, his entire choir threw off their shoes. Imagine some 40 shoes flying through the air. It was a wonderful and funny moment, and, as a result, just minutes after a stunning performance, "Over The Rainbow" seemed like a distant memory.

THURSDAY

Final Night, two-hour broadcast: The Verdict

Clash of The Choirs was clearly the "buzz" of the television world during the week of the broadcast. The network was winning the ratings war for that time slot for the first three nights, and the producers and the network were ecstatic, as the ratings far exceeded their expectations. Remember that "success" on network television is measured in ratings and income from advertising.

Here is something that I find rather extraordinary. The final night was originally scheduled to be a one-hour broadcast. However, the ratings and interest in the show were so high that on Wednesday afternoon the producers and network decided to extend the Thursday night broadcast into a two-hour show. This meant that the directors and producers had to create an extra hour of live TV with just over 24 hours notice. The entire directing and producing staff spent most of the night Wednesday adding an extra hour of live television that they had not originally planned for. This involved asking some of the other eliminated choirs to sing another selection that they had prepared, plus add other segments to fill an hour, yet still keep the show compelling and retain viewers. I was quite impressed with their ability to produce this on such short notice. I must say, many of the people that I have worked with in this particular idiom seem to thrive on these types of pressures and deadlines.

All of the choirs were obligated to stay in New York for the entire duration of the show, even if they were eliminated. So the addition of the second hour provided a wonderful opportunity for the eliminated choirs to get to perform again, even though they were not competing.

The final show opened with all five choirs onstage singing a holiday medley. Our choir was assigned "Let It Snow," and, due to the short notice, I wrote a relatively simple arrangement of that song and taught it to the choir by rote. They learned it and had it memorized in a few minutes.

Three groups remained in the competition, but one more group was eliminated near the start of the final broadcast. I thought Blake Shelton's choir sang well and gave wonderful performances all week, but they were the next group to go. That left two groups in the final competition: Team LaBelle and Team Lachey.

We had two remaining pieces in our repertoire: "Sing a Song" and "What A Wonderful World," and we were thrilled to have the opportunity to perform these songs on Thursday night. Our group loved the message of both songs, and they performed them beautifully. It came as no surprise to me that, even though it was a mellow ballad with a pianissimo ending, "What A Wonderful World" was met with an audience reaction similar to that given to "Bumble Bee." In fact, when Nick joined the choir onstage following the performance, he was visibly moved by the beauty and emotion of the group's performance, as well as proud of their poise and professionalism, and he expressed that to the host. It was a special moment.

The dramatic conclusion of the show involved the two remaining ensembles onstage anxiously awaiting the announcement of the final result. Of course the producers and directors did a wonderful job of prolonging the suspense! From my perspective, I could not have been more proud of Team Lachey. In terms of the singing and performances, they had done all that I asked of them and more, plus they represented Cincinnati with pride and dignity. Regardless of the results of the voting, we had achieved our goal: We sang our entire repertoire on *Clash of the Choirs*.

> Regardless of the results of the voting, we had achieved our goal: We sang our entire repertoire on *Clash of the Choirs*.

However, a general sense remained that Team LaBelle was still the favored choir. Comedian Tracy Morgan was called onstage to announce the winning choir. As he opened the envelope, I think he was prepared to say

"Patti LaBelle," but when he read the results, the words that came out of his mouth were "that choir over there"... pointing to Team Lachey!

The ensuing reactions were memorable, ranging from celebratory elation for Team Lachey to severe disappointment from Team LaBelle. In that moment I reflected on the importance I had placed on both musical skills *and* musicianship in the audition process.

REFLECTIONS

Throughout the rehearsal process and in New York City, I kept referring to the term "six weeks" because that represented the real time from the date of the singers' auditions in Cincinnati, subsequent selection for the ensemble, rehearsal period, trip to New York City, the actual broadcast and then being chosen the winning choir by the American viewing public. Throughout this entire experience there was a prevailing sense of disbelief expressed by the singers ("pinch me") that they were all in New York City and performing on national television. Indeed, they were being a bit spoiled! The choir had all of their expenses paid and their meals catered, and they were given new wardrobes and "star" treatment. From our dressing/rehearsal room we had an excellent view of the Manhattan skyline and the Empire State Building. In order to keep a proper perspective, I kept reminding everyone of our "six weeks," which brought the fantasy back to a grounded sense of reality. When working with an ensemble, I think it is important to deal in real time, whether it is minutes in a rehearsal, how long a selection is, or how many days until the concert. And "six weeks" seemed a perfect way to efficiently sum up all that the choir had experienced, as well as keep them focused on the task at hand and the purpose of their trip to New York City.

The Orchestra

Full accompaniment orchestrations were written for every piece that was performed on the show, and all of the instrumental music was performed live. The 20-piece orchestra included some of the finest studio musicians in New York City, several of whom were well-known. When I first heard the caliber of playing from the orchestra in rehearsal, I could not believe that everything I was listening to was live, and that there were not prerecorded tracks, as it sounded *that* good. The live sound in the studio and the one broadcast on television were run by most of the sound crew from *Saturday Night Live*, so I knew that we had some of the best in the business. The mix, balance, tone and clarity were outstanding.

Thoughts About Celebrities

In today's society it seems that many people are intrigued by (or obsessed with) celebrities and their lives, through media venues including popular culture magazines, tabloids, Web sites, television shows and paparazzi. Although there is a natural curiosity about the lives and lifestyles of the people whom we enjoy as entertainers or admire as role models, I believe it is important to distinguish between the stage persona and the "real" person with a personal and private life, and who puts pants on one leg at a time, just as you and I do. As an educator, I am always much more interested in and fascinated by the "backstage" persona of a celebrity: the person and personality that the general public does not often see. I think it is important to know the core of the person: who they are offstage, as real people, and how they treat and react to noncelebrities.

The "real" offstage celebrities often are those who are confident and secure because they have worked hard and spent years of practice developing their talents and abilities. Then there are those who are mean-spirited, egocentric, self-indulgent and generally unpleasant to be around. My experience with such people is that their unpleasant behavior can most often be attributed to their own insecurity—perhaps because what career and celebratory status they have achieved has not been truly *earned* and therefore not *deserved*.

> The "real" offstage celebrities often are those who are confident and secure because they have worked hard and spent years of practice developing their talents and abilities.

Thoughts on Mr. Lachey

Prior to our first conversation, I had done my homework on Nick Lachey. From all of the reliable sources I could draw upon, there was a universal opinion: Nick is a terrific person, humble and a "regular, nice guy." This was substantiated for me when he called and left a voice message with his cell and home phone number. Our initial conversation lasted about 45 minutes, and I felt I was interviewing him as much as he was me, for I did not want to enter into this project and establish a working relationship with someone that I did not want to work closely with. Nick and I had several interests in common, and it seemed that he also would take his involvement in this musical project seriously and be committed to doing his best.

This turned out to be the case, on all levels. I am happy to confirm that indeed Nick is a terrific person, well grounded, still in touch with his roots, and specifically his hometown of Cincinnati. Maybe it *is* the solid Midwest ethics, but there is no substitute for this winning attitude.

All of the celebrities on *Clash of the Choirs* were contractually obligated to listen to the final callbacks of auditions plus make one other rehearsal appearance with their respective groups, of course with the omnipresent cameras and requisite spotlights and attention. One of the points that impressed me about Nick was that he took a vested interest in our choir, as well as the individuals in the choir. He came to some of our group rehearsals when he did not *have* to, without any cameras or publicity. He wanted to see how the group was developing and progressing, and get a sense of the ensemble, and perhaps more importantly, learn the repertoire.

Knowing that he would be on camera on the live broadcasts, Nick made a point to learn and memorize all of the arrangements that we were performing (including the choreography and the lyrics). In addition he asked for conducting lessons from me on what would be appropriate gestures and directives in front of a live performance of the ensemble. So I taught him the Zegree conducting style, and, from my perspective, he was a terrific and serious student, and he ultimately looked great in front of the ensemble!

This is a testimonial to Nick's professionalism and to his offstage, real-life personality that does not differ from his stage persona. In addition, Nick demonstrated his appreciation to the ensemble on several occasions. Examples of his generosity can be illustrated by the following anecdotes:

On Tuesday night after the second broadcast, when we knew that we were still in the running and that we would be performing again on Wednesday night, Nick brought cupcakes from a wonderful New York City bakery to our dressing room for all of the singers. Perhaps this was a small gesture, but it was a lovely, thoughtful and greatly appreciated one nonetheless.

On Wednesday night, prior to our performances on the broadcast, Nick presented every singer in the group with a present and token of his appreciation in recognition of all of their hard work and efforts. The ladies received matching silver necklaces with the letter "C" for Cincinnati, and the men all received silver money clips. These gifts came from a very well-known jewelry store in New York City made famous in a movie starring Audrey Hepburn that included the work "Breakfast" in the title. The women wore their necklaces from that point on, as a symbol of unity—and, perhaps, good luck!

After the broadcast on Wednesday night, when we learned that we had made it to the final night, Nick came to the dressing room, thanked the group for their hard work and said he wanted to do something for the choir, regardless of the results of the competition. So he invited the entire ensemble (plus their family members who were in New York City) on a private cruise around Manhattan following the Thursday night performance. He chartered a yacht and treated everyone to a memorable evening. This gift was arranged *before* we knew that we had won the entire competition, so winning *Clash* made the cruise that much more of a celebration. A moment that Nick

> I took a step back, watched this scene unfold and experienced the satisfaction that directors can feel, knowing that they made a positive difference in the lives of others and helped create experiences and memories that will last a lifetime.

and I will remember forever took place about 3 a.m., when the yacht cruised to the base of the Statue of Liberty, and Nick and the entire choir went outside on the upper deck and sang "What A Wonderful World." It was a wonderful moment: the inspirational view at the foot of Lady Liberty, and reflections on the fact that these people, most of whom did not know one another six weeks earlier, had worked so hard to develop into an excellent vocal and performing ensemble that brought positive national exposure and recognition to their hometown (not to mention a quarter-of-a-million-dollar prize to be donated to a local charity!). I took a step back, watched this scene unfold and experienced the satisfaction that directors can feel, knowing that they made a positive difference in the lives of others and helped create experiences and memories that will last a lifetime.

Finally, on Thursday night, in the minutes after we were voted the champions on the final broadcast, there was pandemonium everywhere onstage. I was giving and receiving congratulations and also making a point to thank the crew members, directors and producers. I also knew that the singers led by Patti LaBelle were probably quite disappointed. So I made a point to go to their dressing room as soon as I could to congratulate them, offer a few words of appreciation and encouragement and to let them know how much I enjoyed getting to know them and hearing their music. I learned then that despite everything else going on—all of the cameras, media hype and interviews—Nick Lachey had slipped away (without any cameras following him) and had *already* visited their dressing room to offer his words of encouragement. That is something I will always remember, and it is a testament to who the "real" person is offstage and behind the scenes. I knew that I had directed a winner on many levels, and I was *wowed*!

If you are reading this and voted for Team Lachey, I thank you on behalf of Nick, my singers and Cincinnati Children's Hospital!

THE AFTERMATH

Immediately after the results of the show were announced and in the days that followed, I received numerous letters of congratulation. The most common comment from people who were familiar with my work was, "Your group reminded me so much of Gold Company." My response (to myself) was "of course!" As a friend of mine says, "We do what we do." As the director of a collegiate vocal jazz program that has an international following and that many people believe to be among the finest, I say that "if it works for audiences in Kalamazoo, it should work everywhere in America—and beyond!" This mantra has proven to resonate wherever Gold Company has been, and I am glad that the same philosophies and principles worked on *Clash of the Choirs*.

The winning choir enjoyed incredible coverage in the local Cincinnati media that included daily reporting on television and in newspapers while they were in New York. Upon their arrival at the Cincinnati airport, the members of Team Lachey were met by a huge welcoming crowd. It was as if they had just won the Super Bowl—except this was a *choir*! Later renamed Team Cincinnati, they were truly hometown heroes, and were invited to perform concerts at numerous civic and charity events. Highlights included performances at the governor's mansion and the Cincinnati Reds' Opening Day. The group also gave a gala concert for nearly 2,000 people that was sponsored by Cincinnati Children's Hospital. This event also served as the "official" presentation of the $250,000 award to the hospital. Nick Lachey was there to present the check, and I was on hand to serve as the emcee and also play the piano. When I knew that "Unwritten" and "Friends in Low Places" were going to be published by Hal Leonard, I asked if we could have Team Cincinnati make the demo recordings, and I offered to produce the recording sessions. I wanted to give the ensemble yet another opportunity to sing together and get some recording studio experience. So if you have the demo CD of either of those two arrangements, the recording you hear was made by the people who sang it first! Finally, during the rehearsal process and also during one of the "live" broadcasts, Nick had said that if his choir won on *Clash of the Choirs*, he would have them sing background vocals on a song on his next CD. Nick kept his promise and asked me to arrange the background vocals for a song titled "'Til The World Stands Still." I was thrilled that all 20 of the singers were available for the recording session.

Perhaps what pleased me the most was how Team Cincinnati remained an ensemble following the victory. This is something that I would never have

> This is an excellent example of the *positive* force that music can be and what a wonderful impact it can have on a community.

imagined, especially in light of the challenges involved in maintaining a vocal group. This is an excellent example of the *positive* force that music can be and what a wonderful impact it can have on a community. From the onset of the audition process, I sensed that the city and people of Cincinnati were in need of a shot in the arm and a news story with a positive, uplifting message. I believe the victory provided an enormous boost to the spirits of the city, and it could not have come at a more perfect time. It has been announced that Cincinnati will host the World Choir Games in 2012. This is the first time this European-based prestigious choral event will be held in the United States. And what was one of the determining factors on the selection of Cincinnati, according to the festival sponsors and organizers? Team Cincinnati's victory on *Clash of the Choirs*!

I have been asked numerous times my thoughts on how and why we won on *Clash of the Choirs*. Providing a definitive answer is impossible, but I am happy to speculate. I believe our victory came as a result of several factors and circumstances. These include:

1. Our identity as a choir. Our music placed a greater emphasis on group vocals than the other groups did. We were truly a choir.

2. Our secret weapon. There is no doubt that "Flight of the Bumble Bee" had a tremendous impact.

3. Our energy and stage presence. Not only did the group sing well, but they also looked great when performing, and they were having fun!

4. Our diverse repertoire. It was varied, and represented a wide range of styles and time periods.

5. Our wonderfully talented soloists. Even though we did not emphasize solos, we had exceptional soloists within the ensemble, and everyone who sang a solo performed it beautifully.

6. Nick Lachey's popularity as a well-liked celebrity.

7. The hard work and excellent attitude of our singers. There is no substitute for that.

THE CONTROVERSY:
WHY I TOOK THE *CLASH* GIG

I realize some of my choral colleagues scoffed at this project and regarded it with disdain and even some contempt. There was some negative "press" along with less-than-positive comments on Internet chat rooms and blogs. One contingency felt strongly that this television show misrepresented the hard work that goes into the preparation and rehearsal process for a choral ensemble. The producers of the show decided that they would create the appearance that the celebrities had rehearsed and prepared the ensembles for performance. As a result, this could give the impression to the general public that virtually anyone could put a group of singers together and teach them to sing. (In fact, sometimes this *is* the case in our profession!) Although it is true that the celebrities were involved to some degree in the process, each choir had a choirmaster who had the responsibility of rehearsing the ensemble for 40 hours prior to arriving in New York City. Also, I willingly took on the responsibility of arranging most of the choral music for my ensemble. I knew

> One contingency felt strongly that this television show misrepresented the hard work that goes into the preparation and rehearsal process for a choral ensemble.

that this was to be the case when I accepted the position as director of Nick Lachey's choir. I also knew that I would get very little "face time" on television, although I was seen a few times, and my name as well as the other choirmasters' names were listed in the rolling credits at the end of the show. All of these factors were not important to me.

Contrary to popular belief (and what you might imagine), my compensation for all of my time and effort was quite modest (actually, "modest" is a gross understatement!). Just as in one's decision to enter the profession of music education, or even performance: If making large sums of money is your primary motivation, then you should probably find another line of work.

I am curious to know what those in our profession who were negatively predisposed were expecting. A prime-time show on commercial network TV that is predicated on sponsorship and ad sales for revenue, by definition, will attempt to be more entertaining than educational. And the producers will try to appeal to as wide a general audience as possible. Therefore, programming works such as the Bach *B minor Mass* or Palestrina motets would not be possible. In fact, it is *rare* to see choral literature such as this appear on *any* television station (including cable and PBS), and especially rare on network television. So, of course, traditional, classical choral repertoire would never fly on commercial network television—except, of course, "Bumble Bee"!

> I viewed *Clash of the Choirs* as an opportunity to advance general exposure of the choral art and group singing and to upgrade popular choral standards in front of millions of people. What an *opportunity*!

Therefore I understood perfectly well when I accepted the project that the genre was going to be "pop" and all of the attendant styles that can fall under that generic umbrella.

We must realize that although our professional (and perhaps even personal) lives can be all-consumed by choral music, jazz, classical music or musical theater, these styles and idioms represent a very small fraction of the tastes of the mass-consumption general public. I am not getting on a soapbox here, nor advocating one point of view over another as "right" or "wrong." I am simply stating the facts. A statistical survey of record sales and downloads in the past year will offer a graphic illustration of just *how much* on the fringe we are.

I viewed *Clash of the Choirs* as an opportunity to advance general exposure of the choral art and group singing and to upgrade popular choral standards in front of millions of people. What an *opportunity*! I have essentially built my professional career on bringing high quality, artistic and challenging music to the masses and presenting it in an entertaining format—and perhaps even fooling them in the process! One of my favorite comments following a Gold Company performance—keeping in mind that the name and reputation of the ensemble have been built primarily on vocal jazz and on performing some of the most highly artistic and challenging choral literature in the contemporary idiom—is from a person who said, "I don't like jazz, but I like what you do."

So, for those people in our profession who have a less-than-positive opinion about a major television network programming a show in prime time that celebrates choral music, I am curious about your motivation. Plus, who is to determine which *style* of choral music is better than another? We all have our personal preferences for composers, or styles of music. Some people are Early Music aficionados; others like the Baroque or Classical eras; while others prefer Romantic music or music from the 20th century. And, from within the 20th century (and now the 21st) there is a long tradition of non-classical styles including Broadway, country, jazz, pop, big band, gospel, funk, Latin or world music. What is the better dessert: chocolate cake or apple pie? The correct answer, of course, is: *anything* with chocolate. OK, I'm kidding here! Assuming both desserts are made well, the correct answer is a matter of personal preference, and there is

> *Clash of the Choirs* (was) a chance to expose an enormous mass market to the joys of group singing.

no right or wrong answer. Likewise, musical taste truly is a matter of style and personal preference, and, as long as the music has artistic integrity and is performed well, we should all accept and embrace excellence and quality, even if it is not in our preferred style.

Finally, as a self-proclaimed "pied piper" of bringing as many people to quality music as possible (and, in the process, hopefully raising standards and consciousness), I viewed *Clash of the Choirs* as a chance to expose an enormous mass market to the joys of group singing. My thought is that, as a result of this show, even if just 1 percent of the 12 million viewers on Thursday night became motivated to join a school, church or community choir, we now have at least 120,000 more people throughout the country participating in your choirs, and that is a remarkable recruiting statistic that is hard to match.

CHAPTER EIGHT

WOW PERSPECTIVES
(THE INTERVIEWS)

"I'd love to hang out with Mozart, and pick his brain."
—Bobby McFerrin

"For me the most important thing is connection. That means the
connection of the artists to what they are singing or playing—
to the music, to the tune, to the words, and then translating
that connection to the audience." —Fred Hersch

• • •

Thus far in this book you have been unmercifully subjected to my philosophies, methodologies, opinions, rants, soap-boxes, pet peeves—and it is my hope that you have been inspired or challenged in your own musical performance pursuits to *achieve* **The Wow Factor**. Thank you for your patience, tolerance and perseverance (unless you have skipped to this chapter!). As a reward for your stamina and endurance, I would like to offer some opinions other than mine. I asked some friends, colleagues and working professionals to answer a series of questions about *"wow,"* which factors are important to them, and what wisdom they would like to pass on to you. These outstanding artists and music professionals represent many different facets and disciplines of the profession. I hope you will find their responses to be interesting, informative and perhaps inspirational.

Here are the questions I posed:

1) What are the various musi-cal (and other) factors that go into creating a truly "*wow*" performance?

2) Name a memorable performance that made you think or feel "*wow.*"

3) What important values or professional advice would you like to impart to your students, ensembles, or aspiring professionals to help them achieve **The Wow Factor**?

4) What are any audition tips or advice that you give to people doing auditions (for a role in a musical, for membership in an ensemble, for a college music school audition or for any other professional musical opportunity) so that they can "*wow*" the jury, or get the gig? What are the most notable mistakes or assumptions artists/performers/students make before/during/after the audition process?

5) Was there a point in a concert or performance when you realized you were watching/hearing/sensing something truly extraordinary? If so, what and when? As a performer, what sensations and emotions come to mind—what connection with the audience or with each other did you feel? What, if anything, prepared you for this moment?

6) If you could hear any performer (living or deceased) or group "live" in concert, who would it be, and why?

7) How have **Wow Factors** changed in your career? What were they earlier and what are they today?

8) Are there any musical/performance trends or cultural shifts that have impacted "*wow*" either for the performer or for an audience? What, why, how? Are there people who have led the standards of "*wow*" in your scope of music/performance/educating? Who?

Here is the esteemed set of interviewees:

Michele Weir
André Thomas
Ward Swingle
Georgia Stitt
Diana Spradling
Don Shelton
Kirby Shaw

Weston Noble
Tim Noble
Liza Minnelli
Darmon Meader
Bobby McFerrin
Philip Lawson
Tim Lautzenheiser
Nick Lachey
Peder Karlsson
John Jacobson
Mac Huff
Gary Fry
Clare Fischer
Roger Emerson
Peter Eldridge
Eph Ehly
Cedric Dent
Duane Davis
Simon Carrington
Hilary Apfelstadt

Due to the fact that my last name begins with the letter "Z," I have arbitrarily decided to place these interviews in alphabetical order—in reverse!

THE INTERVIEWS

MICHELE WEIR

Author, Arranger, Pianist, Vocalist, Professor at University of California-Los Angeles
www.micheleweir.com

The much more meaningful, "Wow—that really got my attention!" experience comes for me when the performers are communicating emotionally—making me feel something. —Michele Weir

Wow Factors

Certainly I have said "*wow*" about performances that are fantastic in their overall execution—challenging, impressive literature performed with

MICHELE WEIR, cont.

virtuosic mastery, for example. But in truth, this is not what really "*wows*" me on a deep, gut level. The much more meaningful, "*Wow*—that really got my attention!" experience comes for me when the performers are communicating emotionally—making me feel something. This is what is truly inspiring. Whether it be jazz, classical, musical theater, pop, fast, slow, loud, soft, or whatever, for me the stage is set for the ***Wow Factor*** to be present when my emotional side is being touched.

A Memorable Performance

There have been many experiences like this, of course. One example I recall is when over past years I've heard the pianist/arranger/composer Clare Fischer play piano at concerts and clubs: I've actually cried. There's something about his compositions and the way he played piano that really got me out of my head and into my heart. Why did his playing leave such an impression on me? I have no idea. But I do believe the ***Wow Factor*** is not about the instrument, tempo, or complexity of literature: It's something about the communicative way it's being played or sung.

Advice for Achieving "Wow"

In performance, focus on communication. And it's very tough to focus on emotional communication if you're mentally preoccupied with aspects of technique, such as the correct notes, tuning and so on. Therefore, until you're prepared and very solid on the mechanics of a musical performance, you won't have the freedom to express the more soulful side of music! The musical mechanics have to become so second nature that full attention is on expressive communication. Preparation, preparation, preparation first; then, communication, communication, communication.

Audition Tips

Be fantastically well prepared. When a person is fantastically well prepared for an audition of any kind, it is very apparent: not just in the music, but in the attitude and confidence level. Go the extra mile. Do your homework in terms of choosing the right literature, of knowing whom you're auditioning for and what they're looking for, and of practicing intelligently until you not only sound great, but have the personal assuredness that goes along with it. I would also say, don't be shy to let them know that you want the gig, you really LOVE the ensemble (school, show) that you're auditioning for, and are committed to being a positive contributor to their organization.

Everyone wants to work with folks that are reliable, "play well with others" and are simply pleasant to be around!

Sensing Something Extraordinary

There certainly have been a number of times in the past when I experienced a feeling that something truly extraordinary was happening in a performance. One time, for example, was hearing Bobby McFerrin in San Francisco before he recorded his first album, and was still relatively unknown. He was singing "My Funny Valentine" and other standards with a pianist in a small club on a Tuesday night. He was AWESOME. Wonderful. This was before he was doing his miraculous solo voice techniques he is now so known for. Still, in the simplicity of plain ole jazz standard songs, Bobby was so communicative and spiritually focused that I was awestruck.

At other times when I experienced a really extraordinary performance, there were always several common denominators:

- The artist(s) were communicating on an emotional level.
- The artist(s) were being 100% present, "in the moment." (As opposed to being distracted by external performance considerations, such as that key change coming up, and so on.)
- Audience members were drawn in to the focused expression of the performance, and a sense of community developed.

Who Would You Like to Hear?

I think I would've liked to have heard John Coltrane. And many others...

Have *Wow Factors* Changed?

Wow Factors, big and small, are what enticed me to a life in music when I was a teenager, and what keep me there now. When I lose touch with my *Wow Factors* as previously described, music becomes banal: just another job.

Performance Trends and Standard Bearers

I think that there are and have been highly impactful ("*wow*") performances of all sorts, shapes and sizes in any and all genres. I can't think of a particular trend or shift that may have had significantly more or less influence. I would say, though, that certain personal or societal circumstances (a death, a marriage, 9/11, war, a new president, economic struggles, etc.) carry a high degree of emotional charge that can be reflected in music and arts, resulting in "*wow*" performances.

ANDRÉ THOMAS
Conductor, composer, Director of Choral Activities at Florida State University

Love performing and be as prepared as humanly possible. When this occurs, you transcend technique and nerves. —**André Thomas**

Wow Factors
I think when the energy in the performance is simply overwhelming and the music transports you into another dimension.

A Memorable Performance
It was for me at age 16, when I heard Leontyne Price sing live. I had never heard a voice be able to do exquisite pianissimo high singing, plus dramatic forte singing. There were so many exciting timbres of her voice she utilized to express the music. The magnetism she had, from her entry to the stage, where she kept consistent eye contact with the audience, and perhaps one of the lowest curtsies I've ever seen. Once she began singing, it felt as if there was no one in the audience but me. She touched my soul that night!!!!

Advice for Achieving "Wow"
Love performing and be as prepared as humanly possible. When this occurs, you transcend technique and nerves.

Audition Tips
Make sure that you are thoroughly prepared for the audition. Research what they are looking for before you audition. Know your strengths and weakness, so that you can also assess your performance.

Sensing Something Extraordinary
Answering this question is difficult, because for me it is a combination of things: the inspiration I observe on the performers' faces, something that connects with my inner being (i.e., harmony, text, or rhythmic excitement). I think the only thing that can prepare one for that moment is being relaxed and confident enough to experience it. Some people refer to it as "becoming the music."

Who Would You Like to Hear?
Leontyne Price (soprano), Jerome Hines (bass), Eliane Elias (jazz pianist), Mahalia Jackson (gospel singer), John Browning (classical pianist). Each of these performers touched my soul in a special way.

Have *Wow Factors* Changed?

They are still the same. I can respect a performance but not experience that "*wow*."

Performance Trends and Standard Bearers

All of the performers that I listed above, as well as my teachers and sometimes my fellow colleagues.

WARD SWINGLE
Arranger, Founder of The Swingle Singers
www.wardswingle.com

> *Believe completely in what you're doing.* —*Ward Swingle*

Wow Factors

Respect for the score, sufficient rehearsal time, talented performers.

A Memorable Performance

The creation of Luciano Berio's *Sinfonia* in 1970 with the New York Philharmonic and the Swingle Singers, conducted by the composer. There was a dedication and discovery in creating a great work.

Advice for Achieving "Wow"

As a director, it's a good idea to memorize the score, establish a mutually respectful contact with the performers, and get right to work.

Audition Tips

Be prepared. Keep focused on your own performance and that alone. Good concentration can help allay nervousness. Believe completely in what you're doing.

Sensing Something Extraordinary

In the *Sinfonia* mentioned above, there was a common conviction that we were doing something special.

Who Would You Like to Hear?

The early Beatles. They have shaped the listening habits of millions of people.

Have *Wow Factors* Changed?

Wow Factors don't really change. Caruso's singing affects one today just as much as it did a hundred years ago.

Performance Trends and Standard Bearers

The emergence of recording techniques, computer downloading and other technological advances has profoundly affected the definition of a *"wow"* performance, today more than at any other time in history.

GEORGIA STITT
Composer, lyricist, pianist, conductor
www.georgiastitt.com

Your look, your voice, your acting, your energy in the room—all these things combined make up the way that you are perceived as a performer.
—Georgia Stitt

Wow Factors

I think the number one thing that makes a performance a *"wow"* is surprise. I gasp when a performer does something I did not expect him or her to do. I am awed when someone exceeds my expectations—sings more musically, plays an unexpected chord, tells a joke that comes completely from left field. As someone who works in the entertainment industry, I go to a lot of performances each year. The ones I remember and talk about later are the ones that surprised me—both positively and negatively! For me, personally, I really respond when someone has extremely musical phrasing; when a performer shows that he understands a lyric so deeply that he cannot express it without feeling it; and when I stop being aware of the actor "acting" and instead see a character "behaving." I really respond emotionally when a performance resonates truth to me, when it feels inevitable. When I come home at night and can't stop thinking about it—that's a *"wow"* performance.

A Memorable Performance

In 2003 there was a revival on Broadway of the show *Big River*. It was produced by two organizations: the Roundabout Theatre Company, which is a New York not-for-profit theater responsible for several Broadway transfers, and also the Deaf West Theatre Company, based in Los Angeles, and featuring a company of deaf and hearing-impaired performers. Hearing performers sang the show's songs while their hearing-impaired counterparts stood alongside them, sharing the role, performing it in sign language. It was a very theatrical convention and it didn't take long for the audience to accept that the two actors were sharing a role, expressing it in two very different ways.

Near the end of the show there was a full-company number called "Waiting for the Light To Shine." It was filled with passionate, rousing gospel singing and signing. And then, at the climax of the number, breathtakingly, all of the sound went away. The orchestra stopped playing. The singers stopped producing sound. And yet the number went on—choreography, sign language, facial expression. They were still performing the number; we just could no longer hear it. For about eight bars, we were in the world of the deaf performers, sharing their experience. When the sound returned, after about 10 seconds of total silence, I had tears in my eyes and realized I had been holding my breath. Several years later, as you ask me this question about "*wow*" performances, it was the first thing that came to mind.

Advice for Achieving "Wow"

One of the things I tell young musical theater actors over and over again is how important it is to know how you are perceived. If you walk into an audition full of spunk and personality—a born comedienne—and then you open your mouth to sing and it comes out all serious and sad, you might find that the people watching your audition are a bit confused. It isn't to say that funny people can never be serious. It isn't to say that you can't have diverse talents and skills. It is to say that all elements of your performance need to point in the same direction. Your look, your voice, your acting, your energy in the room—all these things combined make up the way that you are perceived as a performer. If you walk into the room thinking you're the leading lady and they size you up instead as the comic sidekick, then things are probably not going to go so well for you. The most memorable performers become iconic. You know when you hire Audra McDonald that you're going to get Audra McDonald. It may well be an emotionally full and comically diverse and gloriously sung performance, but it's not going to be Bernadette Peters. It's going to be Audra McDonald.

That said, once you know how you are perceived, be true to yourself and deliver that consistently. Don't try to be all things to all people. You can't do it. Just be the best, most truthful, most carefully prepared and practiced version of yourself you can be. You won't get every role you audition for. (Even the greatest performers don't.) But, oh, when you do find the role, production, director, composer, vehicle that is right for you, how lucky your audience will be!

Audition Tips

Let's see. Audition tips. Know that your audition starts the minute you walk in the room. It all goes into that assessment of how you are being perceived. In fact, it may well begin even before you walk into the room. If you are grouchy to your monitor in the waiting room, it's likely that that little nugget of info could make it back the show's producers. Being a professional goes a really long way. Do your homework. Know who is watching your audition. Read up on what kinds of shows this theater has done in the past. Does the director have a clear aesthetic, a specific taste, a style? Treat everyone with respect. Be kind and clear to your pianist.

Beyond that, remember that your audition is your time.

Don't start until you're ready. Breathe. We can tell instantly whether or not you have the power in the room. The greatest auditions I have ever seen made me feel like I should have bought a ticket to the performance. They were polished, natural, comfortable and commanding. Now—how do you do that when you're dying of nerves? You breathe. You remember that you chose this profession and that you love performing. You get into the head of your character and you play the action of the scene, the action of the song. You treat yourself with kindness and don't beat yourself up if it doesn't go as well as you'd hoped. There have been times in auditions when I knew the person auditioning wasn't going to get this particular role, but I wrote down his or her info and called later when I had something more appropriate to offer.

At an audition, what I hope to gather from you is this: Are you musical? Are you smart? Are you flexible? Are you skilled? Are you fun to have in the room? Will I enjoy working with you for several months? Are you going to teach me something about the work that I don't already know? Are you going to surprise me? You don't have to show me every single trick you have up your sleeve. Better just to show me that your sleeve does contain tricks, and that if I hire you I will get to spend several months discovering them.

Sensing Something Extraordinary

I suppose we all have a barometer. We know what our level of expectation is. We buy a ticket to see a performance, and we have certain expectations about it before it even starts. You think, "Oh, I love this symphony, I'm so happy I get to hear it performed live." Or, "I love this musical but this is a crazy director; wonder what I'm getting myself into tonight." Or even, "I'm not much for this actress. Hope I don't fall asleep." You can tell from the energy in an audience when people's expectations are being exceeded. For me, as an audience member, I feel it start in my belly. There's a real physical resonance when I am stirred emotionally, when someone states truth in a way I've never heard it stated before, when a musical phrase from a song I know comes out completely different than I'd imagined it to be. I've heard performers describe the feeling they get when they know the audience is on their side. It gives them freedom to make bigger choices, to sing bravely and fearlessly, to take more risks. You can sense, collectively, when that is happening, and I'm really not sure which is the cause and which is the result. But I do think the most engendering thing you can do for an audience is to give them your whole self and hope that they are going to trust it and take care of it. When that happens, it's just magic.

Who Would You Like to Hear?

For me, it would be Leonard Bernstein. Of course I would like to have been in the audience during a New York Philharmonic concert that he was conducting, but even more than that I think I would have loved to have heard him teach. I think if I had been born 40 years earlier, I would have been at Tanglewood every summer, taking his conducting class, watching his performances, playing his music. By all accounts, he was a dynamic performer and a magnetic personality, fully able to express his passion for the music he was creating. Plus—he did everything I aspire to do. He was a composer, a conductor, an educator, a larger-than-life personality, a family man, a pianist, an essayist, and probably a whole lot of fun to have at a party.

Have *Wow Factors* Changed?

I'm not sure if *Wow Factors* have decidedly changed my career, but I do know that the most successes I've had have come from deep soul-searching and really being honest with myself. The hardest, most challenging moments I've ever encountered have opened the most doors for me. I remember standing in the wings three minutes before I conducted an orchestra in performance for the first time. I was sweating, thinking "Why on earth did I agree to do this?" And then the lights changed, the producer shook my hand, and out I stepped to the podium. Two hours later, it was over, and I had conducted an orchestra. *Wow*. Similarly, I recall being the pianist in a rehearsal once when I was not prepared enough and I felt as if I was not playing well. I came home thinking I had probably just hit the ceiling of my abilities, and my conductor said to me, "Instead of complaining about how you can't do it, how about practicing until you can do it?" *Wow*. One of the most important things I am currently gathering about myself and my career is the fact that I am in charge of it. It's a huge thing to realize. If you want your music to be recorded, you record it. If you want to write a musical, you write it. Instead of waiting for someone to give you a break, it is possible for you to put all the pieces into place so that the break becomes inevitable. *Wow*.

Performance Trends and Standard Bearers

Oh, I think everything in life comes and goes in phases. I'm not sure I can comment on cultural trends except to say that there are some years when there seem to be a lot of puppets on stage or other years where every show breaks the fourth wall and makes self-aware musical theater jokes. Some years seem to be filled with comedies; other years are heavy with serious and epic musicals. There are those who follow the trends and those who break the trends. But, in keeping with all of my comments above, I think the visionaries are the artists who continue to stay true to themselves and create a body of work over the long haul that is consistent in its voice but diverse in its subject matter and execution. Some examples of these kinds of visionaries: Julie Taymor, Stephen Sondheim, Patti LuPone. And the younger generation: Adam Guettel, Rob Ashford, Gustavo Dudamel, Eric Whitacre, Kelli O'Hara, and so many others.

DIANA SPRADLING
Professor of Jazz Voice at Western Michigan University
Author of *Jazz Singing: Developing Artistry and Authenticity*

In my mind, "wow" performances tend to be occasional, sometimes random and wonderfully surprising, and usually do not happen in every performance situation. —*Diana Spradling*

Wow Factors

Live "*wow*" performances are no accident, particularly in this age of technology. We are led to believe that at any given time anything can be perfect. Using overdubbing, editing, delete buttons, etc., the media have prepared us to expect (what appears to be) a very high percentage of flawless performances, and that has created certain standards of perfection in our minds that in reality are not actually being reached.

In my mind, *"wow"* performances tend to be occasional, sometimes random and wonderfully surprising, and usually do not happen in every performance situation. The more seasoned I have become as a teacher/ conductor, the fewer *"wow"* moments I experience. I'm sure this is because my music education, music experiences and musical maturity have caused me to raise my expectations significantly. I recognize that many audience members seem to be able to enthusiastically choose at least one moment of *"wow"* in every performance they attend, but I believe that is largely because in most audiences the state of intellectual and cultural diversity and variety of personal taste is influenced as much by the entertainment factors as by the artistic sophistication of the performance.

That being said, I believe that music listeners, teacher/coaches, performers, composers, arrangers and conductors experience and evaluate performances with many different and often individual degrees/levels/stages of

- musical and intellectual sophistication,
- cultural filters,
- standards of excellence,
- personal taste,
- interest in capital "A" art,
- interest in capital "E" entertainment,
- awareness/recognition and understanding of authenticity,
- and personal and professional expectations,

not to mention some sense—be it conscious or unconscious—of prioritization of the importance of these factors from their individual points of view.

Balancing the interplay among musical and nonmusical elements requires informed and demanding leadership, extremely detailed rehearsals/ preparation, constant repetition, determined focus and precise results, all of which can lead to a *"wow"* moment. Furthermore, I don't believe that all of these factors are activated at once. The performance/concert/show should flow between and among these elements for a "complete *wow*" and not just one or two tunes with "occasional *wow*" factors.

DIANA SPRADLING, cont.

Musical factors (not in a particular order) might include but are not limited to:

- dynamic nuances
- volume or intensity
- clarity of execution
- rhythmic vitality
- resonance in the sound
- delivery of lyrics
- appropriate phrasing
- unified text treatment (vernacular or formal)
- appropriate use of vibrato
- appropriate choices and execution of articulations and inflections
- appropriate/intended and steady tempos
- keys that promote healthy vocal technique in different age groups
- the tessitura of a tune
- intonation
- balance and blend among singers and between singers and instrumentalists
- expressing the intent of the composer/arranger
- a hip dance break
- high physical and vocal energy
- an artistic scat solo
- an artistic scat chorus
- healthy vocal timbres that are not imitative or "covering" someone else's sound
- a truly entertaining performance that captivates an audience (owning the room)
- "no louder than lovely"
- synergy on the entire stage
- sophisticated/polished stage presence
- program notes or an emcee that prepared the audience for what they are about to see and hear

Nonmusical factors might include

- attention to detail—degrees/levels of flawlessness
- not everything is predictable
- always some thread of elegance
- the "focused hush" of the audience
- the size and condition of the room (lighting, temperature, visibility, acoustics)
- the mood of the audience (hungry, drunk, cynical, etc.)
- the hour of the day
- the age(s) of the audience
- choice of outfits/costumes (somebody's outfit too tight or pants too short)
- lack of individual ego apparent on stage (single-minded)
- honest and sincere interaction with the audience
- a high quality and "efficient" sound system
- a sound engineer who understands "who decides who decides"
- a bit of novelty; a fresh idea
- well-intentioned and well-placed humor
- an audience feeling "better" at the end of the performance than they did when they arrived

A Memorable Performance

I can immediately think of three; all of the audiences were multicultural in makeup; and all three venues were SRO. The performers were Van Cliburn, piano, at Coral Ridge Presbyterian Church in Fort Lauderdale—the televised one with a full orchestra and a 200-voice choir; Leontyne Price, soprano, at Miami Dade Auditorium; and Curtis Stigers, jazz singer, at an International Association for Jazz Education conference in New York.

Van Cliburn played an all-Debussy recital. A close friend gave me a ticket for my birthday. We sat in the fifth row where I could clearly see his hands. I couldn't get over how large his hands were (a 13-key extension), and when he raised them off the keyboard his fingers kept hitting the wood panel behind the keys. That distraction lasted only about eight measures into his first piece because I was quickly swept up into the music: the colors of the chord clusters, the resonance ringing from the elegant Steinway grand, the elegant and flawless playing. I almost (almost!) forgot <u>he</u> was there! There was total silence in that acoustically brilliant sanctuary—no one moved, no one coughed—it felt as if no one was breathing! I learned much about Debussy and the way I listen that day. I was reminded of how many rules of "traditional" music theory he broke as a composer; I was jolted by so much asymmetric phrasing; I experienced abrupt mood and color swings; and I found myself envisioning some of the Impressionistic paintings of Monet, especially the ones he painted from the balcony of a room in the Savoy Hotel in London. I truly was swept into an altered state of consciousness. I almost found the applause intrusive! Van Cliburn let the piano speak the music… he was a mere conduit. It was a stunning moment. Debussy's music was more than composition. It was Art. I can still put myself in that room and in that performance.

> *I truly was swept into an altered state of consciousness.*
> *I almost found the applause intrusive!* —**Diana Spradling**

Leontyne Price is my absolutely favorite soprano of all time. She made her debut as the first African-American woman to sing at the Metropolitan Opera during my first year of teaching. I dedicated the largest bulletin board in my classroom to her. I left that tribute up for an entire semester!

I was living in South Florida when she performed a recital in the gigantic hall known as the Miami Dade Auditorium. Having grown up in the segregated South, that recital event was the first time I had ever attended a program where well over half of the audience was African-American. I knew when she elegantly walked onto the stage that I was about to witness an artistic awakening. She sang for about an hour and a half—sang six encores but the audience wouldn't leave—so she finally left the stage. After that recital she received every patron who wished to meet her. I got her autograph and looked into the face of beauty. Her skin was flawless and her color was peachy brown; I was in the presence of a stunning and noble woman. She seemed to carry that air of nobility all the time, on or off the stage. I was so overwhelmed I could hardly breathe. To this day I can remember being at that performance. The hall seated about five or six thousand and my seat was about three-fourths of the way back. The room was as still as the church where Van Cliburn played. Her technique was flawless, her appearance was flawless and her musicianship was flawless. Every note she uttered was voluptuous, powerful, sensitive, and poignant … and she made it all look and sound effortless. The audience was in a trance! Needless to say, so was I. I don't remember what she sang but I remember how she sang. It was so brilliant and I felt as if she were singing to me. A few years ago, at age 69, she went on a national farewell tour and stopped in Kalamazoo to sing at Miller Auditorium. She sang high D's as if they were in the middle of her range and again took the stage with nobility and elegance. After the performance I found out from one of the stagehands that she was deathly ill and was under doctor's care, full of meds and physically exhausted. No one had a clue. She sang through that illness as if it didn't exist. She's the ultimate pro and continues to pride herself in maintaining exquisite technique. What courage. What wisdom. What dedication.

And finally, Curtis Stigers. His singing is so intimate I am always convinced that he can read my mind and that he must be singing just to me! Every time I hear him it's the same reaction. He's incredibly consistent. He uses many vocal timbres to tell his stories and he may well be the only singer alive whose "raw" sound does not interfere with my enjoyment of his performance. When he's onstage, if he were to announce that the sky was falling I could believe him! I've heard him live several times in different settings and he never disappoints. The emotional shadings in his sounds are unbelievably convincing. I see tears in people's eyes when he sings. I have no idea if he's ever had acting lessons, but he's a word magician and understands the power of words. Where has he learned that kind of sensitivity? He must have a huge imagination and be an avid reader of good literature. I've never had a chance to ask him.

All three of these people command my attention and my respect … and I'm not easily impressed these days. Their art is honest, earnest and inspired, and they keep delivering at a superior level all the time. That's a *wow*!

Advice for Achieving "Wow"

The music is always more important than the performer.

Honesty and sincerity cannot be manufactured—audiences pick up on fakes very quickly.

The more prepared you are, the less likely you'll make mistakes.

The best way to win an audition is to practice auditioning.

It's not the mistakes you make, it's how you handle them.

You're only as good as your technique.

Be proud but never be satisfied.

DIANA SPRADLING, cont.

What you focus on determines how well you perform.

You don't own a tune until you've performed it 200 times.

Audition Tips

Your audition begins when you step onto the stage/into the room. How you walk, how you carry yourself, what you wear all matter. You are a package, not an item. Since you often speak before you sing, your voice needs to be well pitched and "musical." Your speaking voice reflects your singing technique. Being ill doesn't matter to the panel of judges. They will have a preconceived notion of what THEY are looking for; if you don't fulfill their preconceived notion, you won't get the part no matter how well you perform.

When the feelings of "I'm not ready" or "They'll hate me" start creeping into your mind before you step onto the stage, you've lost your focus and the gig.

Sensing Something Extraordinary

As a member of an audience:
Chills;
Hair standing up on my neck;
Mesmerized;
No one else seems to be in the room but the performers and me;
The audience is frozen in time.

As a performer:
A moment that seems to be frozen in time.

Have *Wow Factors* Changed?

During my 43 years of teaching at every level but elementary school, my knowledge of what I need to teach, how much I should expect and how I set standards of excellence have changed dramatically. In the earlier years I was more concerned with parents and administrators buying into the value of a music education and students loving music. Now I am focused on quality issues and just how much my students understand the value of these issues. Early on, entertainment mattered more than Art, and now craft and Art matter more than entertainment. Earlier, participation mattered more than the craft. Now craft matters more than participation.

Somehow we've come to equate quality with elite in our society. That says to me that the suggestion of sustained excellence is neither considered nor possible by a majority. I beg to differ. Maybe the number of times we experience "*wow*" is lower because we as leaders in the field haven't insisted on sustained excellence.

Performance Trends and Standard Bearers

Leaders, performers, educators who set and expect high standards of excellence; who can think outside the box and never accept second best; who maintain/sustain excellence; and who are superior musicians in their own right:

> Gene Puerling
> Mark Murphy
> Robert Shaw
> Fred Waring
> Luciana Sousa
> Steve Zegree

Trends or cultural shifts that have impacted "*wow*":

> Disney Entertainment.
> Modern group vocal jazz – The Real Group; The Manhattan Transfer, New York Voices, Take 6.
> Las Vegas – no longer just a place for gambling and movie stars.
> Crossover singers.
> American Idol – anyone can win; no need for agents, managers up front.
> Satellite Radio and TV, more of everything available more quickly.
> The iPod – downloads increase emphasis on intimate listening.
> Computer downloads—if it's recorded it's probably available!

DON SHELTON
Singer and Saxophonist
The Hi-Lo's! and The Singers Unlimited

It is important to relate to the audience and bring them along with you on the musical journey. —*Don Shelton*

Wow Factors

First off, I have always believed that a performance must begin with an "onstage" look by the individual or ensemble—as in walking onto the stage confident and focused but pleasant-looking to the audience. And next comes opening with a spirited piece that says to the crowd that we are glad to be here and listen to this. By good preparation and lots of rehearsal, the performer/performers should have some good things to display such as blend, pitch, feel and, of course, crisp entrances and overall togetherness. By doing an up-tempo piece and then a nice ballad of sorts with good harmonies and a chance to show that balance, blend, etc. ... the audience should begin to get the idea that the performance is becoming a "*wow*" one. Certainly passion and emotion are the most important factors for an artist to bring to the performance.

A Memorable Performance

1. Maureen McGovern in Palm Desert. The Annenberg Theatre at Eisenhower Medical Center. Solo performance with only a fantastic pianist to accompany her. Every piece was meticulous in artistry ... a riveting performance for sure.

2. From my personal experiences with The Hi-Lo's! One was in Germany at a NATO Base in 1962 when the audience was just amazing in helping us to rise to the occasion and bring an extra bit of magic to the evening.

3. Another was in Denver, Colorado, at Taylor's Night Club in '63 with a similar audience of real devoted fans who just sparked us to another level of performance. In reality it seems that the audience can give incredible incentive to artists when they just anticipate something beyond the ordinary. Perhaps by reputation or whatever...

4. The Hi-Lo's! in 1988 at La Mirada Performing Arts Center receiving a standing ovation as we walked on stage ... spine-tingling to say the

least … and we geared our performance up many notches for sure. Amazing to have experienced that.

Advice for Achieving "Wow"

Practice, practice and know the material very well. Look like you are having FUN! It is important to relate to the audience and bring them along with you on the musical journey. Achieving something not expected is very good as well.

Audition Tips

Have confidence by good preparation and by being rested and in good shape are all contributing factors in performing to a high level. A good attitude and being very cordial as well as taking any direction well are also important. No ego trips are a must. Being humble but still businesslike with a degree of true confidence will go a long way toward showing who you are. Being arrogant is a "no-no" for sure. A know-it-all is not what will win over any judge or jury. Play or sing your very best even when faced with a mistake or two … carrying on the very best you can is also important. Be as relaxed as you can … Many intangibles are at play during the process and are sometimes not in the control of the artist. Being personable is always a must.

Who Would You Like to Hear?

1. Frank Sinatra. 2. Stan Getz. 3. Stan Kenton Band of '53 4. Woody Herman's Band, '61, because they are the epitome of incredible exciting music and full of "*wow*"!!

Have Wow Factors Changed?

I think they have changed dramatically due to more technological advances in electronics and special effects. … People expect much more, and it takes more to "*wow*" the audience.

Performance Trends and Standard Bearers

I think The Hi-Lo's! was a "*wow*" group for its time … possibly The Singers Unlimited too … certainly New York Voices are! And many of our past heroes, like great instrumentalists/vocalists Coleman Hawkins, Harry James, Benny Goodman, Artie Shaw, Ella Fitzgerald, Peggy Lee, Sarah Vaughan, Carmen McRae, Charlie Parker, Stan Getz, Alfred Gallodoro and others. This has been fun to do!

KIRBY SHAW
Composer and arranger
www.kirbyshaw.com

The United States is the world center of "wow"! —**Kirby Shaw**

Wow Factors

- Talent
- Demonstrating a knowledge/understanding/mastery of what's gone before.
- Discipline
- Attention to detail
- Audience rapport
- People skills

A Memorable Performance

Louis Armstrong—San Jose, California Civic Auditorium, 1954. I was an eighth-grade trumpet player. Hearing Louis' crackling tone and free-spirited, happy improvisation turned me upside down, and made me realize for the first time that the melodies I was beginning to play by ear on my horn really mattered. To this day, I have more of his recordings in my listening library than any other artist.

Advice for Achieving Wow

In addition to question #1 (above):

Get your own personal act together; be the best person you can be (be authentic); don't waste time covering your inadequacies; if you blow it, apologize and move on. Carry a questioning mind with you in all things musical, as in what is it about a particular artist/ensemble that makes it worthy of your study? If it's good, steal it! From a musical standpoint, be able to musically and aesthetically analyze and know what you're hearing and seeing. Do your homework!

Audition Tips

Be prepared—musically, facially and physically. This will alleviate the fear factor and eliminate the need for excuses. For a musical theater role, do research on the role for which you're auditioning. If it's the lead role in *Annie*, a red wig can help! Don't be late to your tryout. Don't ever underestimate the importance of "people skills."

Sensing Something Extraordinary

I believe that great performances are perceived immediately. The artist's mastery is so complete that it's impossible to miss. In an outstanding performance, all involved can have a sense of being at one with the universe.

Examples (in addition to question #2, above):

1955 Jazz at the Philharmonic with Ella Fitzgerald, Oscar Peterson, Stan Getz, Coleman Hawkins, Joe Jones, Ray Brown, Roy Eldridge—my first-ever concert of giants of jazz!

1956 Maynard Ferguson Birdland Dream Band. I'd never heard a trumpet player that could play so accurately at a stratospheric level before. It was also my first exposure to the sound of West-Coast-style Big Band arrangements.

The 1968 Buddy Rich Big Band playing "West Side Story" medley live in Seattle—Don Menza doing "circular breathing," Al Porcino on lead trumpet, and the amazing Buddy Rich himself. With the exception of the Benny Goodman's band arrangement of "Sing, Sing, Sing," this is truly one of the best Big Band arrangements I've ever heard, and an absolutely electrifying performance! My ears rang for days!

Carmen McRae in concert at College of the Siskiyous in 1976. Her sassy yet warm vocal mastery of her material, her ability to make every individual in the auditorium feel like part of a warm community and her careful, yet effortless attention to the text (consonants) and vocal phrasing forever changed the way I thought about performing vocal/choral music!

Any solo vocal performance by Bobby McFerrin. With his virtuoso performances, this man, more than anyone, has given all humanity permission to "play" with their voices and break free from the written page.

Torvill and Dean's "Bolero" in the 1984 Olympics. Within the strict rules of Ice Dancing they raised the artistry bar higher than it had ever been raised before.

Any performance of Cirque du Soleil. This organization had the wisdom to question/analyze/reform every aesthetic aspect of the "circus" genre and take it to an unequaled level of excellence! We can all learn from their heightened sense of analytical curiosity.

Who Would You Like to Hear?

Paganini, Liszt, Nijinsky, Farinelli, Caruso, Art Tatum, Clifford Brown, Django in Paris. Unequaled technical mastery of their instruments.

Benny Goodman's 1937-1938 Carnegie Hall concert. Top arrangements (Fletcher Henderson) and top players (Benny, Harry James, Gene Krupa). The legendary swing-band at its peak—the recording only hints at the excitement in the hall!

Charlie "Bird" Parker. Unequalled technique *and* incredible lyricism in his melodic lines at any tempo. His musical influence cannot be overstated.

Duke Ellington Live At Newport 1956. Paul Gonsalves' 27 choruses, Cat Anderson playing lead trumpet, the legendary Duke Ellington at the helm and an ecstatic crowd. A legendary moment in jazz history!

Maria Callas. She gave her all in every performance.

Steve Ray Vaughan. For my money, easily the greatest blues guitar player who's ever lived.

Have *Wow Factors* Changed?

For me, the "*wow*" factor has evolved over time. In my grade school days, I was "*wowed*" by almost any musician who could play music at a higher technical level than I (instrumental or vocal). I also inherited my father's "question everything/is this as good as it can be?" way of looking at things. As I gained in knowledge and ability, I started noticing aspects of musical performance that "*wowed*" me: technical virtuosity, unique tone quality, singing styles, musical genres, facial animation/physical presence, audience rapport, tune selection, lyrics, grooves, changes that singers make to individual notes (inflections), phrasing, set pacing, concert attire, stage lighting and vocal registers. I like to think that aesthetic discernment increases with knowledge and understanding. Additionally, I find that the more I learn about musical perfection when attending a performance, the harder it is to be thrilled. But best of all, when I happen upon a really great performance, the aesthetic satisfaction is most sweet.

Performance Trends and Standard Bearers

The United States is the world center of "*wow*"! Blues, spirituals, ragtime, Dixieland, swing, bebop, folk, bluegrass, progressive jazz, rock-and-roll, jazz-rock, acid-rock, heavy metal, funk, cabaret, musical theater ... the list goes on. Over time, each has had its influence on other music, and all are still going on right here and right now. For me, the single best/most important cultural influence on American popular music has been/is the influence of Black America. This music, more than any other, has a freedom of utterance that has allowed for limitless creativity and melodic expression to occur.

People who, for me, have led the standards of "*wow*"? There aren't enough pages in this book for me to name all the people who've helped me gain in the "*wow*" level of musical understanding, but here are a few:

All of the artists/groups mentioned previously

Choral arranging: Gene Puerling. He raised the bar on advanced choral harmony and vocal blend.

Vocal groups:

The Four Freshmen. Early modern jazz giants, they sang swingin' close-harmony arrangements and were their own band at the same time!

The Hi-Lo's! Early modern jazz giants—how can you lose when Clark Burroughs is singing lead tenor!

Lambert, Hendricks and Ross (Bavan). Improv can be the centerpiece for success.

The Swingle Singers. Creative, elegant and accurate!

WESTON NOBLE
Conductor, Johnson Professor Emeritus of Music, Luther College

We never know when an individual has a "wow" moment, but it can come at any time, from any rehearsal. —*Weston Noble*

Wow Factors

Almost invariably, the acoustics in a room will have an effect. If you have the right acoustics, "*wow*" moments can come much faster. If the singers cannot hear from one side to the other, it will be difficult from a group to achieve "*wow*." It doesn't have to be the epitome of perfection or technically perfect for there to be "*wow*."

A Memorable Performance

My very first "*wow*" moment was as a student—a freshman in high school—rehearsing with my high school band. On Saturday we had gotten a rating of 3 at a festival (we weren't very good!). On the following Monday, the director's mood in rehearsal was also not very good. I was struggling, playing my metal clarinet with a #2 reed. We were rehearsing the "Light Cavalry Overture" by Von Suppe, and I will never forget the moment when the brass came. It was 8:20 a.m., May 4, 1936, in Riceville, Iowa. It doesn't have to be a Robert Shaw/Brahms *Requiem* to be a "*wow*" moment. We never know when an *individual* has a "*wow*" moment, but it can come at any time, from any rehearsal. Look what that moment did to my life.

A "*wow*" moment that affects everybody in the group is rare. So it's most often an individual experience. So many circumstances are variables that can affect the group (if someone has a headache!), so everyone will react differently and individually, within the group.

In my 57 years of teaching at Luther College there were some "*wow*" moments where everyone experienced the "*wow*." In 1959, at a performance of Nordic Choir in Albuquerque, everyone had a "*wow*" moment—the acoustics were great. Also, in 1985 at the ACDA [American Choral Directors Association] National Convention in Salt Lake City when the Nordic Choir performed right before the Mormon Tabernacle Choir. When I conducted the Luther Band at Lincoln Center, we opened with the "Festive Overture" by Shostakovich and the audience was already applauding at the final cutoff of the final chord of the piece. And that was just our opening number!

I'll never forget the first time I heard the Samuel Barber "Adagio For Strings"—that magnificent F major chord. And I'll never forget the first time I heard the Bach "Air on a G String." I was in high school at a summer camp, listening on a small radio.

Advice for Achieving "Wow"

First and foremost, above all, they [musicians] must be willing to be totally vulnerable. Vulnerable first with yourself: You must be in touch with your soul. You must be vulnerable to what the score is saying and with the depth of the emotion and whatever the composer wants. As a director, you must be willing to be vulnerable with your group. Some of my most wonderful memories are when I cried in front of my group. You cannot predict when something like that will happen.

Audition Tips

A face that reflects the mood of the text is so important in an audition. One of the most notable mistakes is when a person is trying too hard to impress, as opposed to just showing sincerity.

Sensing Something Extraordinary

Well, Nordic Choir always held hands during performances, and that was a great means of communication within the ensemble. Sometimes a squeeze of one hand to another in the middle of a piece can be great communication. Also, sensitivity is so important. Extraordinary can be a chord that is *so* in tune that it resonates a great sound, or an incredibly effective moment in the rhythm, when everything is in sync.

Who Would You Like to Hear?

There are three [I'd like to hear again]:

I recently heard the Mormon Tabernacle Choir Christmas concert "live" in Salt Lake City. There were 1.2 million requests for tickets and they gave four sold-out performances in a concert hall that seats 21,000 people. So there was a "*wow*" even before the concert began.

Hearing [Robert] Shaw doing Bach when his Chorale was on tour at Luther. His inner pulse was so unbelievable that I had to get up and walk around—I just couldn't sit there. Fortunately I was sitting in the back row!

Hearing Fred Waring and The Pennsylvanians singing "O Holy Night" on the radio. I suppose that would have been Shaw, too. Howard Swan would always ask where people had a great choral experience. He thought everyone has their own inner ear and what you hear in your inner ear is probably different than what someone else hears. Swan believed that most people have a great choral experience in their college choir. But I never sang in a great college choir, so the inner ear for me was hearing Waring on the radio—and Robert Shaw was influencing my inner ear then.

Have *Wow Factors* Changed?

I think "*wow*" moments are harder to get the longer you are involved in music. Maybe we get more fussy as we get older, but those moments become more rare. Earlier in my career those moments were just more spontaneous. But then the technical side becomes more involved. You learn more, so as time goes on, making a "*wow*" moment can become more difficult, because we become so technically oriented. That gets in the way of spontaneity.

Performance Trends and Standard Bearers

Absolutely! Ask how many CDs your choir kids own. Kids today are *so* aware of recordings. They know all the artists and groups. The technology available today has created a situation where critical thinking and judgment have improved. It's a very positive thing. Great performances are available on TV.

I think about the Shaw recording of the Rachmaninoff *Vespers*—and it was all done in one take. Simply unbelievable—his ability to translate the emotions of the score and his musical sensitivity within him in a performance. Also Helmut Rilling for his live performances and his incredible knowledge of Bach. And Howard Swan—his ability to verbalize the trends and schools of thought and the *reasons* for them. He was a great verbal communicator. He could synthesize thoughts like nobody else. And Leonard Bernstein—I *loved* his lack of restraint when he was conducting.

TIM NOBLE
Metropolitan Opera Baritone
Distinguished Professor of Voice, Indiana University

*Open your soul and give of yourself, and then, and only then, will you even have a chance at achieving the **Wow Factor**.* —*Tim Noble*

Wow Factors

The *Wow Factor* is something that for me is truly difficult to define. The *Wow Factor* or "it" is really an intangible that seems to transcend (for instance, for a singer) technique, talent, voice quality, style and musicianship. I have heard performers who have all of the above and still don't manage to create the *Wow Factor*. So then, what is it? For me the *Wow Factor* in any performance is the one thing that transports the listener to another place, that raises the hair on the back of your neck, that reduces you to tears, that communicates beyond all of the aspects that make the performance, but still embodies them. Can it be taught? No. Does every performer have the ability to create the *Wow Factor*? No, but in performance I have heard groups of performers, none of which individually necessarily are blessed with this ability, but collectively create magic. I have also seen performers who have maybe captured this rare phenomenon on an occasion, only to spend the rest of their performing lives trying to re-create that moment and never succeeding. When it does happen, one thing is for sure, and that is that the audience has heard truth.

A Memorable Performance

It hasn't happened often, but listening to Olga Borodina sing Delilah at San Francisco Opera a few years ago comes to mind. Placido Domingo in the last act of *Otello* at the Metropolitan Opera some 15 years ago. Sarah Vaughan singing "My Funny Valentine" in a 4 a.m. show at Caesar's Palace in Las Vegas in the early '70s—utter perfection! Listening to Janos Starker and Rostropovich rehearsing next door to my studio at IU—beyond heaven!

Advice for Achieving "Wow"

Become the best that you can be at your craft. In other words, prepare yourself for performance by being the best that you can be technically, mentally and musically, and when you are performing, total concentration is an absolute. Open your soul and give of yourself, and then, and only then, will you even have a chance at achieving the *Wow Factor*. Many artists strive for perfection, and of course I don't think that it is ever achieved, but the attempt will certainly be appreciated by the audience. Remember, what you give will come back to you many times over.

Audition Tips

I think auditions are probably the most difficult situation to perform in, because they are so often sterile and devoid of the human condition. Again, concentration is the key to a good audition. If you are worried about what the judges or adjudicators think, you are already in a negative mental place and you probably won't be successful. Students and professionals often think that because a judge yawns, writes something down or cuts you off, that means that you have failed. Many times this is certainly not the case. When I auditioned for Maestro James Levine at the Metropolitan Opera, I recall that I screwed up the words in the "Catalogue" aria from *Don Giovanni*, actually inserting names of pasta rather than the correct Italian words. After the aria I heard Levine say, "So you like pasta, do you?" At that moment I knew that my brief career in opera was over and so I immediately left the theater, and thanked my stars that I knew how to tend bar. After a few drinks at a pub in NYC, I got a call from my frantic manager asking why I had left the theater so hastily, as Maestro Levine wanted to hire me. Go figure. So, go about the business of performing, using the tools that you have, and simply commit to the performance. If you are involved in your performance, rest assured that the judge/auditioner is involved as well. Remember that when you audition, the people who listen to you want to hear something *good*. Give it to them, and for cryin' out loud, don't worry about a mistake here and there. An honest mistake will almost always be forgiven.

Sensing Something Extraordinary

This would have to be a performance of *Simon Boccanegra* that I sang in Stuttgart with Georg Solti conducting. I wasn't feeling particularly great, and we were given only one intermission, as it was in concert. In complaining about the shortness of the intermission to the maestro, he simply told me that he would pull me through the night. Now here was a man well into his 80s, who by his sheer will and strength helped me to sing as well as I probably ever did. The result was a standing ovation of some 20 minutes. What prepared me for this moment was all of my training and experience, but the maestro allowed me to reach deeper than I ever thought possible. It was an amazing evening, I have to say.

Who Would You Like to Hear?

I would love to be able to hear Sarah Vaughan and Leonard Warren live. Miss Vaughan, I worked with and listened to, and her impeccable musicianship, vocality and heart produced amazing performances. Leonard Warren, for my money, was the greatest baritone of all time. The voice alone had the *Wow Factor*, and his artistry is beyond comparison in my book. As for groups, you would be hard pressed to find anything better than The Hi-Lo's! I never got to see them perform, but it would sure be something to hear and see.

Have *Wow Factors* Changed?

Wow Factors are pretty much the same, just different artists. The human condition does not change. I do think that the *Wow Factor* has become more visual in recent years. This is not to say that there are not great musical performances, but audiences today tend to dote on what a person looks like as well as what they hear. Conductors, pianists, concert artists, singers and groups have gone for a hipper, less traditional look, hoping to appeal to the audiences of today. For bad or good, there are so many types of entertainment available to the public at large, particularly at home, that there is a lot more commercialization of the arts. Personally, I don't care for it. If a baritone can sing "Largo al factotum" on a trapeze and it is good, then what the heck.

Performance Trends and Standard Bearers

In my musical sphere, I would say that many musicians, actors and singers have led the way in this area. In opera, Placido Domingo, Carol Vaness, Verdi, Puccini, Nicola Rossi-Lemeni, Richard Bradshaw, Renee Fleming, Luciano Pavarotti, Kurt Herbert Adler, Jean Pierre Ponelle, Mirella Freni and Virginia Zeani come to mind. Musicians who have been and are torch-bearers include Fred Waring, Janos Starker, Dave Baker, Sir Georg Solti and Robert Shaw. Other names that I have known and worked with would be George Abbott, Harold Prince, Irving Berlin, Johnny Carson and Bob Hope. Educators (that I have known) that have led and helped create the standards of the *Wow Factor* in my musical sphere would be Nicola Rossi Lemeni, Don Neuen, Dr. Steve Zegree, Dr. Charles Webb, Menachem Pressler, Dave Baker, James Noble, Bob Austen and Carol Vaness.

LIZA MINNELLI
Singer, dancer, actress
www.officializaminnelli.com

I want to act each song like each song is a complete story.
—Liza Minnelli

Wow Factors
Work your ass off!!! And then work it again! That's it!

A Memorable Performance
Charles Aznavour, New York City, when I was 17 years old. I saw him and I thought, "That's what I want to do. I want to act each song like each song is a complete story."

Advice for Achieving "Wow"
Be prepared. Because when luck meets preparation, you win! If luck comes along and you're not prepared—that's it.

Audition Tips
Research the role you're going for and find a song that has humor in it, and that is like the part that you want to play, so that they can picture you in that part. Also, don't waste your time, find out first if they're looking for a blond or brunette!!

Who Would You Like to Hear?
Charles Aznavour and Pearl Bailey, because they both put so much thought and truth and heart into their performances.

Have *Wow Factors* Changed?
When you first start out, you are like a wide spotlight, and as you learn more and you experience more, you try and pull that spotlight down to a laser beam, so that if you threw your arms way out to the side, as you go on you find out that you can just toss your hands and it means the same thing.

Performance Trends and Standard Bearers
Eddie Cantor, Georgie Jessel, Johnson and Olson, Lou Holtz, The Howard Boys, the Cohans and Foys, and that singing fool Al Jolson.

DARMON MEADER
New York Voices, composer, arranger, saxophonist
www.darmonmeader.com

...auditions are not a place to try something new, like a new piece you are working on. Go with the tried and true even if it's old news to you.
—Darmon Meader

Wow Factors

Well, I'm going to answer this from the music geek side of things. As a performer, New York Voices has given me a musical backbone. I find I really need to think about and remind myself that vocal music is a performance art and not just notes on a page. I have to work on really being a performer— being visual and really connecting with the audience. With that in mind, the first thing is really knowing your proverbial "stuff." Just really being conscious that we know our notes and having confidence in what we sound like. With that together, then we can really perform well, we can connect with the audience and put on a good show. But without that backbone, the rest of it doesn't really happen. Then the next step is reminding myself how much vocal music, whether it is classical, jazz or pop or whatever, is a visual connection to the audience. It's different than if you are just playing saxophone in an orchestra or where it's just about a sonic experience.

A Memorable Performance

One that comes to mind as an audience member is a Yellowjackets concert; the "*wow*" was just how polished and musical the performance was. That these four musicians all individually are very competent musicians became a much stronger "thing" when connected together. From a compositional standpoint, from an interactive standpoint, from a musicianship standpoint, everything was just so... I mean, it jumped off the stage. It was at an IAJE [International Association for Jazz Education] convention, maybe in Chicago.

Advice for Achieving "Wow"

If you are an aspiring vocalist in particular: I'm always encouraging vocalists to develop a well-rounded musicianship so they have the backbone we were just discussing. So they understand not just the melody of the song or just the lyrics, but knowing harmonically what the song does so that you have the confidence to explore the song in different ways and find new ways to interpret the melody and those types of things. Oftentimes we know that as singers we can—we tend to in this day and age—be concerned about what the visual elements are, but really being a strong musician is equally important. As an aside, I find it interesting that once in a while we have an opportunity to actually hear pop singers *live*, and hear them really sing, like at sporting events or on *Saturday Night Live* singing live (versus on a track). It's kind of hit or miss as to which ones can really sing as strongly as they present themselves on their recordings. I had an interesting experience a while ago meeting Katerina Valente—a woman now in her 70s who is very famous in Europe and who also made quite a few appearances in the United States on variety shows in the 1960s. On shows like the *Ed Sullivan Show*, one minute she would be singing and dancing—live with the band—and she's just wailing, and then she's dancing, and then another minute she would be playing the guitar. All this crazy stuff. Live. Talk about a **Wow Factor**: This is a person who had all of that knowledge.

Audition Tips

Auditions are not really part of my scene, but I would say auditions are not a place to try something new, like a new piece you are working on. Go with the tried and true even if it's old news to you.

Sensing Something Extraordinary

A performer live: When I read that question, I first thought of being in the TV audience with someone like Katerina Valente.

Who Would You Like to Hear?

From a jazz standpoint, Ella Fitzgerald in her prime. Charlie Parker in his prime.

Have *Wow Factors* Changed?

How have *Wow Factors* changed? That's very interesting to me. Early on, I think that on my saxophone, influences were Coltrane. My early arranging and performing aesthetic was the higher-faster-louder syndrome. And you hear that on early NY Voices recordings; it's very aggressive from an ensemble standard. And then, over time, the group has grown and shifted to something more sophisticated in our music. And it is as much about the melodic content in the song. There is more subtlety in the arranging and hopefully also the arranging has embraced the lyrics more and so that translates to a little bit more of an emotional connection to the music and not just technically challenging.

Performance Trends and Standard Bearers

Cultural Shifts: Unfortunately the thing that comes to mind is more of a negative than a positive with the way music has evolved from a pop standpoint. There's a further and further disconnect between real music performance values and just creating a visual element (with visual being such a large part of it). Then you also include all the technology you can take advantage of in as many ways. You can take people that don't really sing that well and make them sound like they *do* sing well and then you put them on stage and you have them lip sync their own recordings. And then if the individual is a great dancer and visually interesting to look at, you then have a pop star. Whereas, 20 years ago there was still the sense that if you could sing *and* you had all these other elements—great. You had to be able to sing to be able to make it. If you couldn't sing, then it didn't matter how good the visual performance was. So that's the thing I find a little disturbing. Somebody like you or I who understands how all that works, we can kind of separate our sense of "who's got it" and who doesn't—but the average person on the street doesn't know. It is what it is.

The opposite of that is that when the New York Voices go into a TV appearance or something where we are outside of our normal jazz element and we work with people who are just mildly stunned that we can sing like we do. Because the singing is so much more sophisticated than what they typically see in their day-to-day experience.

On the other hand, one of the things that does continue to grow is a strong education. A lineage of the educational side of music in American culture is something that does not seem to be diminishing. That we can introduce young people to good music, whether it's classical, jazz, theater—all those things we seem to embrace in our culture, on the education side of things. This is not the case even in some European countries, even if they are culturally oriented. It's good to see we haven't lost that.

BOBBY McFERRIN
Singer, conductor, recording artist
www.bobbymcferrin.com

Everyone has butterflies—just make sure your butterflies are flying in formation. —**Bobby McFerrin**

Wow Factors
I think it is honesty. I think what *wows* people is seeing something that is genuine, and something that has integrity. When you notice people really being themselves—and that is hard to define—but you know it when you experience it. There is something about their personalities that is sharing their gifts with you, and doing it in such a way that you are really emotionally moved, and sometimes you can even feel it physically, like when you get goose bumps.

A Memorable Performance
The first time I heard Miles Davis I left the concert molecularly changed! It was February of 1971. The band included Keith Jarrett, Jack DeJohnette, Gary Bartz and Airto. I never approached music the same way after that. I was literally stunned and after that I kind of "got" what improvisation was all about. I had no expectations going in to the concert. I didn't know what Miles was doing. I didn't know much about his repertoire. I was not a fan and I didn't own any of his albums. I think I went just because I was trying to impress my date!

Advice for Achieving "Wow"
It all comes back to being yourself. Sometimes kids think that in order to make it they have to sound like everybody else. But the secret of making it and longevity in the business and success is *not* sounding like anyone else—and sounding like *you*. When I discovered that I was a singer, I spent two years deliberately staying away from listening to singers. Because I knew that if I did that and if I found singers that I really liked a lot, that I might try to imitate that singer. I'm very impressionable that way. I had to find out what I sounded like so I didn't dare listen to a single singer, because I had found my sound, and I found what I was going to work on, and I stuck with that.

Audition Tips
I remember being scared to death before auditions, and being really nervous, which made me try a little too hard. I was super self-critical about every little

move that I made. I tell people that it is good to feel nervous going into an audition because it means that you really care about what you do and you want to impress people, and you want them to like you. I actually stopped touring for a period in my career because I was *not* nervous and I felt as though I did not have the "juice" to perform well. Everyone has butterflies— just make sure your butterflies are flying in formation. Just try to harness your nervous energy as best as you can and don't let it get the better of you. Remember that the goal is to get the gig, but if you don't, it doesn't mean that your life is over.

There are TV shows that show people auditioning, and these people have invested so much of their time thinking "This is my one opportunity, my one chance," and if they don't make it they go away despondent, thinking that they've blown it, and that they will never get the chance to be what they want to be, like that is the *only* opportunity that they have, and it's not at all. Sometimes I just want to meet those singers and shake them and say, "Wake up. This is just a single opportunity and there will be many down the road, and maybe this isn't the *right* one for you."

Sensing Something Extraordinary

Again, being in the audience and seeing Miles Davis perform "live." Also, when I first experienced conductor Carlos Kleiber. When I first saw him conduct on television, I thought that I was observing something really profound, and I had never thought that way about other conductors. To me, there was no conductor who conducted like Kleiber. Even Bernstein, as wonderfully marvelous as he was. I couldn't believe what I was seeing, because [Kleiber] embodied the music so deeply that literally, if you turned down the sound, you could almost guess what he was conducting, because you could hear the music out of his body. That was an amazing experience for me. I was really moved. And the fact that we exchanged letters for a few weeks was very, very interesting. I still have his letters. I keep them with me and read them occasionally, especially when I become despondent. When I am working with an orchestra and we are not connecting at all, I will pull out his letters for encouragement.

Those experiences are becoming more and more few and far between. I think I had more when I was a young music student and going to different concerts. Back in the late '60s and early '70s, when jazz and rock and Third World music—music from Africa and India—were starting to meet and greet one another and started to fuse. I was a composition student in those days, so

I was trying to throw everything into the mix and see what it would sound like. There was a lot of experimentation, and I kind of miss that.

I haven't had one of those "*wow*" experiences in a long time, but you know what (and this is not to butter *you* up), I had a "*wow*" experience the last time I worked with you and Gold Company. It was this moment when we had done whatever we had rehearsed and I just walked up to the pianist (the rhythm section was really groovin') and I said, "Now just play something, completely unexpected, you decide what you want to do and I'll see if I can find my place in it. And he played something that I really didn't know, but I remember that afterward I thought "*That* was really hip and happening—that was so cool." I often think about that moment—and I didn't realize it until the piece was done and I was able to reflect on it. It threw me into a place that I didn't expect. It was like going back to place that you had been, but hadn't visited in a long, long time.

Who Would You Like to Hear?

I'd love to hang out with Mozart, and pick his brain. I'd like to be in a room with him and say, "Mozart, what could you do with this theme…" then sing a couple of bars and just watch him take it and do something with it. He is the musician that I would really love to have spent some time with. I was not a Mozart fan until I started studying his scores, and then standing in front of an orchestra and having to tell them not only *what* to play but *why* to play it a certain way. There are so many places of discovery in his music.

Have *Wow Factors* Changed?

Wow Factors have a lot to do with the audience that I'm working with, and I'm at this stage in my career where it is all about interaction with the audience. More than being a solo artist, though that is part of it. I've gotten into inviting individuals, people out of the audience, literally to come up on stage to sing with me. Sometimes it takes real coaxing and sometimes I'll just hold the microphone out and there will be 20 people waiting for their chance to come up onstage. Every once in a while someone will come up and sit down on stage with me and blow me away and I'll think, "Wow…what are you up to, and who are you?!" But I also have to give credit to some kids who may not sing very well but you can tell their heart is so into it, and people fall in love with them just because they can tell that they are giving their best and they have the courage to try. So that *wows* me more than anything.

BOBBY McFERRIN, cont.

Performance Trends and Standard Bearers

The inundation and the amount of music that is available through the Internet has lessened our capacity to be surprised by things. Our brains have become so saturated and everything is so easily available at our fingertips that the search and the intensity of the search have diminished. So now we don't have as many "*wow*" moments, or we have them but we don't recognize them as easily, because there are so many of them. We can't appreciate them like we used to.

For me, Keith Jarrett. To this day, I'm still amazed at his musicianship. His left hand in particular—his harmonic sense knocks me out. There are a few musicians, like Chick Corea and Keith, who really have their own harmonies and "stuff" that we normal musicians wouldn't even think of, or wouldn't even know how to begin to even get there. I love Keith's compositions and his writing and I hope that at some point he will do some more and come up with more original material.

PHILIP LAWSON
The King's Singers, arranger
www.philiplawson.net

> *Know your game so you can walk on the stage with confidence.*
> *—Philip Lawson*

Wow Factors

Obviously you need to be totally prepared musically to do the job onstage, so that the audience feels comfortable that you know what you're doing! The confidence that you know how to do the job will communicate itself to the audience.

We, in the King's Singers, don't have at our disposal the massive wall of sound that would be one of the main **Wow Factors** in a rock concert, so we try to make our sound as blended and beautiful as possible, and often we will get the biggest feeling of "*wow*" from an audience after a soft, still piece that is perfectly blended and in tune.

That said, when we have started a concert with "serious" music and we get to one of our most entertaining encores ("Crocodile Rock," "Nella Vecchia Fattoria," "If You're Gonna Play in Texas," etc.), the scream that frequently happens as the piece finishes is quite loud and certainly makes you think "*Wow!*"

A Memorable Performance

If we're talking about King's Singers performances, then the recent three Christmas shows called "Rejoice and be Merry" we did with the Mormon Tabernacle choir in their 21,000-seat Convention Center, with every seat taken, must get a mention. Just an awesome response from the audience.

In 1996 we performed in a football stadium in Korea to 40,000—with a 10 million live TV audience—and for obvious reasons that was "*wow.*"

We did a tour a few years back with the great pianist Emanuel Ax. Just to be sharing the stage with someone of that stature really helped us perform at our best.

Shortly after 9/11 we did a tour of the States and decided to open each concert, unscheduled and unannounced, with a soft *a cappella* rendition of "The Star-Spangled Banner" in memory of those who lost their lives. At every single performance everyone immediately stood up as we began, and that was "*wow.*"

Advice for Achieving *Wow*

As I said before, know your game, so you can walk on stage with confidence and be able to devote enough attention to communicating musically with your audience, rather than being wrapped up in the music itself.

Audition Tips

Don't be too pushy. Guys have walked into our auditions giving the impression that they are well on the way to getting the job before they've sung a note. It's an instant turnoff! If you're good enough you'll get the job.

Sensing Something Extraordinary

I was asked back in 1985 to turn pages for Geoffrey Parsons, accompanying Janet Baker. There was no rehearsal so it was a bit nerve-racking. I had not been a particular fan of her voice until that evening. The timing, the technique and the timbre were all spectacular, and the two of them held the audience spellbound throughout.

Who Would You Like to Hear?

The Beatles—why do you think?!

Have *Wow Factors* Changed?

The *Wow Factor* with the King's Singers has increased as more people get to know the group—the reception we get as we walk onstage is very gratifying, and is certainly more than when I sang with Salisbury Cathedral Choir, though having said that, sometimes singing full-on with the organ playing fortissimo does have its own *Wow Factor*!

TIM LAUTZENHEISER
Author, professor, motivational speaker,
Instructor at Ball State University
www.attitudeconcepts.com

Choose to understand before being understood. —*Tim Lautzenheiser*

Wow Factors

The human creature responds to a vocabulary it understands, recognizes, and can comprehend. From a musical standpoint, the *Wow Factor* (it seems) needs to be a banquet of different flavors that stimulate the listener's emotions. We always want the listener to feel a part of the performance in some fashion, and so it affords the chance for happy, glad, sad, bittersweet, humorous, gentle, etc.

A Memorable Performance

It was a performance of the Ball State University Singers many years ago. They were doing one of their spring concerts and the pacing of the show was perfect, from lots of dancing to a poignant rendition of "Someone to Watch Over Me" that was a left turn from the rest of the performance. There was something for everyone, and it wasn't forced in any fashion. Great singing, appropriate choreography and tasteful programming. *Wow!*

Advice for Achieving "Wow"

Choose to understand before being understood. Get behind the eyes of the audience when planning the program. Run everything through the "Will this connect with them?" filter. We often do what WE LIKE, and it is important to present what is most attractive to the audience. We don't have to sidestep the chance to stretch them to new levels, but we cannot afford to lose them in the process. People embrace familiarity.

Audition Tips

We all like different things, but one commonality is the ABILITY TO BE YOURSELF. Is it genuine, is it real, is it an extension of the performer, rather than some artificial effort? The uniqueness of the individual has to be evidenced. Of course all the qualities of being musically competent are an assumed, but what gives the audition a flavor of BEING REMEMBERED? Therein lies the key to attracting the eyes and ears of the adjudicator.

Sensing Something Extraordinary

The MAGIC that takes place when there is a connection with the audience may be unpredictable; it seems to be something we simply KNOW. There are times the program works, and there are times it doesn't work. Countless factors play into this, but when it does take place, it is a signature moment.

From a viewpoint of logic, it is when all judgment is suspended and there is sense of safety to simply be ourselves. There is not a need to convince, persuade, impress, but simply BE; to communicate the reality of who we are through music, and the listener eagerly stands alongside and enjoys the gift.

Who Would You Like to Hear?

Barbra Streisand, always convincing. Oscar Peterson, a genius at work—no wasted effort. Nat King Cole, gentle art gushing forth at all times.

Have *Wow Factors* Changed?

In the early years I would try to program *Wow Factors*, almost manipulate things to be *Wow Factors*. The "YOU'RE GONNA LOVE THIS!" theme got more energy than simply being sensitive to what others would enjoy. Much like the mother who force-feeds the child, the best nourishment comes from having the child want the meal.

Performance Trends and Standard Bearers

Having been a student of Don Neuen, all of the "*wow*" was based on solid musical fundamentals. Now, things have progressed dramatically over the years, but that still seems to be a cornerstone of great performances.

Many have taken the art form to a new level. Stephen Zegree has set the bar MIGHTY HIGH for all of us, and people point to his work at Western Michigan University as the model for this aspect of musical performance. I WOULD AGREE. His blend of the best of the old and the joy of the new is unprecedented. BRAVO!

NICK LACHEY
Singer, recording artist, producer

> *Don't ever walk out of an audition and wish you had done*
> *something more—leave it all on the table.* —*Nick Lachey*

Wow Factors

As a performer, I think it has to start with a good song. You can have the best singer in the world, but if the song is not very good, he or she will not reach that "*wow*" place. To me, the melody is the most important thing.

A Memorable Performance

As a performer, it was the Michael Jackson 30th Anniversary tribute concert at Madison Square Garden in New York City. I was with 98 Degrees and we sang "Man In The Mirror" along with Usher and Luther Vandross. That was one of those moments when it all came together. It could not have been more special than performing with Luther and Usher, especially Luther, and to have a great song, and to sing it for Michael Jackson as he sat there and watched. Luther was such a great singer and it was so effortless for him. He had one of the greatest voices I ever had the chance to work with.

As an audience member I have seen Sade in concert twice. Each time I saw her I was blown away. She's the most mesmerizing and enchanting performer I have had the pleasure to see "live." I'm a huge fan of her voice, but when she is onstage she has such a huge presence that it's literally hypnotizing.

Advice for Achieving "Wow"

It probably goes without saying, but as a singer, your voice is your instrument—it is your life. You need to take care of it accordingly. So, as a singer there are certain sacrifices you have to make, in terms of lifestyle, in order to take care of your voice. Celine Dion is an example of someone who is almost fanatical about taking care of her voice.

Also, you also have to train, and to take care of your voice the way athletes take care of their bodies—the way a pitcher takes care of his pitching arm.

Audition Tips

Don't ever walk out of an audition and wish you had done something more—leave it all on the table. You have one opportunity to impress the people who are casting. Just one chance to make an impression, so don't miss your opportunity to make that impression.

Also, make sure you give the impression that you are enjoying what you are doing. Whether it is a casting director or the audience in a Broadway show, they are going to enjoy your performance. If your enjoyment doesn't shine through, then they will not be able to enjoy it either. You've got to show the joy in what you do, and leave it all on the table. Don't hold back.

Sensing Something Extraordinary

As a performer, you have to be prepared for an extraordinary moment every night. If you are on a tour, you must be prepared physically and emotionally for a great performance. Some nights will be better than others; some crowds will be more engaged than others. There definitely are those special moments or special performances where you are on the top of your game, singing well and performing well, and the audience is more passionate and you can feed off their energy, enthusiasm and love.

Who Would You Like to Hear?

I would have loved to hear Led Zeppelin "live" in 1975. If there is ever a reunion tour, I will definitely be in the front row. On a totally different level, I never had the chance to hear Pavarotti sing "live." That would have been a concert that I know I would have enjoyed.

Have *Wow Factors* Changed?

No, I don't think those factors have changed. When you are on stage and you are singing well, and you hit your high note effortlessly, and you are on top of your game and the audience is outstanding, and the house is sold out—there are those moments. When they happen, you know it. And that is what makes it all worthwhile. It's like hitting that one great golf shot. As a performer, it's those moments that we all strive for. I felt them early in my career with 98 Degrees and I felt them on my last solo tour. The audience changes, the music changes but those moments stay the same.

Performance Trends and Standard Bearers

From a technical aspect, in-ear monitors have been a huge advancement for singers. Being able to hear yourself when you sing is a fairly important part of the equation. Also there are much more pyrotechnics and video in concerts today that make them more spectacular and impressive and grand, but at the end of the day, for me, it still comes down to the music and the talent of the performer. I'd rather go see The Eagles sing for 2½ hours on stools than see a lot of performers with fireworks and big sets.

Culturally, I love the fact that more soul-based music has become more mainstream. There used to be black radio and white radio and now those barriers have come down a bit, which I think is great. It's definitely a great thing for music. One part of the *Wow Factor* that we have lost a little bit is the showmanship of classic performers like The Rat Pack. The sophistication and the showmanship that they brought to their performances—I don't think you see that as much anymore, which is a shame because that is part of a great performance as well. That is something that I wish we would see more of. Ne-Yo is a good example of a contemporary performer who has embraced that showmanship dynamic.

In terms of an educational inspiration, my high school choir director was a huge inspiration and had a huge influence on me. For a young kid, it is really important to be taught by someone who has a real passion and love for music, as that is contagious. In terms of other artists, I had the chance to sing with Stevie Wonder. To be in the studio with him and to sing "live" with him—those are "*wow*" moments. No matter what happens for the rest of my career, no one can take those special moments away. And I'll be honest, winning *Clash of the Choirs* for me was a "*wow*" moment. People still come up to me and tell me "Flight of the Bumble Bee" was the most amazing thing they have ever seen.

So I've been blessed. There are definitely a handful of moments I can look back on and really appreciate as being "*wow*" moments in my career.

PEDER KARLSSON
The Real Group
www.realgroup.se

> *Say "yes" to what you hear. If you miss a note, forget about it and move on to the next musical phrase.* —*Peder Karlsson*

Wow Factors

For me, the artists' ability to respond to the here-and-now is essential. To just repeat what they have learned in the rehearsal room doesn't do it for me.

Such an ability requires a lot of practice, of course. Practice and then forget what you have practiced—isn't that what they all say??

I also appreciate an artist who has developed his/her technique to a point where you don't hear the limitations and you get as close as possible to "pure spirit."

A Memorable Performance

Right now I remember:

Rajaton at Amazing Voice 2008, in Seoul, South Korea. (a vocal festival where The Real Group were artistic directors)

Nicolaus Harnoncourt conducting Chamber Orchestra of Europe. That was in Cologne, I think in 1999.

A concert with Prince in Stockholm a couple of years ago.

You're asking me why? I would think, a total dedication to exploring the core of the music, at the same time as giving attention to detail. Inspiration combined with ability and beauty.

Advice for Achieving "Wow"

I have a theory that there are four dimensions of artistry that each performer develops over time, each person developing a certain distribution between the four:

Spirit—the ability to inspire.

Feeling—the ability to connect emotionally to the moment, to the music, and to one's fellow musicians.

Intelligence—the ability to reflect upon one's art, with a detached perspective.

Technique—the ability to master the physical relation to one's instrument.

Intelligence and Technique are taught at schools. For those dimensions, going to a school can be helpful.

Spirit and Feeling are the two most important factors. You have to explore those dimensions on your own, with your fellow musicians in the real music life, outside of the school environment—in my humble opinion and experience.

Each dimension can be (and needs to be) developed by everybody. A person who feels that he/she is not so strong in the "Spirit department," for example, can increase the amount of inspiration by seeking such experience.

The journey never ends. You will never be perfect in any sense.

Audition Tips

I don't have much experience of auditions, but I would say:

Be very well prepared.

Be on time.

Be friendly.

Sensing Something Extraordinary

This question has to do with the very reason I am a musician, I think.

As a performer, when the music is going in a direction that you didn't plan before, but intuitively you know it is appropriate for the moment, and you can feel that all the musicians are connected somehow, that is when you make Music. This happens in many gigs with The Real Group. I guess that's the main reason why I have stayed with the group for so long.

You have to know the music and your fellow musicians very well to get to this point. And you need "split vision"—an ability to know what you do at the same time as being 100 percent aware of what is happening around you.

I think the audience can feel when the musicians are connected this way, that we are all sharing a unique moment.

You need a truly positive attitude to get there, and must drop any analytical or critical awareness. Say "yes" to what you hear. If you miss a note, forget about it and move on to the next musical phrase.

If you like to analyze, record the gig and do the analysis later.

Who Would You Like to Hear?

Mozart's and Bach's improvisations.

Jesus Christ talking.

William Shakespeare's plays, as performed by his theater group.

Frank Zappa.

The Beatles.

Weather Report when Jaco Pastorius was in the group.

Joni Mitchell in the late '60s.

Charlie Parker and Dizzy Gillespie jamming at Minton's Playhouse.

Aretha Franklin in the mid- or late '60s.

…and a bunch of other stuff!

Have *Wow Factors* Changed?

I guess I was more into impressing the audience with my abilities when I was younger.

I was also very interested in checking out where the beautiful women were seated, in order to know where I wanted to direct my full attention.

These days, I just go onstage and focus on the music itself, and where it takes me. That is what I am there to do; it gives me sense of purpose, and it gives me something back. The audience response is important, of course, but my focus is to be within the music first.

Performance Trends and Standard Bearers

I guess you're talking about how a performer is affected by considering his/her relation to what is currently Hip or Trendy or considered Cool. And, "did I have any sources of inspiration?"

Well, you know, I think it is fair to say that I never did anything because it was considered hip, not in my music, or general behavior, clothing or anything. I have been like that since childhood. And I do have a problem with respecting people who are mainly oriented toward the current trends. I grew up in the '70s and liked the Beatles, jazz and classical music, while my peers were all into Kiss, Sweet and Abba. I thought their perspectives were narrow.

If you just go for the trends, your perspectives will always be very limited. It is not important what your classmates say. Don't listen to them. It is a cliché—but here it is—follow your heart instead!!! Your classmates will respect you for going your own way. And your life will be more interesting.

> *It is not important what your classmates say. Don't listen to them.*
> *It is a cliché—but here it is—follow your heart instead!!!*
> *Your classmates will respect you for going your own way.*
> *And your life will be more interesting. —Peder Karlsson*

JOHN JACOBSON
Music educator, author, choreographer, choral director
www.johnjacobson.com

> *When the curtain has gone down, no one will long remember*
> *the names of the songs, the soloist, the clever staging, the expensive*
> *costumes, but they will remember how the performance made them feel.*
> —*John Jacobson*

Wow Factors

From my point of view, the most important factor in creating a *"wow"* performance, or at least a *"wow moment"* in a performance—be it musical, staging or otherwise—is the creation of an emotional experience through your efforts as a performer or musician. This experience could be a second or an hour but, in the end, it is what separates art from noise and memorable performance from tedious exercise. It is often difficult to label what is art/ music and so on and what does or doesn't qualify. To me the most basic question is "How does it make me feel?" When the curtain has gone down, no one will long remember the names of the songs, the soloist, the clever staging, the expensive costumes, but they will remember how the performance made them *feel*. Still remember, a *"wow"* can be soft as well as loud, subtle as well as flashy, obtuse as well as obvious. And everyone in the audience and onstage may very well experience a different kind of *"wow"* at the same moment. But alas, some kind of feeling ought to be the goal.

As a choreographer/choral director, I have always looked for opportunities to create these special "moments" on stage that the audience will take home, due to the emotion it made them experience. I want belly laughs as well as tears; comfort as well as angst; bawdiness as well as a soaring spirit. How do you do that? Ah, that is the challenge of the artist.

I spent a year of my life working in Japan and made of lot of friends and learned a lot about *"wow."* In Japan, they talk about building a Buddha. Anyone can build a statue of a Buddha. But until that statue is given a heart, it is just a pile of brick and mortar, bronze or jade. The builder, the follower, someone has to assign that Buddha something to make it play a broader role. Some believer has to give it a heart.

In a way, I think that building a musical performance is much like building a Buddha. Almost anyone can put elements together: tone, melody, harmony, diction, perhaps staging, costumes, lighting and so on. But until that combination of elements is managed in a way to make real emotion happen, I believe, we have created nothing more than a Buddha without a heart.

"If it ain't got heart, it ain't art." I believe this.

A Memorable Performance

There are so many. But one in recent pop/Broadway culture comes to mind immediately. It occurs both in the Broadway stage version and in the movie version, so many people have borne witness to it, and I hope they will see my point. It comes near the end of the first act of the musical *Dreamgirls*, where the character Effie sings "I Am Changing." If you haven't heard it and/or seen it you must be living under a rock. Really. A big rock.

I was lucky enough to see Jennifer Holliday perform it in the original Broadway production when I was 2—OK, 22—and of course I've watched and heard Jennifer Hudson in the movie version. They were both phenomenal.

So, the gist is that she is being dumped by the Dreamgirls performing trio and her boyfriend all at the same time. She tells them in gut-wrenching song that frankly "She's Not Going!" It is as dramatic a moment in theater as you will ever get, right up there with Oedipus Rex gouging his own eyes out and Medea chowing down on her own kids. I will concede, that the singing of this song is a "*wow*" moment in and unto itself. But, what sends me soaring is what happens next. Just as she finishes this song and the audience begins to scream, stomp, reel and applaud, the rug is pulled out from under her even again. The stage in the live performance is pulled back with her still on it and reaching for help. She disappears. In the movie, it is similar as she fades away. She is replaced with the "new" Dreamgirls in their first performance without her and she is not missed. They steal her applause just as they have stolen her job, her love, her life. It is breathtaking and perfect staging. It is a "*wow*" on top of a "*wow*" and I, for one, will forever remember it.

Advice for Achieving "Wow"

Never forget the privilege it is to have an audience/listener of one or a million and one. These human beings gave up their time, their energy and their ears to hear what you have to sing, say, dance or play. That should never be taken lightly. All you can do to pay them back is to do your very best, not just in the performance itself, but also in all of the hard work leading up to that moment. Rehearsal is the rent you pay to earn attention. It's a small price to pay for gigantic rewards. It's all about preparation.

Earn their attention through your dedication to your art. Then, once you have it, sing, play, dance, paint, act or whatever with something to say.

Take care of yourself physically and emotionally. Get your training. Take it seriously. This may be your one chance. Make "*wow*" happen and you will earn the right to dance another day.

Audition Tips

Be prepared. Do your homework. Get your training.

Like any profession or avocation, the more prepared you are, the better your chances of success and the more rewarding the experience. Learn as much as you can about the role or ensemble you are auditioning for. Know as much as possible about what the audition audience is looking for and be realistic about whether or not you fit that bill. Never take it as a validation or judgment of your talent and training if you don't get the job or even if you do. Never resent those that do get cast, when you don't. Your time will come. Don't quit.

Sensing Something Extraordinary

I believe that in the most "*wow*-ing" performances that I have ever witnessed, the single most consistent element has been the "genuine factor." Does the performance seem real? Do I believe it? Are they performing for me or for themselves? Do the performers see it as their responsibility to reach out across the footlights to touch me or do I need to go to them?

There is a term not often used but always apparent in the arts. It's called phenomenology. It's a long word that basically asks the questions, "How long does a song, dance, or act feel?" It has nothing really to do with actual time. We have all sat through performances that seem like two hours when they are only 20 minutes in reality. (I've written a lot of those 20-minute productions that seem like two hours!) We have also witnessed those that seem like an instant and perhaps went on for hours. It is not necessarily a reflection of the work's merit. It's just a phenomenon. But it brings to mind a production I saw years ago in New York by the Royal Shakespeare Company of Charles Dickens' *Nicholas Nickelby*. It was something like eight hours long. No kidding. There was a dinner break! Or you could have the option of seeing the first half one night and the second half the next. When it was over, it seemed both like I had been living with these characters for a lifetime and just an instant. It was, well, phenomenalogically phenomenal. (I totally made that long word up.) Nonetheless, I believe here is why it was so.

Everyone involved did their part as dedicated artists. It started with a classic story adapted by writers who had studied their craft for years. It was matched with acting, staging, lighting and stagecraft executed by one of the most well trained ensembles the world could put together. It was an eight-hour "*wow*" that I wanted to go on forever.

Yes, there was a moment when I had a hint that this was something special. It was confirmed when after eight hours of theater, I would gladly have sat through it again, starting immediately. I sensed that all or most of the audience would have stayed there too.

Who Would You Like to Hear?

Nina Simone. When I hear "Lilac Wine" I am not the same…every time.

Have *Wow Factors* Changed?

As a younger person, I think I would always listen to or watch a performance and be thinking about how I might do it differently or even how I would feel if I were doing the performance. Even as an audience member, it was mostly about me. Now, I believe I am more able to let myself be audience, let myself be taken for a ride, let the "*wows*" happen to me as opposed to trying to make them happen myself.

Performance Trends and Standard Bearers

Oh, I think there have been huge shifts. Thank goodness. How boring it would all be if our arts were not dynamic. Most obvious, it seems, is in the awareness and influence of global music on all of us. With the expansion of the Internet, ease of world travel and a myriad of other reasons, we are all so much more aware of the music and other art forms from other parts of the world. As we hear it and embrace it, it changes our own artistic expressions and individual as well as collective experiences. It can't be helped. I think that's thrilling.

I was recently in Suriname at the top of South America and a woman I met there said, "Here we believe that when you walk into a room and everybody is dancing on one leg, don't be too quick to dance on two." From this simple statement I think she was telling me to Watch, Listen, Experience and Learn from all that have come before you and who share this planet with you. Then when you dance, on one leg or two, you will be part of that enlightened community of people who reflect universal truths through your art. In my book, that's a pretty big "*wow*."

MAC HUFF
Composer and arranger
www.machuff.com

Prepare and rehearse to the point that no one is
aware of the preparation. —*Mac Huff*

Wow Factors
An honest connection from the material to the performer to the audience.

Performance is coming from a point of passion and inner joy.

Prepare and rehearse to the point that no one is aware of the preparation.

The perfect meeting of instinct and experience.

Surprise!!

A Memorable Performance
Ella Fitzgerald at the Hollywood Bowl—need I say more? Nelson Riddle conducted. The voice, the setting, the songs: It was magical.

Cleo Laine in Santa Fe—by accident. She sang in a small old mission. I'm a huge fan and she was in great voice. She was having as good of a time as I was. She sang 2½ hours. It was nirvana!

Harvey Fierstein in *Torch Song Trilogy*. It was art that spoke to me and my life. It did what true art does. It reflected inward.

Rent on Broadway. It was new, it was timely, it was ingenious, it was real.

Oscar Peterson. Late in his career, he played a few small clubs in the Marina in Los Angeles. I stumbled upon the club where he played three 50-minute sets. It was one of the most exciting musical experiences of my life.

Advice for Achieving "Wow"
Respect the material you are performing.

Prepare, prepare, prepare.

Always search for the essence of anything you perform. Seek the truth as you see it.

Your craft is to create an emotional bond with the audience. If you are craft-driven, the "*wow*" takes care of itself.

Audition Tips
Be prepared.

Know yourself and as others see you.

Practice auditioning.

Practice being confident.

Understand NRFTP (not right for the part). Auditions aren't about good and bad. They're about right or not right for the hire.

Sensing Something Extraordinary

Now I'm speaking as an arranger: If you're talking timing, "*wow*" usually happens in structural moments. Openings, End of Act (or section), Return of Material, Closings, and the three-fourths point of any evening of entertainment (the 10:30 number)—a concept developed by Richard Rodgers that still holds true today! Of course, surprise can happen anywhere and will usually create a "*wow*" moment.

Who Would You Like to Hear?

I think hearing performers early in their careers is a fascinating thought. They operate so much more on instinct instead of education or experience.

The Beatles in 1964.

Arthur Rubinstein playing Beethoven.

Mary Martin doing South Pacific.

Barbra Streisand doing Funny Girl on stage.

Janis Joplin in the '60s.

Ella Fitzgerald in the '40s.

Have *Wow Factors* Changed?

As a writer, my goal is to constantly find new ways to "*wow*" an audience. It is a never-ending search. In some ways, to "*wow*" an audience hasn't changed that much through time. Uniqueness and honesty with your art is universal and will always occur. Also, once you learn that "*wow*" is subjective, the goal is to stay true to yourself and your craft.

Performance Trends and Standard Bearers

There are obvious advances in electronics and recording techniques that allow for more "*wow*." I love the fact that young artists today can self-publish and sell their songs through the Internet (iTunes, CD Baby, etc.). More people will develop as true artists rather than "marketable business models" (as was many times the case with a big label selling CDs). I guess I figure the more true artists getting their music out there, the better the chance for "*wow*" to happen.

FRED HERSCH
Composer and jazz pianist
www.fredhersch.com

I don't go to hear music to be impressed. It's not like a "talent show."
I go to hear music to be moved. —**Fred Hersch**

Wow Factors

For me the most important thing is connection. That means the connection of the artists to what they are singing or playing—to the music, to the tune, to the words, and then translating that connection to the audience. Because if a performer is not connected and it is just mannerisms or on the surface, it is very hard to grab people's attention. You have to bear in mind that certain people are not capable of appreciating a *"wow"* performance, and for them, anything that looks and sounds reasonable is going to be fine. But to those of us who are discerning, what makes the difference is that I want to feel that person's connections. I don't want to feel they are just going through the motions or phoning it in. It should be vital. If it's improvised music, I want to feel like I'm hearing something that is different from the way they have played it any other time—something that's fresh, not rote, not like the album—and that they are taking chances. I give more points for taking chances and crashing and burning than for playing it safe. This idea of connection is particularly important for vocalists. I find sometimes singers choose material that they can't really relate to. Or they sing it because they think that's what jazz singers are supposed to sing, but they don't really understand it; and they can't relate to it personally. It's like an actor taking on a role that is not suited for him/her. Once you are connected with your material, it's easy to bring the audience in; you don't even have to work at it, because they will be feeling that connection. You won't have to work with a lot of gestures and mannerisms and shtick, etc. It just grabs them immediately just by its connectedness.

A Memorable Performance

I can think of two in recent months. One was a house concert in a loft in SOHO, a benefit concert for Classical Action. It was violinist Christian Tetslaff and pianist Alexander Longuich—it was Beethoven sonatas. From the first note of the first piece to the last note of the last piece, there was a sense of freshness, of pure music, of focus, of beautiful ensemble. And I felt that the music was really speaking to me. It was very easy for me to hear it.

Neither of these performers is flashy even though both are virtuosos—it was all about the music.

The other was a set at a concert at The Jazz Standard in NYC with pianist Benoit Delbecq. A very interesting character—he's one of the world's most interesting users of the inside of the piano. He does all sorts of amazing things inside the piano and processing the piano on recordings in interesting ways. But this was just an acoustic jazz trio setting. He has this way of playing melodically and harmonically without it being jazz. It's improvised. And the format you think, OK, it's a jazz trio. But he doesn't reference chords, really. It's just these free, very interesting melodies. Some are rhythmic, some aren't. But it was a fascinating concert. It didn't degenerate into jazz nor was it blips and blops, like cliché-free music. It was lyrical and it was interesting, and it was beautifully played, and he was focused completely. He has a very unique and personal language that really knocked me out.

Advice for Achieving "Wow"

Everybody needs to spend the time necessary to get deeply into whatever it is that they are performing. Carefully consider the tempo; consider the arrangement, if there is one. Carefully consider, for a vocalist, what tempo and key are going to best suit the words. I don't go to hear music to be impressed. It's not like a "talent show." I go to hear music to be moved. I want to feel something, to be stimulated. If I go to a great concert, it gets me thinking. Other times if it's just a lot of "showbiz" it's like going to see an action movie—it's fine, but typically there is not much to talk about afterwards. But if you go to a challenging film with two other people, all three of you can have different reactions and you can talk about it. It stimulates something. So while you have to be a good performer, you need to take the time to be secure with what you are doing—so when unexpected things come up, you won't be panicking.

Audition Tips

Put your best stuff out there first and turn up the wattage, especially in music theater auditions, because you want them to remember you! Even if you don't get the part in this audition, they may remember you for another part in another show. We've heard stories about people auditioning for one role and then they were cast in another role where they were more "right" for that character.

Make sure you play what you do best. Keep it real. Show your confidence and some energy—not nervous energy, but confidence and a mature presentation of whatever it is. Don't try anything too technical unless you have absolutely mastered it. You have to allow for adrenaline and nerves. If things come up that are unexpected, don't panic; be able to roll with it. Also, do your homework. Find out what they are looking for. What is the style? What are they expecting?

Sensing Something Extraordinary

Great performances happen in real time so there is a flow about it—like in a great acting performance, like Sean Penn in *Milk*. I was never thinking that I was watching Sean Penn; after a few minutes he was Harvey Milk. I think great actors are able to inhabit a character. Sometimes they'll get into it with something physical that helps them achieve the character. In music, let's say an hour of music, or a set or a half of a classical concert, there will be a point at which I get into a flow space, where time stands still. I'm just completely involved in the performance. I am not thinking about what's in my e-mail inbox, or looking at my watch. I'm really there with it. I've gotten older and I've seen a lot of music. So it takes more and more for me to really get to that place—to where it's really "*wow*." And I think because it takes place in real time, there will be patches where you are really involved and in other parts, where it's just nice. It is very rare that a set of music can sustain completely. But there are those stretches, where you are with the music. Everything extraneous is dropped away.

As a performer, I love getting to the place where there is nothing but the music. That is the reason why I close my eyes when I play: to eliminate visual distraction, so that I will not have any distractions.

Who Would You Like to Hear?

If I could hear anyone "live," I think it would be the Miles Davis Quintet, with Ron (Carter), Tony (Williams), Herbie (Hancock) and Wayne (Shorter). They are all such strong stylists and they all took such amazing chances. It's jazz on the highest level, both intellectually and emotionally. It's very sophisticated and it's deeply swinging and deeply connected to the roots of jazz. I'm sorry that I never saw Thelonious Monk play. I did see Duke Ellington, but I would have loved to see Monk play "live." I would have loved to hear Louis Armstrong in his prime. Or to hear Ornette Coleman in the late '50s when he came to New York and turned the jazz world upside down. As a child or as a teenager, I got to see Horowitz, Rubinstein and David Oistrach, some of the greatest classical musicians.

Have *Wow Factors* Changed?

When I first started out as a jazz pianist, it was like learning a foreign language. I was happy when I could get through a tune without turning the time around or when 50 percent of the phrases were swinging. Or when I discovered a new ii-V-I, it was like the doors of heaven had opened up. Now it's different. I am playing with musicians at a much higher level. I feel like I'm really getting off with the music. I look for that openness and also depth in the players I work with. And I look for sound. The bass players and drummers I work with are sensitive to sound. It's like dating in high school—everyone seemed attractive then! As we get older, we get more specific in our tastes. It can't be just anybody. Likewise if I am playing a solo, I need a good piano and a room that has some great acoustics in it.

GARY FRY
Composer, arranger, music producer
www.garyfry.org

I have experienced many "wow" concerts that were imperfect musically, but filled with energy and emotion... —Gary Fry

Wow Factors

In my personal order of importance, they are:

1.) **Energy.** This requires performers who are committed to the music and who have an overriding desire to communicate it to the audience. There is no equivalent substitute for "being there" with great performers and great music.

2.) **Artistry.** This means executing the musical demands with precision and attention to detail. Why isn't this #1? Recordings are generally excellent in this regard, but they cannot match a live performance with energy as described above. And I have experienced many *"wow"* concerts that were imperfect musically, but filled with energy and emotion; likewise, I have experienced many concerts that were very precise and well-executed musically that left me cold and untouched. Guess which I prefer....

3.) **Eye appeal.** Sometimes, it's enough to see passionate performers who are demonstrative in their interpretation, but more and more in today's culture, additional visual interest (movement, changes of location within the venue, projection of visual images) can make the difference between "good" and "great."

A Memorable Performance

I'll go "way back" to the first performance I saw and heard that was so exciting that I still recall it intensely after more than 35 years. My high school jazz band attended a concert by the rock/fusion/trumpet group called Chase in 1971 at the University of Iowa. The concert opened in total darkness with just Bill Chase's unbelievable high "screech"-register trumpet wail piercing the anticipation in the auditorium. It was electrifying, and only built from there as four virtuoso trumpets (plus rhythm section) displayed their considerable skills in high-energy (there's that word again) musicianship that had the audience not only standing in ovations from the first number on, but standing on their seats with wild excitement by the end.

Advice for Achieving "Wow"

1.) **Practice.** Develop your musical performance skills and the consistency that separates average from outstanding performers.

2.) **Analyze.** Listen carefully to the music that excites you, watch carefully the performers that engage you visually. Don't just enjoy it; *understand* it.

3.) **Go for it!** Show your passion; take the risk that demands your total commitment in every way.

4.) **Follow your passion but respect your audience.** Always ask yourself: What am I giving the audience that is unique and valuable to them?

Audition Tips

1.) **Overprepare.** Thoroughly master any known audition materials, then go beyond them to understand their context. If you're auditioning for a show, can you speak about it intelligently? Could you perform another piece from the show if asked? If you're auditioning for an ensemble, do you know something about it—previous performances, ensemble history, or typical repertoire? Not only is it impressive to be conversant in the aspects beyond the audition materials, it also gives you an even more solid foundation in understanding your audition materials and gives you confidence and poise.

2.) **Don't apologize for anything!** The single most common mistake, I believe, that performers make in auditions is making excuses for the quality of the audition, sometimes even before they do anything. ("I usually have the ending high B-flat, but I have a cold," etc.) Just do your best and let the chips fall where they may. The people judging your audition don't need to have deficiencies pointed out to them.

The single most common mistake, I believe, that performers make in auditions is making excuses for the quality of the audition, sometimes even before they do anything. —**Gary Fry**

3.) **Underpromise and overdeliver.** Perhaps not as applicable to auditions as to other professional situations, such as submissions "on spec" for potential projects. Let's say you're a composer, and an advertising agency is looking for music for a particular commercial. They might approach several composers or music companies to ask them to submit sample ideas for the commercial. If they ask for a demo track by Tuesday, can you not only meet that specification but provide two different tracks by Monday? This requires a realistic assessment of your own capabilities, and sometimes the ability to "push the envelope" and work a little harder, stay up a little later, or enlist additional assistance to show that you're the best choice for a particular gig.

4.) **Be personable, positive and enthusiastic.** In many situations, the abilities of those auditioning might not be markedly different, and it comes down to this: Which person seems to be the most enjoyable to work with?

Sensing Something Extraordinary

Two things come to mind:

Virtuoso moments of great difficulty that are beautifully negotiated by the soloist or ensemble—often involving the "risk-taking" mentioned above. Can the performer hit that high note? Sustain that long note? Maintain tempo and rhythmic accuracy at breakneck speed? When challenges like those are met, it's like (to use a sports analogy) watching the motorcycle daredevil successfully jump the chasm—tremendously exciting and thrilling. And (2) the sustained absence of blemishes (musical or emotional) that might spoil the overall effect of the performance. This is more like realizing that you have a no-hitter going into the seventh inning: From that point on, the excitement builds as you realize something special is happening. If you can get all the way through to the end, it's a huge "*wow*"!!

GARY FRY, cont.

Who Would You Like to Hear?

I have three composer-conductor heroes, two of which I have had the great pleasure of meeting and watching perform (in this case, conducting their own works). John Williams is my greatest inspiration, obviously still living and conducting, and I have met him and experienced several of his performances. Leonard Bernstein is deceased, but I had a similar privilege when he was alive. Jerry Goldsmith, however, is now deceased, and I never had the opportunity to experience his music "live" under his baton (which admittedly was a pretty rare occurrence). So he would top my wish list in that department.

Have *Wow Factors* Changed?

Of the *Wow Factors* I mentioned above (energy, artistry, eye appeal), only the eye appeal has changed *significantly* over the course of my career. The rise of multimedia, the proliferation of all kinds of visual/aural entertainment options, and the ever-changing technology that allows more visual effects in concert have all impacted the concert experience. Without the eye appeal, it is much harder today to have the audience experience a "*wow*." It can be done, but takes even more energy and artistry. And audience perceptions of energy and artistry have changed somewhat, though not as dramatically, because of the exposure to and ready availability of displays of talent on television, radio and the Internet. Today's musical performers continue to push the boundaries of what is considered virtuoso (just as athletes continue to break seemingly unbreakable world records). For example, singers such as Bobby McFerrin, Mariah Carey and Christina Aguilera have brought "vocal gymnastics" to the public in a way that has changed perceptions of what the human voice can do. On the educational side, groups such as Western Michigan University's Gold Company (with their annual big show that incorporates not only great musical artistry but amazingly varied visual interest), or the Percussion Scholarship Group of inner-city kids tutored by percussionists from the Chicago Symphony (integrating technology such as percussion-based MIDI instrument triggering) continue to amaze and delight audiences with all three of my "*wow*" factors.

Performance Trends and Standard Bearers

There are actually lots of performers who come to mind that have changed standards of virtuosity: Victor Wooten on the bass, for example, or the Turtle Island String Quartet in jazz/chamber music fusion, or Take 6 in close harmony ensemble vocals, or Thomas Newman in integrating electronic textures into traditional orchestral film music. The list could go on and on, but it still boils down to performers who have worked tirelessly to achieve musical artistry, and the "*wow*" of experiencing that energy and passion. That is why, I believe, that even in the YouTube era there will continue to be a premium on the live performance of music.

I'm honored to be asked for input for your book alongside the likes of Weston Noble, who conducted the Iowa All-State Chorus in 1971, when I was the first ever to be selected from my tiny high school. The Iowa All-State concert always provided a "*wow*" moment for the audience with their traditional closing: the singing of "The Battle Hymn of the Republic" with orchestra (Carmen Dragon's wonderful arrangement) as a GIGANTIC American flag unfurled on the rear wall of the stage behind the performing forces. Sounds corny, but few times have I seen such a large percentage of an audience wipe away tears.

CLARE FISCHER
Composer, arranger and pianist
www.clarefischer.com

When a performance exudes maturity, that can only come as a result of
deep heartfelt contemplation. —*Clare Fischer*

Wow Factors
Absolute musical integrity is a must, but it's also the emotional content that will get the listener.

A Memorable Performance
Taking my children to see Duke Ellington perform "live" in L.A. with his Big Band around 1970. His sax section was irreplaceable.

Advice for Achieving "Wow"
There is only one level and that is professional. You must do whatever is required to achieve that in every performance.

Audition Tips
Anybody can show off with flashy displays, but when a performance exudes maturity, that can only come as a result of deep heartfelt contemplation. That person will stand out.

Sensing Something Extraordinary

When you are reduced to tears by the sheer beauty of what you are hearing.

Who Would You Like to Hear?

To be able to hear J.S. Bach take a melody and improvise what amounts to a spontaneous composition is the most amazing thing I can think of.

Have *Wow Factors* Changed?

Audiences tend to be fickle. I've been lucky enough, in that many musicians attend my concerts, so that I can just be myself.

ROGER EMERSON

Composer, arranger, educator, Instructor, College of the Siskiyous
www.rogeremerson.com

> *My advice to students always includes passion,*
> *musical integrity, 100 percent effort, and communication*
> *of the song's idea or intent.* —*Roger Emerson*

Wow Factors

For me, musical accuracy is an important part of "*wow*." Since I am an "intuitive" musician at heart, I hear balance and blend, and I know when chords are just plain wrong. It is *so* important that attention be paid to the accompaniment (rhythm section/horns) portion of the ensemble. They must feel totally integrated in the performance. The second factor is "energy." I have seen accurate performances that do not move me, and less accurate ones that do, go figure. The third is obviously "the visual." Most ensembles sound better once you put them in a uniform or costume, or at least "seem" to sound better. Fourth would be programming. Good songs—well arranged and appropriate to the group's skill level—and proper pacing are essential.

A Memorable Performance

Real "*wow*" does not occur for me very often, but I can name two off the top of my head. In the early '80s I was judging a college show choir at Iowa City, I believe, and they performed "Corner of the Sky" from *Pippin*. Not only was it a great arrangement, beautifully sung, but I remember a group move to "the corner of the stage," which was so beautifully and movingly appropriate that it made the hair stand up on my arms! The second was at Yoshi's (a jazz club in Oakland) with the New York Voices. The entire show was the epitome of musicianship, a culmination of artistry. Stellar arrangements by Darmon Meader, flawlessly executed in an effortless but honest manner. For me, it doesn't get any better.

Advice for Achieving "Wow"

My advice to students always includes passion, musical integrity, 100 percent effort, and communication of the song's idea or intent. I also want them to be literate musicians. An understanding of the part that they play in the harmonic fabric is really important. I encourage them to sight-sing and play as much piano as humanly possible. Listen to jazz as much as they do their familiar "pop" artists. Sing every chance that you get. Be grateful! Many people would give anything to have their talent.

Audition Tips

Audition advice: Avoid the obvious. Make a real effort to find great tunes that are buried in shows. Check out all of the off-Broadway shows for gems. Do less, well. I can tell in the first few measures if a student is ready for my ensemble. Sell the song. What is your face saying? Avoid being "pitchy" at all costs. Sing your strength. If it is pop, do pop; Broadway, do Broadway; jazz, do jazz, etc. Don't show them what you cannot do.

Sensing Something Extraordinary

I am usually taken by a performance from the downbeat. My gut reaction is then either reinforced by continued excellence or diminished by a spotty performance.

Who Would You Like to Hear?

I have been so fortunate to hear many of my favorite groups live. I would go see New York Voices again in an instant. I love James Taylor, but was not *wowed* by his performance recently. I'd like to see Earth, Wind and Fire live as well as Gordon Goodwin's Big Phat Band. Great tunes, arrangements and performances are part of all four in my opinion.

Have *Wow Factors* Changed?

I don't think "*wow*" has changed much for me. Again, I am moved most by truly well-written songs, skillfully arranged, honestly and accurately performed. My barometer is usually a huge smile on my face, a groove to my body, and the hair rising on my arms. I recently saw *Spring Awakening*, the musical, in

ROGER EMERSON, cont.

New York. It was truly a *"wow"* moment, very visceral. Duncan Sheik is a very inventive writer: tasty arrangements and letter-perfect performance. *Wow*!

Performance Trends and Standard Bearers

I think that *"wow"* exists in small doses everywhere. I am not a fan of rap; however, I thought it was used beautifully by Lin-Manuel Miranda in *In The Heights*. I was equally moved several years ago by the simplicity and musicality of "Bist Du Bei Mir" performed by the Toronto Children's Chorus—in unison!!! I have been, of course, influenced by my mentor, Kirby Shaw. His attention to detail, while maintaining the sense of joy in the performance, is exemplary. Steve Zegree, with his artful blend of jazz and show. Darmon Meader, quintessential musician and arranger as well as a great performer. Eric Whitacre—and his polychordal textures—truly refreshing aurally.

> *I think that "wow" exists in small doses everywhere.*
> *—Roger Emerson*

PETER ELDRIDGE
New York Voices, composer, arranger,
Instructor at Manhattan School of Music
www.petereldridge.com

> *Rule number one—know your material backward and*
> *forward so that you can do your very best and be*
> *comfortable as possible… —Peter Eldridge*

Wow Factors

I think one of the major factors of *"wow"* potential is when a performance has that perfect mix of vulnerability, mastery and musicality—when all three of those elements come together. The artist has done his or her homework and is completely comfortable with the material being performed, confident in having studied the complexity and nuances in the music, and the technical production is unhampered (that the artist makes it look "easy"). I think the ***"Wow" Factor*** comes when you feel like you get to know the person (or group of people) performing, that they let you in, almost as though you feel like you're sitting across a table from them and they are telling you something quite personal. At least in terms of great singers specifically, I think the audience really yearns for that connection, whether consciously or unconsciously.

A Memorable Performance

Most recently I saw (and sat in on) a set by jazz singer Kate McGarry and her incredible band at Joe's Pub in New York City. Kate was in particularly good voice that night and her performance felt so real and expressive, in the pocket and in the moment. She let the adoring audience in to a place that felt private but comfortable, and each musical moment that passed felt completely new and spontaneous from Kate (as well as the interplay amongst the band members). Each phrase and every lyric was an expression of how she was feeling as a person at that specific moment in time. She was energetic but still not trying too hard, ultimately just being an extension of herself. Each song she sang had its own particular vibe or personality with obvious attention to detail. She really understood and "lived in" each song she was singing, its harmonic structure and the specific rules and freedoms involved. When she would add a vocal embellishment or change something rhythmically, it was never at the expense of the lyric—it was enhancing the lyric. She never added anything superfluous or "showy," she just sang from a decidedly deep and open place. The audience just went crazy for her because it was just so real.

> *Each phrase and every lyric was an expression of how she was feeling*
> *as a person at that specific moment in time.* —*Peter Eldridge*

Advice for Achieving *Wow*

To this question I would say try to find something unique and special about what you do that no one else does, whether it's in your sound, in the way you communicate and connect with the audience, whether it's your lyric interpretation or how you orchestrate your material, or finally, choosing the repertoire you feel really represents who you are at the stage of life that you are in. Especially if you're doing a standard that's already been done so many times—you have to find something (perhaps in the arrangement, or in the groove or meter) that makes the song yours no matter how many times a person in the audience has heard it prior to your version. You don't necessarily have to reinvent the wheel every time. Sometimes a great standard is a great standard and it swings really hard and that's enough, but finding something new in some small detail of the piece can really make it feel like a totally new experience emotionally for the listener. And speaking specifically of groups,

I really do feel that a group of singers can have as much real emotion and personal interaction with an audience as a solo singer can. It might take a bit more work, but it is absolutely possible.

Ultimately, I think it is about individuality and confidence. Nothing translates to an audience like someone who really believes in what he or she is doing, even when the music that is being shared is perhaps "inaccessible" or takes a lot more concentration on the part of the listener.

Audition Tips

Being on the jazz voice faculty of the Manhattan School of Music, I continue to be surprised at how often people are simply underprepared for their audition. Rule number one—know your material backward and forward so that you can do your very best and be comfortable as possible in that sort of situation. And let's face it, auditioning is rarely an easy thing to do, so know your stuff before you walk in the room. You can tell pretty instantly if the singer knows his or her stuff or not, or if they are second-guessing themselves.

Sensing Something Extraordinary

Yes—you can almost feel a transcendent and collective lifting of souls—almost like an amusement park ride—that's the biggest payoff for an audience. It's ultimately why people go out and hear live music—for that collective experience of transcendence through music.

Who Would You Like to Hear?

The Archies—no, wait a minute, they weren't real, were they?

Have *Wow Factors* Changed?

I think when I was younger the *Wow Factor* would come from a "faster, louder, higher" angle (for lack of a better comparison, sort of like those folks on *American Idol*)—those devices that might be a faster "payoff" with an audience and try hard to impress, but now that I am older and have a lot of performances under my belt, the *Wow Factor* comes from a deeper place. It's more about feel, honesty and an emotional connection. From an audience perspective, it's those artists who pull you toward them, not the ones who knock you over the head with their talents.

EPH EHLY
Conductor, Author, Professor Emeritus,
University of Missouri-Kansas City

Emotion is easier to enact because it is more innate to the human spirit.
To enact good technique requires more disciplined practice.
Therefore, technique is practiced in a more objective way
while emotion is encouraged in a more subjective manner.
"Wow" requires a balance of the two. —**Eph Ehly**

Wow Factors

At the least, experiencing *"wow"* is encountering the unexpected. At the most it's encountering the unbelievable.

Predictability breeds monotony. Monotony breeds boredom. Boredom, or "Ho-hum," is the opposite of *"wow."*

"Wow" begins with programming. Avoid the predictable. Open the program with something astonishing. This may be either astonishingly strong and fast or astonishingly soft and subtle.

What follows should be strikingly different, i.e. fast followed by slow or two slows balanced with two fasts. The design of the program may be recognizable and develop a theme or tell a story, but the result of the musical choices should be unpredictable. (It's not easy to design a *"wow"* program.)

Technique alone can become a *"wow"* factor on an intellectual level, but not necessarily on an emotional one.

Emotion alone can become a *"wow"* factor on an emotional level, but not necessarily on an intellectual one.

Emotion is easier to enact because it is more innate to the human spirit. To enact good technique requires more disciplined practice. Therefore, technique is practiced in a more objective way while emotion is encouraged in a more subjective manner. *"Wow"* requires a balance of the two.

Under the umbrella of "Technique" are multiple basic fundamentals, of which *tone quality, diction, dynamics, breath management, pitch and rhythm* demand near-perfection to qualify as *"wow."*

Other technical factors, such as *balance of parts, phrasing, interpretation, etc.*, can and should be addressed prior to rehearsal, because the **Wow Factor** must exist in the leader/teacher/conductor's imagination before it will be brought to fruition in a performance.

EPH EHLY, cont.

A Memorable Performance

There have been a great many. Some of the incredible performances of Gold Company left me saying "*Wow*! How do/did you do that?"

The Mormon Tabernacle Choir's performance in the Disney Hall in L.A. during the National ACDA Convention left me saying "*Wow*!" That was as perfect as a choral concert can be.

"*Wow*" performances have been given by children's choirs like Jean Ashworth-Bartle's Toronto Children's Chorus or Henry Leck's Indianapolis Children's Choir. I have said "*wow*" after hearing a young girls chorus from Sweden, a boys choir from Japan, numerous middle school choirs and many fabulous high school choirs such as Ben Keller's Lakes High School Choir from Lakewood, Washington, doing Eric Whitacre's "Leonardo Dreams of His Flying Machine"; or Neil Hendricksen's Woods Cross High School Choir from Woods Cross, Utah, whose sense of pitch was so remarkable it made me say, "*Wow*." Then, of course, there are the professionals, like the Kansas City Chorale, under the direction of Charles Bruffy, who give consistent "*wow*" performances.

Advice for Achieving "*Wow*"

"*Wow*" materializes when details are perfected.

- "ART" consists of details.
- Details are not trifles. Be self-critical.
- Don't believe only what your audience says. Be your own critic.
- Address each basic fundamental and analyze your result. Every fundamental element that is ignored WILL BE WEAK.
- "*Wows*" are rare.
- Not every performance has to be a "*wow*." If they were, then there would no longer be a "*wow*."
- "*Wow*" is something to strive toward. It should be the means to the end, but not the end itself.

Audition Tips

Do not assume that your talent will carry you all the way.

Talent without discipline is like owning a horse, but not knowing how to ride.

Excuses like "I have a sore throat" or "I didn't have time to practice" are like climbing onto a saddle without a cinch. Chances of slipping off are a hundred to one.

PREPARE!

Sensing Something Extraordinary

I am seldom prepared for a moment of "*wow*." Perhaps it's the skeptic in me.

Judgment is usually reserved for proof; proof that the basic elements of technique are addressed; proof that the performers' emotions are deep-seeded; proof that the music material is age-appropriate; and proof that there is a keen sense of timing.

(Notice, I did not mention proof of talent. Great effort by the initiate can be more astonishing than mediocre effort by the professional.)

The "feeling" of ensemble may be a subjective element but it is real. When performers subordinate themselves for the benefit of the whole, amazing results can be expected.

Man was meant to commune. I doubt there will be solos in heaven. People, together, accomplish much more than they can alone. When people empathize with one another, using the tools of pitch, rhythm, etc., it creates an aura that in itself communicates with an audience.

I doubt there will be solos in heaven. —Eph Ehly

Human #1 has an experience and shares it through words. Human #2 enhances the words with music. Human #3 serves as an instrument to communicate to Human #4, the listener. Thus the circle of sympathetic communication is complete. If all steps are done in an effective manner, all four will experience "*wow*."

Who Would You Like to Hear?

Everyone.

Live concerts bring a dimension to the performance that a recording, even on video, cannot.

Have *Wow Factors* Changed?

In the mid-20th century, there was more emphasis of appreciation on the composition and its communicative spirit than on the performance. With the advent of electricity came special effects. The invasion of special effects has been so invasive as to dull the senses of perception, requiring ever-increasing sensational results. What society has gained from "perfection," it has lost in innocence.

Performance Trends and Standard Bearers

I will let persons of the 21st century discuss the questions posed in #8.

CEDRIC DENT
Take 6, arranger, Professor of Music at Middle Tennessee State University
www.take6.com

If you give your all, 110 percent in the preparation stage, you can then "enjoy the moment" when your opportunity comes. **—Cedric Dent**

Wow Factors

Once my wife and I went for breakfast at Golden Corral, an all-you-can-eat buffet-style restaurant. One of the employees cooking made-to-order omelets stood out from everyone else working in the restaurant. Not only did the omelets taste good, but they also looked wonderful. He also went the extra mile by coming from behind the grille and bringing the omelets to our table. It was obvious that he took pride in his work. He had an infectious smile and a twinkle in his eye as he placed the plates before us. The icing on the cake was that every so often he would stroll by tables of satisfied customers, winking at them while asking "is it right for ya?" His charm was magnetic and customers were instantly drawn to him, tipping him over and above the normal tip that they left on the tables. My point is that he had *je ne sais quoi*—that special intangible thing that distinguished him from the other employees. Likewise, performers must constantly ask themselves, "What is it about what we do that distinguishes us from other performers?"

Additionally, there are three other factors that go into creating a truly *"wow"* performance: preparation, preparation and more preparation. In other words, people are always *wowed* by excellence and you can only attain it with a strong work ethic. As an example, when I joined Take 6 in 1985, I can count the number of performances in the first two years on one hand. In fact, we all committed to giving up weekends to rehearse. At that time, most of us were college students and rehearsing on weekends meant essentially no social life. I remember several of us bringing girlfriends to rehearsal from time to time in an effort to spend time with them.

A Memorable Performance

My first encounter with the Thomas Whitfield Company occurred while I was a college student. It was a live performance in Detroit, Michigan (my hometown)—a *"wow"* performance that changed the way I think about music. His sound was a proportional blend of jazz and traditional gospel that was *sui generis*. He was supremely gifted as a pianist/organist, vocalist, songwriter and vocal arranger. Simply put, he was a genius.

Advice for Achieving "Wow"

Identify an artist (or several artists) whose performances *wowed* you. Analyze that artist's performance style identifying specific "*wow*" elements that you can emulate and incorporate into your personal performance style.

Audition Tips

You've heard it said that to be successful it's not what you know, it's who you know. That statement is inaccurate because it's both. Take 6's success is due in part to influential musicians like Stevie Wonder and Quincy Jones who took an interest in our music early in our career. But that came after years of hard work—what I referred to earlier as "preparation, preparation and more preparation."

If you give your all, 110 percent in the preparation stage, you can then "enjoy the moment" when your opportunity comes. Whatever happens after that is destiny. No need worrying about what may go wrong. In fact, lack of preparation and the guilt associated with it is manifested in worry and fear.

Sensing Something Extraordinary

The point in a performance when you realize you are experiencing something extraordinary is when the audience and performer are in sync. As a performer, you can sense when you have the audience in the palm of your hand. Audience members may sit on the edge of their seats and mouth the lyrics during the performance with wide-eyed attention. They may wipe away a tear or nudge their friends at times when they are especially *wowed*.

Who Would You Like to Hear?

I wish I could have experienced a live performance by Ella Fitzgerald. The precise intonation, unique phrasing and vocal agility on her live recordings boggles the mind. In my opinion, Bobby McFerrin is the only other jazz vocalist in her league, who, by the way, has worked with my group Take 6 both live and in the studio.

Have *Wow Factors* Changed?

When I was younger, virtuosity was everything, both as listener and performer, sometimes to the detriment of musicality. Inexperience usually manifests itself in this kind of imbalance. I often tell my music-arranging students that inexperienced arrangers tend to pack every trick they know into a single arrangement, creating musical oversaturation. This is because they want to be heard and respected and thus have something to prove. They seek adulation and approbation and lose perspective on what is most important in a musical arrangement. An experienced arranger conserves musical ideas, is more likely to repeat an idea with variation than to continually add new ones. Now that I'm older and more experienced, I'm willing to sacrifice virtuosity for nuance and emotional content. I not only want to hear the music but feel it too.

Performance Trends and Standard Bearers

Regarding educators that consistently create "*wow*" performances—choral directors in particular—two come to mind immediately. Patrick Gardner was on faculty at the University of Michigan when I was a student there in the early '80s and he was awe-inspiring to sing for as well as to watch. He once said in a conducting class that there are generally two types of conductors. The first type is skilled in preparing an ensemble for performance but is not necessarily exciting to watch. His ensembles are so well-prepared that they can usually perform well without a director in performance. The second type of director does an average job of preparing his ensembles but is so exciting to watch that singers are inspired to perform brilliantly. Patrick Gardner was unique in that he possessed both skills. The other choral director is Stephen Zegree. Watching these two directors and listening to their respective groups is bound to give most people goose bumps.

Other performers that come to mind are the five guys that I stand next to onstage—Claude, Mark, David, Joel and Alvin, collectively known as Take 6. After 20 years, I am still *wowed* by their innate talent and commitment to excellence. What's more, one of these guys—Mark Kibble—is my favorite vocal arranger. How many folk can say they sing in a group with their favorite arranger? After more than 20 years and a Grammy nomination for my own arranging, I am still learning from the best!

DUANE DAVIS
Professor of Jazz Voice, Western Michigan University
www.wmugoldcompany.com

All this is to say, the extraordinary often is unexplainable.
—Duane Davis

Wow Factors
The bottom-line factors that can contribute to a *"wow"* performance are ownership and honesty. Ownership simply means having total knowledge of the music at hand. Without that, it would be quite difficult to expect one to reach the level of honesty.

A Memorable Performance
Patti Austin recently joined the Grand Rapids Symphony Orchestra in a tribute to Ella Fitzgerald. As I think about the elements that made that performance head and shoulders above the ordinary, the following thoughts come to mind. Patti knows her instrument. There was not one moment in that performance where I felt uneasy about her vocals. Another factor that can be attributed to this *"wowing"* performance was totally knowing and delivering the lyrics to the point where one could think they were written for her. A third factor is the air of confidence and sophistication in the performance and the interaction with the audience. And the final factor is how well the music was arranged for the artist, orchestra and her rhythm section.

Advice for Achieving "Wow"
Be here and now.

Audition Tips
The obvious advice cannot be overstated. A great attitude and personality will open doors. However, it should be noted that once the door is opened, the individual's skill and preparation (or lack of) will come to light. Always be prepared. The second thought is, "Do not assume anything." Always stay positive. Do not bring attention to or make excuses for mistakes.

Sensing Something Extraordinary
Whether I am conducting, performing or listening, I know that I am experiencing something extraordinary when there is a synthesis of the head and soul, aesthetics, acoustics and the re-creation or creation of the inspired

moment. All this is to say, the extraordinary often is unexplainable. One just knows that something extraordinary is occurring.

Who Would You Like to Hear?

Nat "King" Cole offered the listener so many sides of excellence. To overcome so much and sound so contrary to the challenges that he had to face is pretty admirable.

Have *Wow Factors* Changed?

Simply stated, life has allowed me to see the "*wow*" in the subtle. The "*wow*" has more depth today than it did 40 years ago.

SIMON CARRINGTON

**Conductor, founding member of The King's Singers,
Yale University Professor Emeritus
www.simoncarrington.com**

For me the truly extraordinary moments come when the dynamic is soft and the listener feels he or she can almost reach out and touch the sound.
—Simon Carrington

Wow Factors

Having listened to rather too many beautifully blended but otherwise uncommunicative performances by all kinds of distinguished choirs these past several years, I would suggest the following "*wow*" essentials:

Singers (solo or choral) must think consciously about the meaning of every word they sing, as they sing it. Good singing and rhetoric are inextricably intertwined. Rhetoric is the art of using language effectively and persuasively, and every singer has the responsibility of persuading the listener of the importance and emotional significance of the text being interpreted. Unlike orators, singers have the added benefit of beautiful music to help them be persuasive.

A Memorable Performance

This may sound a bit rarified but I remember being greatly moved when, as a small boy chorister, I first heard a recording of Henry Purcell's String Fantasias—yes, I know, no words and no singers!

There is something about Purcell's control of tension and relaxation (i.e. dissonance and consonance) that made my hair stand on end then and still does now 55 years later!

Advice for Achieving "Wow"

The technical aspects of your performance need to be as refined and as well-executed as possible for obvious reasons, but your singers must always remember that audiences are listening to the performance for the first time and yearn to be on the edge of their seats waiting for your <u>spontaneous</u> reaction to the music being sung.

Tips

Even the most hard-baked jury member or audition panel will respond favorably to emotions simply expressed and effectively communicated. There is no need for stylized (or indeed ham) gestures, but not only your voice but also your eyes must communicate the pain, the joy, the melancholy, the elation, the grief, the happiness and the countless other emotions being expressed by the poet through your singing.

Sensing Something Extraordinary

For me the truly extraordinary moments come when the dynamic is soft and the listener feels he or she can almost reach out and touch the sound. These moments require enormous concentration on the part of performer and singer alike—the kind of concentration that's less fashionable these days because of the easy availability of relentless amplified noise.

Who Would You Like to Hear?

The focus of my work has been on Early and Contemporary classical choral music since I began my teaching and conducting career, so this remark will seem rather out of bounds. But I would love to have seen and heard live The Hi-Lo's! singing Gene Puerling's arrangement of "Cockles and Mussels," which had such a powerful effect on me on first hearing—along with perhaps the Deller Consort singing the Tallis *Lamentations*!

Have *Wow Factors* Changed?

Returning to my own world, I would quote the huge changes in the understanding of style that have taken place during my career, particularly in the field of Early Music. Clarity, color, dexterity and flexibility are ingredients in the ***Wow Factor*** that have blossomed greatly these past 40 years. Intensity and expressivity of vocal line have eased out opulence of tone; nuance and elegance in many different genres have finally undermined weight and hefty vibratos. There are still well-intentioned teachers trying to squeeze the last drop of power and resonance out of voices that are light and delicate by nature, but there are now soloists and choirs of all shapes and sizes singing with simplicity and elegance and placing the emphasis where the *Wow Factor* lies: the combination of an expressive text effectively set to music.

Performance Trends and Standard Bearers

As his contemporary with whom I made much music as a student, I quote the conductor John Eliot Gardiner as one of the first of his generation of musicians to place the emphasis squarely on intensity and expressivity and the use of the text as the guiding light to all choral interpretation. Although I quoted a wordless piece by Purcell in an earlier answer above, there is no doubt in my mind that the words must lead the way in our performances if the audiences are to sense the *Wow Factor*—the music will follow.

HILARY APFELSTADT
Director of Choral Activities at The Ohio State University

> *If we could all learn to rehearse in performance mode,*
> *I think we might accomplish more polished and fulfilling performances.*
> *—Hilary Apfelstadt*

Wow Factors

Musical spontaneity—or the sense of it—makes a performance sound fresh and exciting.

A Memorable Performance

I remember hearing the Indianapolis Children's Choir sing at a national ACDA convention years ago and thinking it was truly a wonderful performance because of that very characteristic. There are others, of course, but that stands out to me. The most outstanding, however, was a concert in Cincinnati by the Dale Warland Singers during their last tour. It was spectacular—a warm tone, fluency of line, beautifully shaped phrases and impeccable intonation. They sang as one. I remember being spellbound, wishing it would never end. My students talked about it for months afterwards.

Advice for Achieving "Wow"

If we could all learn to rehearse in performance mode, I think we might accomplish more polished and fulfilling performances. We have to strive for excellence as a basic foundation (notice I do not say "perfection," which is so elusive as to be defeating sometimes when we struggle to pursue it). We have to strive to express the text in a way that honors the poetry and the composition.

Audition Tips

First of all, be prepared musically 100 percent. Second, focus on expressive presentation—communication is key.

Sensing Something Extraordinary

I think this can happen for performers and conductors when we sense we are really in sync with each other and with the music. We can tell when we know what we are doing is really expressive and we feed on that, working individually and collectively to continue it. It's the concept of "flow"— complete immersion in the process.

Who Would You Like to Hear?

It would likely be some of Bach's Sunday services—what did those choirs really sound like?

Have *Wow Factors* Changed?

They have changed as I have become more sophisticated musically. What might have *wowed* me as a youngster is different from what moves me now. I understand now more the pure beauty of a stellar unison line sung perfectly in tune by children; years ago, somehow, I took that for granted. I am moved more now by the wonderful complexity of impeccable choral singing because I know more how elusive that is after working toward it for decades!

Performance Trends and Standard Bearers

I think our culture demands more "glitz" now than ever before. It seems as though things have to be more colorful, more fast-paced, more technically stellar, etc. Have we lost the ability to value simplicity in excellence? I think we can be too concerned about "packaging" and not enough about substance in our society, and when that creeps into the arts, it isn't necessarily a good thing.

CHAPTER NINE
CODA

Simply stated, life has allowed me to see the "wow" in the subtle.
The "wow" has more depth today than it did 40 years ago.
—*Duane Davis*

When the curtain has gone down, no one will long remember the names
of the songs, the soloist, the clever staging, the expensive costumes, but
they will remember how the performance made them feel.
—*John Jacobson*

• • •

We have covered a lot of ground and explored a multitude of elements that all combine to create **The Wow Factor.** I hope the following short list reminds you of some of this book's salient points that will help you, your students *and* your ensembles to create "*wow*."

How do you get to Carnegie Hall?

Don't be a **but**.

Don't go to your face.

Do your homework.

Avoid excess verbiage.

Figure out how to make them thirsty.

Develop a philosophy *and* a methodology.

A as in attitude.

Old-fashioned values.

Be humble.

Keep an open mind.

The only constant is change.

What is the secret shortcut to get to be good?

We perform the way we practice.

The joy of frustration.

Be open to self-assessment, re-evaluation and criticism.

No excuses.

Appreciate your collaborative musicians.

Personal hygiene is your friend.

Repetition, repetition, repetition—but keep it fresh.

The more you perform, the easier it becomes.

Think outside the Bachs.

Do what you do well, and do it with conviction.

Never say never—never rule out a possibility.

Secret blend of intellect and emotion in performance.

I also hope you enjoyed reading the perspectives of the wonderful group of music professionals whose responses to my questions appear in Chapter 8. Even though they represent diverse and varied backgrounds and experiences, the interviews revealed a notable set of common and recurring "*wow*" principles and inspirational themes.

Find your own voice.

Technique first, then expression.

Be prepared.

Be authentic.

Feel it.

Connect to your music.

Exude energy.

Surprise.

Communicate.

Be a nice person; be friendly and cooperative.

If you found any of the ***Wow Factors*** contained herein to be a bit overwhelming, that's OK! I certainly understand. When you experience a "*wow*" performance, you now know that it does not happen by luck, coincidence or random happenstance. Instead, there is most likely a healthy combination of forethought, vision, practice, attention to detail, expenditure of energy, high artistic standards, inspiration, sweat, passion and humor.

All of these factors are available to you and are attainable. Do they involve hard work? Yes! Will they require effort? Of course! Is the process always a pleasant experience? Perhaps not!

Is it worth it? Absolutely and unequivocally!

Only you can choose how much effort and energy you are willing to expend in the pursuit of excellence and *"wow."* It seems that in our society today we are constantly barraged with mediocrity and averageness, from the expectations that are placed upon our students to the majority of programming that can be found on television. As a result, people often have the notion that talent and hard work are overrated, and that fame can be easily acquired, even when it is not earned or deserved.

I have made the conscious choice that I will not settle for lackluster effort or "just OK" from my students. Simply put, anything less than their very best is unacceptable. I encourage you to consider adopting the same winning attitude and to employ the ***Wow Factors*** that apply to you, your students and your ensembles. The results of your efforts will be both rewarding and motivating. After all, what have you got to lose? Remember, you cannot lose something that you did not have in the first place.

I wish you all the best in your pursuit of personal and professional *"wow,"* and I take comfort and satisfaction in knowing that your commitment, effort, enthusiasm and positive attitude will all combine to make our world a better place.

GOLD COMPANY AUDITION FORM

One who can properly fill out an audition application ranks higher in the audition process than one who cannot!

● ● ●

GOLD COMPANY PROGRAM
WESTERN MICHIGAN UNIVERSITY
www.wmugoldcompany.com

Audition and Interview Form

Audition pieces 1._____

2._____

NAME _____

BIRTH DATE _____

SCHOOL ADDRESS _____

SCHOOL PHONE _____

E-MAIL _____

Parent Name(s) _____

Parent Address(es) _____

HOME PHONE _____

1. Are you currently enrolled at Western Michigan University?

_____

2. Total number of credits you are registered for this semester

_____

3. Are you on probation of any kind? (specify)

   _____

4. Your major _____

   Class year _____

5. GPA_____

6. High school attended _____

7. High school music director _____

8. Hometown newspaper (full name & town) _____

   _____

9. I am auditioning for:

   ❑ SINGER   ❑ INSTRUMENTALIST   ❑ AUDIO TECHNICIAN

10. Previous choral experience:

11. Previous jazz experience:

12. Previous show choir experience:

13. Which instruments do you play, how well, and how long?

14. List voice teachers and length of time with each one:

15. List any prescription medications you now take, indicating condition for which you are being treated:

16. Do you have perfect pitch? _____

17. Do you transcribe jazz music?_____

18. Do you compose popular music? _____

19. Do you arrange jazz and/or pop music?_____

20. Are you interested in a leadership position in either group?_____
    Explain:

21. List dance experience:

22. List choreography experience:

23. List theater experience:

24. List other music ensembles for which you're auditioning or plan to participate in:

25. List any additional special talents, abilities, and/or interests, such as juggling, magic, storytelling, creative writing, etc.:

26. Will you be on campus all year? _____

27. Are you willing to participate in extra rehearsal as the need arises?

    _____

28. Exactly why are you auditioning for one of these groups?

29. Describe your music theory background and skill level:

30. Anything further you'd care to add?

31. Will you accept a position in either ensemble? _____
    If not, then which ensemble?
    ❏ Gold Company only   (or)   ❏ GC II only

Your height _____   Weight _____

T-shirt size _____

Sweatshirt size _____

Female dress size _____

Male jacket size _____

Male waist size _____

Male inseam _____

I usually sing:
❑ soprano   ❑ alto   ❑ tenor   ❑ bass

Your highest note _____

Your lowest note _____

ABOUT THE AUTHOR

Dr. Steve Zegree is the Bobby McFerrin Professor of Music at Western Michigan University, where he teaches classical and jazz piano; directs Gold Company, an internationally acclaimed jazz vocal ensemble; and performs as pianist with the Western Jazz Quartet. Recognized as one of the most respected vocal jazz conductors and educators in the world, Dr. Zegree is also active as a conductor, clinician, and adjudicator. His career as a pianist and conductor includes performances on five continents. His former students are among today's leaders in jazz and pop performance, Broadway, recording studio production, writing, arranging, singing, and music education.

Gold Company and Dr. Zegree's vocal jazz program at Western Michigan University have won more than 50 Student Music Awards from Down Beat magazine. His ensembles have performed at MENC National Conventions, IAJE International Conferences, the World Symposium on Choral Music and several major jazz festivals, and with artists including Bobby McFerrin, Janis Siegel, Jon Hendricks, Darmon Meader, Mark Murphy, Don Shelton and Bonnie Herman.

Dr. Zegree auditioned, arranged for and rehearsed Nick Lachey's "Team Lachey," the winning choir on NBC's *Clash Of The Choirs*. His choral arrangements have been published by Hal Leonard, Warner Bros., Alfred Publications and Shawnee Press, and he has produced several recordings including *Mark Murphy Sings the Nat King Cole Songbook*, which received a Grammy Award nomination. His piano CD, *Steve Zegree and Friends*, is released on the Sea Breeze Jazz label. His highly acclaimed first book, *The Complete Guide To Teaching Vocal Jazz*, is published by Heritage Music Press, a division of Lorenz Music Publishing. Dr. Zegree is a Steinway Artist.

PRAISE FOR
THE **WOW** FACTOR

MICHELE WEIR
Author, arranger, pianist, vocalist, educator

I am really impressed with Steve's new book, *The Wow Factor*. To the best of my knowledge, there is no other publication out there with so much hands-on, no-nonsense and very pertinent advice for students, teachers, and pro musicians about topics ranging from preparation to professionalism, and everything in between. This book is going to be extremely useful for students as it speaks to areas of their study and preparation that are often overlooked in music education programs: how to audition, choose a university to attend, begin preparation for a music career while still in high school, practice effectively, prepare a resume, and much more. It is equally useful for teachers for the same kinds of reasons: this book offers a wealth of practical advice for achieving maximum effectiveness.

The Wow Factor left me with the feeling of, "I wish someone had told me all of this when I was a student (teacher, or aspiring professional)." This is a useful publication!

Steve is a long time friend, and I've always admired his work. The evidence of his tremendous experience and expertise is quite apparent in the quality of the ensembles he directs, particularly, Gold Company. Steve really knows what he's talking about in music and music education, and *The Wow Factor* is truly a gold mine of wisdom and good information.

In short, the scope of the book is awesome, the writing style is to the point and fun at the same time, and the topics are extremely pertinent for teachers, students and professionals.

BOBBY McFERRIN
Singer, composer, conductor, recording artist

I really don't think anyone else could have written this book. Steve's group, Gold Company, has consistently been the high bar for excellence, and whenever I've had the opportunity to work with them, I often find myself lost in the land of "WOW-ness." Bravo Steve!!!

NICK LACHEY
Singer, songwriter, actor, producer, television personality
(*The Wow Factor*) gives a lot of great insight and of course, I especially liked the chapter on *Clash of the Choirs*. It was fun to read and recall that great experience.

TIM LAUTZENHEISER
Teacher, composer, author, consultant
WOW! After reading and re-reading Dr. Steve Zegree's new book, *The Wow Factor*, my first and lasting reaction is: WOW! Dr. Zegree blends his own successful musical/educational journey into a blueprint-of-success relevant to every teacher, parent, administrator, PERSON. While the content area is MUSIC PERFORMANCE and performance preparation, a simple change-of-the-noun makes it applicable to all areas of life where EXCELLENCE is the foundation of any/all achievement. As with everything produced by Dr. Zegree, the final product warrants a standing ovation. Simply put: WOW!

JOHN JACOBSON
Composer, author, educator, conductor, choreographer, director, speaker
When the folks at Hal Leonard Corporation sent me the galleys for Dr. Zegree's new book I read it all in one sitting. Then I flipped back to the front and read it all again. After finishing the second go at it, all I could say was…you guessed it…WOW! An exceptional read, full of invaluable advice, inspiration and know-how gleaned from Steve's many years as an artist, conductor, educator and "WOW-er!" *Def. n.* One who "Wows"!

MAC HUFF
Composer, arranger, conductor, producer
Wow! Steve Zegree's *Wow Factor* is fantastic. Comprehensive, smart and imaginative, it breaks down the nuts and bolts of performance preparation like no other text I have ever read. Whether you are a student, music educator or professional musician, there is something here for you. The interviews and quotes are fascinating and fun. Steve's consummate approach as a musician and educator is insightful and inspiring, raising the bar for all who strive for that ultimate, wow performance.

ROGER EMERSON
Composer, arranger, educator
The book is a "must read" for every educator and student performer! A wealth of great ideas and inspirational commentary. All I can say is "wow"!

EPH EHLY
Conductor, author, educator
WOW! What a book. Reading Zegree is like having your own personal tutor. Here is a textbook that deserves a place in the library of every serious performer and teacher of music. An examination of this thoroughly comprehensive document will leave one with the ultimate impression, WOW! What a book.

CEDRIC DENT, PhD
Professor of Music, Middle Tennessee State University
Member of the Ten-Time Grammy Award-Winning Vocal Group, TAKE 6
Steve Zegree is a gifted music educator and performer whose passion for his calling leaps from the pages of this book. Performers, educators and students alike will benefit from this practical guide on how to create "wow" performances. From elements such as rehearsal techniques and stage presence to programming a concert and preparing for auditions, Steve covers everything needed to transform average performances into "wow" performances. Prepare to be inspired!

HILARY APFELSTADT
Conductor, educator
The WOW Factor is a very practical, readable book that every choral musician, novice or professional alike, can expect to find interesting, informative, and useful.

Steve Zegree writes in a conversational tone and literally, "tells it like it is." Students can expect to find information about audition preparation and many other aspects of the professional world. His "Old-Fashioned Rules to Live By" in Chapter 4 may be second nature to the boomer generation but are not so to college students, yet the commonsense advice Zegree offers will enable them to handle the complexities of the professional world and should be required reading in every college methods course. Every page of this book has valuable insights gleaned from the author's career as a performer, arranger and teacher. Although much of the context relates to vocal jazz and the author's experience with the outstanding collegiate ensemble, Gold Company, the practical suggestions are applicable in many other contexts. Zegree challenges musicians to make performances more engaging, a lesson we all can learn, regardless of the style of music presented.

I found the chapter on *The Clash of the Choirs* very revealing in terms of what it says about public perceptions of ensemble singing. We need to understand that audiences have changed and while we are not slaves to their taste, we need to recognize and try to understand them.

The final chapter, a compilation of interviews with a variety of seasoned professionals, adds further credence to Zegree's own ideas by supplementing and complementing them. I highly recommend *The WOW Factor*; despite the title, there is nothing gimmicky here. There are no quick answers; the value of a good solid work ethic permeates every page of the book. This is honest, direct, and informative advice presented in the spirit of generosity as a seasoned professional offers his perspectives to the reader.